D1548604

THE
GOLDEN
GONG

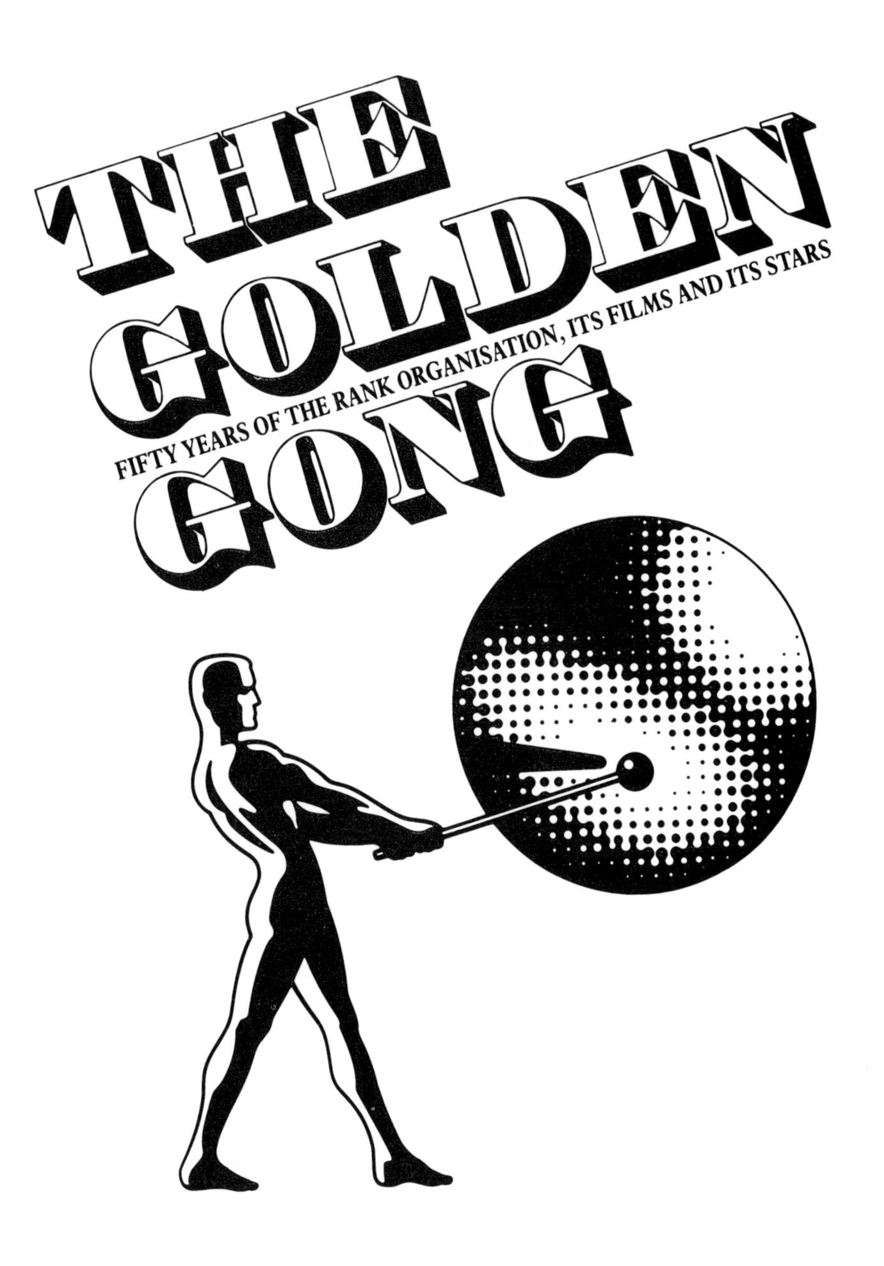

Quentin Falk

Foreword by Michael Caine

COLUMBUS BOOKS
LONDON

This book was produced in collaboration with Euro Center Productions as a companion to the BBC TV documentary also entitled *The Golden Gong*

First published in Great Britain in 1987 by
Columbus Books Limited
19-23 Ludgate Hill, London EC4M 7PD

British Library Cataloguing in Publication Data
Falk, Quentin
The golden gong: fifty years of the Rank Organisation, its films and its stars.
1. Rank Organisation——History
I. Title
384'.8'0941 PN1999.R37

ISBN 0-86287-340-1

Designed by Brian Davison

Phototypeset by Falcon Graphic Art Ltd
Wallington, Surrey

Printed and bound by R.J. Acford
Chichester, Sussex

Contents

Foreword

Even if I had never made a picture for the Rank Organisation, I'd always remember the company. When I was 17, I had a job as an office boy at its South Street headquarters and Mr Rank had me fired for smoking in the toilet.

Many of the war films seemed to be directed by a man called Lewis Gilbert, who was to play a very big part in my life when he directed *Alfie* and *Educating Rita*. When you're a kid and going to the cinema, how could you ever even dream you'd end up being in a film made by this or that company? Those logos are like fantasies as you watch them. They don't really exist until you suddenly find yourself one day in an office or at Pinewood Studios.

When I was a youngster I used to go every Sunday to a place called Clubland run by a Reverend Butterworth and he used to show Rank's religious films at the place all the time. I think that's where I first learned to act.

Later, I used to go to the cinema sometimes seven days a week. In those days your British film industry was, basically, the Rank Organisation, so I grew up with The Man with the Gong. Think of all those Margaret Lockwood and James Mason films, not to mention some great wartime pictures . . . those all came from Rank.

The first film I ever made for the Organisation was *The Bulldog Breed*. Norman Wisdom was the star and I had a tiny part. I was a sailor and Oliver Reed played a teddy boy, but because Norman was the star we never got to meet him.

The Ipcress File was the big break for me, though – it was the first film where I actually got billed over the title. I went on to make a lot of pictures for Rank at Pinewood. It's always been my favourite studio and it also has the nicest restaurant.

My hero in British films is definitely Johnny Mills. He's one of the few people I can think of who can play convincing working-class as well as toffee-nosed parts. Perhaps Dickie Attenborough too. Everyone else, especially in those days, tended to sound very 'french windows' and all that, if you see what I mean.

Years ago Johnny did a marvellous film for Rank with Robert Newton – *This Happy Breed*, written by Noel Coward and directed by David Lean – and he was perfect as an ordinary working-class guy. Bob Newton tried to be working-class but it didn't work. He came out sounding slightly pissed.

The company also had a great casting director, Weston Drury. He had to be. He gave me a part.

The only thing I was disappointed about was that I was never chosen for the Charm School. I always thought I was a pretty charming guy, and yet I was passed up for the school year after year. I remember there were people like Patricia Plunkett, Susan Shaw, Maxwell Reed, Roger Moore, Joan Collins, masses of them. I used to look at them and think, 'What do you have to do to have charm?' After all, all the girls I used to go out with would say, 'You're very charming'. But I used to say, 'I can't be. I can't get into the Charm School.'

Rank's horizons were much more confined to Britain in those days than they are now. But the British film industry has always been held in great esteem in Hollywood. You have to remember that ninety per cent of all Hollywood executives used to live in Chester Square, London, when they were here during the 'sixties. The Americans have never seen their industry as just the 'American film industry'. They brought in people from all over the world and have also gone out everywhere. The British must do the same thing – think of it as an international business.

Of course, there's still an emphasis on casting with an eye to the American box-office. There has to be. I remember when I came to England to make *Educating Rita*, everyone in Hollywood said, 'Who's in it? Why are you doing it?' I told them I'd be working with a wonderful girl who was totally unknown in the US called Julie Walters, and that the script had a universal theme – of a woman trying to better herself – and that was good enough for me.

My latest film for Rank, *The Fourth Protocol*, is an international picture and also has a universal theme, so we're hoping it'll have just as big an impact, though it's a very different film.

Yes, on reflection, I've been involved with Rank, one way or another, all my life. It seems a long time since the day when J. Arthur caught me with a cigarette in the toilet . . . Who'd have guessed that from such beginnings I'd have started a life-long relationship with Rank?

Introduction

Before television began to consume so much of our post-war lives, my cinema-going was dominated by 'The Man with the Gong'. All my subsequent love of cinema – and that of many others too, if they're not too proud to admit it – was predicated by those magic words 'The Rank Organisation Presents'.

What followed, within the confines of my own particular dream palaces, the Odeons Swiss Cottage and Haverstock Hill, shapes a general, if necessarily idealised, knowledge: about the war, via the exploits of Kenneth More, Virginia McKenna and Peter Finch in *Reach for the Sky, Carve Her Name with Pride* and *The Battle of the River Plate*; about motor-racing, in *Checkpoint*; hospitals, in the *Doctor* films; the police, in *The Long Arm* and *Violent Playground*; and nuns, in *Conspiracy of Hearts*. Classics were made flesh in such films as *A Tale of Two Cities* and *The 39 Steps*. We were an uncritical, ever-rapt audience.

Later, television and more discriminating cinema and film theatre visits inevitably revealed other cinematic pleasures. But not least of these was Rank's legacy, rich as a result of an earlier, unprecedented helping of creative freedom handed to Britain's finest film-makers, among them Lean and Neame, Powell and Pressburger, Launder and Gilliat and Carol Reed. Ealing Studios, too, survived and flourished thanks to a generous deal initiated by the Organisation.

From the 'sixties, as the Organisation became more embroiled in diversification and retreated further and further from its involvement in the creative side of film-making, the name Rank became cinematically unfashionable. Then it merely represented one half of a stultifying exhibition duopoly.

When the company actually went back into production – abortively, as it proved – towards the end of the 'seventies, the cynicism was tangible. Today, as cinema attendances seem to be rallying, Rank remains firmly ensconced in the industry with cinemas (though far fewer in number), studio, healthy distribution – from theatrical to video – and, in a low-profile way, production. Mr Rank, who got the ball rolling and the spools turning 50 years ago, would probably approve.

Quentin Falk

CHAPTER 1
Flour Power

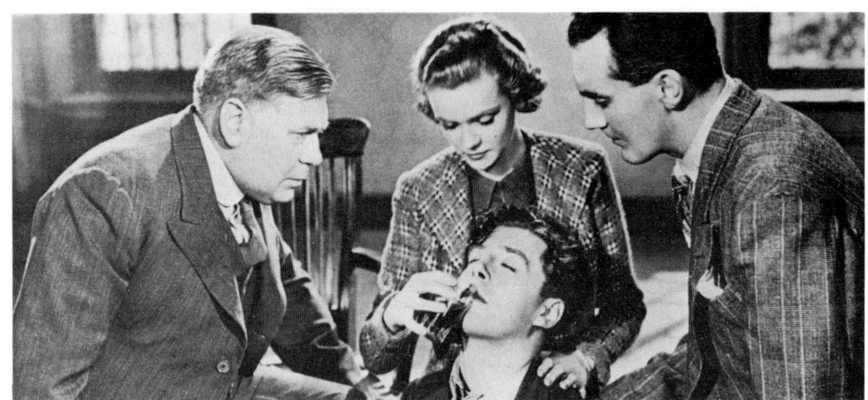

Previous page: Ralph Lynn, Tom Walls and Chinatown friend in *Stormy Weather*, a typical Aldwych farce adaptation; a trio of Hitchcocks – John Loder and Sylvia Sidney in *Sabotage* (above left), Robert Donat and Madeleine Carroll in *The 39 Steps* (above); and (left), Nova Pilbeam administers aid in a tense scene from *Young and Innocent*.

One day, in the late summer of 1938, at Pinewood studios, during the making of Gaumont British's *Climbing High*, its star, Jessie Matthews, noticed a tall dark man standing at the back of the set watching the filming. Like many other stars, she disliked unidentified visitors coming on to the set during shooting, so she mentioned it to the director, Carol Reed, who asked his assistant to tell the stranger to go away.

Reed's 'gofer' asked the man if there was anything he wanted.

'No,' he replied pleasantly, 'nothing in particular.' And the visitor walked away without any trouble at all.

'Did you ask his name?' said Reed.

'Yes,' replied the assistant, 'I believe he said it was Rank.'

J. (Joseph) Arthur Rank, born in Hull in 1888, public school-educated and heir to a flour and milling fortune, would probably have favoured such anonymity. After all, as Miss Matthews and her co-star, Michael Redgrave, were going through their romantically comic paces at Pinewood their tall visitor was already, and with great single-mindedness, on his way to becoming one of the most powerful men in British filmland. Even the site of the cinematic frolicking between two of the country's most popular performers was now part of his gathering film empire.

Yet what possible interest could film-making, with its crucial triumvirate of production, distribution and exhibition, have had for this rather puritanical industrialist, already inordinately wealthy and well into middle age by the early 1930s?

The man who was to tell his biographer, 'I am in films because of the Holy Spirit', and spent his Sunday afternoons teaching in a Sunday school, took his first steps in filmland directly as a result of his Methodism, enacted with all the vigour of a born-again practitioner after a period of disillusion with the faith. Why not, he thought, use the most contemporary forms of communication to spread the word to the largest number of people? With that end in view, he first bought *The Methodist Times*; later, his interest turned towards the possibility of evangelism via films.

Impressed by a 23-minute religious film called *In Our Time*, written and directed by one Aveling Ginever and featuring a Voice that intervenes in a quarrel between two men of different classes and proposes faith as a solution, Rank commissioned Ginever, a former journalist and advertising man, to make a film for his recently formed Religious Film Society. The result, with material partly supplied by Rank himself, was *Mastership*, shot in a week at Merton Park Studios, 22 minutes long and costing a little under £3000. Featuring Vi Kaley and Dorothy Vernon, the film showed a wrangling family re-united after hearing the reassuring words of a saintly slum preacher.

Now, with the bit between his teeth, Rank even ventured for the first time into Wardour Street, where he struck a deal with Gaumont British to make, initially, three films for his Society. In the year *Mastership* was first shown (1934), he also formed what was to be his first commercial film-making venture, British National Films.

With his partners Lady Yule, a widow

(Above) Jessie Matthews and Michael Redgrave in *Climbing High*; (right), Geraldine Fitzgerald and Niall McGinnis in *Turn of the Tide*, Rank's commercial début.

who had been left about £15 million by her jute magnate husband, and John Corfield, whose film experience seemed to consist of, to date, an £8000 'quickie', Rank embarked on his first film to be made not, as in the past, for church halls, but for the cinema. This was *Turn of the Tide*, a suitably moralistic tale about two Yorkshire fishing families whose feuding ends in marriage. Costing about £30,000, with locations filmed near Whitby, Yorkshire and interiors shot at British & Dominions studio, Elstree, it had a good, solid British cast: Wilfrid Lawson, Niall McGinnis, Sam Livesey (father of Roger) and newcomer Geraldine Fitzgerald. The critics seemed to like it ('one of the best English films I have yet seen', wrote Graham Greene) and the film even won a prize at the Venice Festival.

But good reviews were not enough for Rank. He wanted the film seen by as many people as possible and he was far from pleased with the efforts of the distributor, Gaumont-British, to maximise the returns. When Corfield approached the Ostrer brother-run circuit on behalf of Rank, he was apparently told by Mark Ostrer, head of theatres, 'I've never heard of [Rank] and I don't want to hear of him.' Such a stance was shortly to rebound on him rather badly.

The answer, Rank was told, to cracking the industry was not just to make films which one hoped would be successful, but also to have complete control over their distribution and exhibition. To start up his own 'vertically integrated' operation, he would first need the finest film salesman in Britain.

The man in question was undoubtedly Charles Moss (C.M.) Woolf, then managing director for the Ostrers at Gaumont-British. Get Woolf to set up a new distribution company and, at one stroke, you have not only got a good man but you have also pulled out the mainstay of Gaumont, which is then likely to fall into your hands too: this it did, though perhaps not as cold-bloodedly as this scenario might seem to suggest. Woolf, quite independently, it seems, had a major disagreement with the Ostrers and resigned. But when he set up his own company, General Film Distributors, one of the prominent backers was none other than J. Arthur Rank.

John Mills and Nova Pilbeam in an early Gainsborough title, *Tudor Rose*.

According to Sir John Woolf (who as plain John would become joint managing director of GFD after the war before leaving to start his own company, Romulus), son of C.M., the true making of GFD was a tie-up with America's powerful Universal Pictures.

'Carl Laemmle, who owned Universal, had run into difficulties and the company was going bust. When this became known, a syndicate was formed in America to take Universal over. My father heard about it and joined the syndicate. Because of my father's involvement in this, GFD got the distribution rights to the Universal films.

'Remember the first three films which turned up from Universal – they would have saved Laemmle if he had got them out in time. One was *Showboat*, a huge success, the second was *My Man Godfrey*, with William Powell and Carole Lombard, and the third was a little film with a girl nobody had heard of: the girl was Deanna Durbin and the film was *Three Smart Girls* and it became an absolute sensation.'

A year after the formation of GFD, Gaumont-British was in deep financial trouble. It was heavily committed to film production and its overdraft was growing. British films were failing to make substantial inroads into America while American films were exerting more than their usual stranglehold over the business in Britain. *Plus ça change . . .*

To the rescue came, ironically, C.M. Woolf, who, with the backing of Rank and his associates, would take half the risk of continuing some of G-B's production commitments, most of which, it was demanded in return, should be undertaken at Rank's new studio, Pinewood. By the turn of the 'forties, Rank had taken over Gaumont completely, except for the minority interest of Twentieth Century-Fox, which remained a thorn in Rank's side for years.

If Rank had achieved his goal of being able to distribute and show films, there was then the small matter of also trying to make a few good films to feed the system.

An American commentator of the time noted: 'I have seen three types of films made in England: the imaginative film drawn from the works of H.G. Wells; the spectacular historical film; and the comedy drama with which various names are associated.'

The writer might have been referring almost solely to the output from the flamboyant Alexander Korda, who, with his close-knit expatriate Hungarian entourage, was fashioning such gems as *Things to Come*, *The Man Who Could Work Miracles*, *The Private Life of Henry VIII*, *Rembrandt* and *The Ghost Goes West*.

In addition to Korda, who was also build-

Will Hay gets his nose tweaked by Jimmy Hanley in *Boys Will Be Boys*; (far right), Margaret Lockwood shows concern for Hugh Williams in Carol Reed's *Bank Holiday*; (below), dressing-room tension in *The Arsenal Stadium Mystery*.

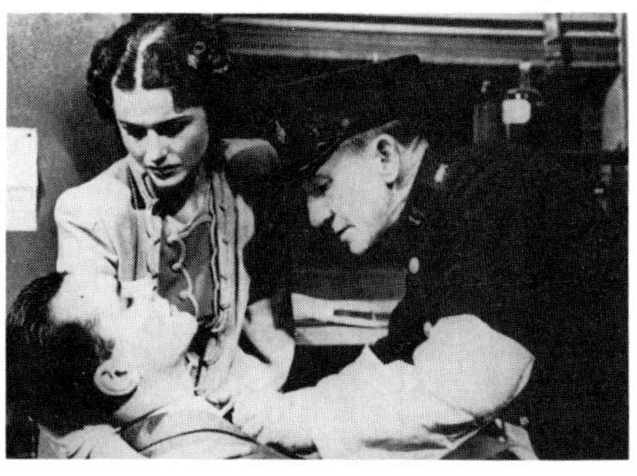

Professor Henry Higgins (Leslie Howard) corners Covent Garden flower-seller Eliza Doolittle (Wendy Hiller) in *Pygmalion*.

ing grand studios at Denham, there were Hitchcock, Herbert Wilcox and Anthony Asquith. Beyond that, there was little else apart from 75-minute adaptations of Aldwych farces.

GFD's initial investments were all, recalls Sir John Woolf, 'pretty disastrous'. *Moscow Nights* – retitled, prophetically, for the USA *I Stand Condemned* – with Laurence Olivier and Penelope Dudley-Ward, and directed by the normally reliable 'Puffin' Asquith, proved a real stinker and almost drove GFD out of business.

The company's first big success was its fourth film, *Limelight*, backstage *schmaltz* directed by Herbert Wilcox, with Anna Neagle (later to become Wilcox's wife) and Arthur Tracy.

While Rank was properly aware of the talented Hungarian, Korda, in opposition, he was also about to acquire his very own East European, the extraordinary Gabriel 'Gabby' Pascal, who hailed from either Hungary or Transylvania, depending on which version you believed of his famous line-spinning.

Just as Rank was in films 'because of the Holy Spirit', Pascal believed it was his divine right to make films from the works of George Bernard Shaw and had, astonishingly, convinced the playwright of such. Sir John Woolf recalled, 'I remember Pascal coming into my father's office to sell him the idea of making *Pygmalion*. Pascal – he was wearing mauve spats with purple buttons – had come straight from buying the rights from GBS and he had to borrow from Shaw to pay the fare to see my father.'

Weighing it all up – a low level of public interest in the classics, Pascal's inexperience and so on – C.M. Woolf rejected the idea. Separately, Pascal arranged a meeting with Rank who, not knowing of C.M.'s opposition, said yes, but only if the producer could arrange a completion guarantee – a sum of money that would be readily available if the agreed budget was exceeded. Pascal concurred and Woolf later waived his objections.

Released towards the end of 1938, *Pygmalion*, co-directed by Leslie Howard and Anthony Asquith – making amends for *Moscow Nights* – and starring Howard and Wendy Hiller, was to become the largest moneymaker of 1939 and earned five Oscar nominations, including one for the original author, Mr Shaw himself.

Rank needed his flour power at the end of the 'thirties to add just one more 'arm' to the foundation of his rapidly increasing film empire – a cinema circuit (Gaumont-British would not be finally accessible for a couple of years yet, and ABC, the other main circuit, would always remain an implacable opponent).

In pre-war years, a familiar slogan became known across Britain: 'Oscar Deutsch Entertains Our Nation' – ODEON for short. Son of Central European Jewish emigrants, Deutsch was born and brought up in Birmingham, where he was at school with two other filmmen-to-be, Michael Balcon and Victor Saville. While they went into production, Deutsch interested himself with the exhibition side of the business. He built his first theatre at Brierly Hill and also controlled others in various parts of the Midlands.

The Odeon dream itself, and the name, was hatched in the Birmingham suburb of Perry Barr in 1930. With the technical expertise of a right-hand man, Sidney Swingler, who helped develop a sound system that would go into all Deutsch's subsequent cinemas, and the initiative of a young illustrated-sign manufacturer called Pearce, who came up with a distinctive logo, the first Odeon opened.

The name itself came from Greek amphitheatres named Odeions, was also redolent of those pioneering 'nickelodeons' from the earliest days of movie-making and, perhaps most seductively, contained the initials of Oscar Deutsch's name.

From 1933, Deutsch concentrated the building of his bold art deco circuit (Perry Barr, and earlier acquisitions, officially joined the group two years later) in and around London, pretty much in concert with the construction of new Underground stations. As a station opened, so an Odeon went up. He cornered outer London, too, and the South Coast – five in the first year, seventeen in the next; no less than 36 new cinemas opened in 1937, including the flagship Odeon, Leicester Square.

Towards the end of 1938, Deutsch was contemplating a takeover of Gaumont-British which would have given him control of over 600 cinemas, easily outflanking ABC's 474, but like ABC earlier, he was foiled in his bid because of a complicated share structure.

Only months after this, Rank was firmly ensconced on the board of Odeon, having helped arrange finance. This was sorely needed as Deutsch's expansion plans, continuing apace, were being hampered by both lack of funds and a shortage of steel and other essential materials, diverted in the build-up to war.

When Oscar Deutsch died in 1941 (almost exactly a year prior to C.M. Woolf's passing), his wife inherited the stock and sold it to Rank, who by now had also become chairman of Gaumont-British.

'How,' asks Rank's biographer, Alan Wood, 'had the Rank Empire been built? By deliberate planning, by sheer good fortune, by the guidance of God?

'It was said of the British Empire that it was acquired in a fit of absent-mindedness: though one could hardly go so far as to say this about the Rank Empire, it certainly suggests comparison by the apparently fortuitous, haphazard and higgledy-piggledy nature of its growth.'

CHAPTER 2

Magic Mansion: Pinewood 1

The Gong Men

Britain seemed awash with film studios in the 1930s. There were the new Ealing studios, Sound City at Shepperton, Lime Grove, British & Dominions and Amalgamated at Elstree, Twickenham, Teddington, Hammersmith, Wembley, Denham, of course, Islington and Shepherd's Bush, to name just a few. The size and quality, however, varied enormously, from purpose-built to cramped and squalid.

Shooting at B & D's facility on *Turn of the Tide* clearly had not impressed Mr Rank, who thought the process wasteful when filming had to be suspended while a new set was being erected. Why, he asked his partner John Corfield, don't we build a new, more spacious, one? It just so happened that Charles Boot, head of the building firm of Henry Boot & Son, also had the ambition of giving Britain a really well-equipped, logically planned and modern film studio. He had his eyes on Heatherden Hall, a 156-acre estate near Iver Heath, Buckinghamshire – some 25 miles west of London.

The mansion, built in 1840, had been variously tenanted over the years, by numerous luminaries including the great Test cricketer, Ranjitsinghi. In 1916, a rich Canadian, Lieutenant Colonel Grant Morden, bought the Hall for £300,000 and added a few extras, including marble bathrooms and an indoor swimming-pool. In what today is the club bar, the 1921 Irish Free State Treaty was signed. Along with so many other rich speculators, lost a fortune in the Wall Street Crash of 1929 and had to quit his lush estate.

For less than a tenth of what it had cost the Canadian to purchase, the Hall fell to Boot and soon he had combined with Rank to form a new company, Pinewood Studios Ltd: 'pine' presumably from the pine trees in the vicinity, 'wood' as in Hollywood.

Previous page: Alastair Sim and Sally Gray in *Green for Danger*; (left), an exotic twirl from Anna Neagle in *London Melody*, her first film, completed at Pinewood.

Cecil Parker, Claude Rains and Vivien Leigh in *Caesar and Cleopatra*.

It was a workmanlike, if less than inspiring, choice of name, which rather baffled the distinguished American critic Gilbert Seldes. He wrote at the time: 'I read that a new studio was being opened in England and that it was hoped that this studio would turn out English pictures and would show Hollywood how good pictures could be made. In its physical equipment this studio used all the latest machinery developed in America and elsewhere, but its soul was to be everything that Hollywood is not; it was not to suggest Hollywood in the slightest degree – and they named it Pinewood!'

While under construction, Pinewood's fold was joined by B & D, its studios at Elstree having, somewhat fortuitously, been gutted by fire. The autocratic Captain Richard Norton (later Lord Grantley), who had been, briefly, in charge of production at B & D, moved south then west of Elstree to become Pinewood's first managing director.

By 30 September 1936 all was ready for the complex's grand launch. *The Daily Film Renter* headlined with a special supplement: 'Hundred-Acre Pinewood Studio Opening Today at Iver Heath: Eight Modern Stages and Striking Production Facilities.' There were congratulatory advertisements from stars Jessie Matthews and Sonnie Hale, producer-director Harold Huth, producer Ivor Montagu, Bestlab, General Film Distributors, Simplex Projectors, Western Electric Recording and Pyrene Fire Appliances.

A transformed Eliza Doolittle (Wendy Hiller) gets the attention of Leslie Howard and Scott Sunderland (Colonel Pickering) but meets the disdain of others in *Pygmalion*.

A stirring message from Captain Norton concluded: 'Pinewood provides a working place and a dwelling-place in which its inhabitants can take a pride; and in that knowledge it is *our* pride to offer it as a venue for the making of films which will have every possible chance of furthering the prestige of British production.'

The first film to be completed at Pinewood, although it had been started at the now defunct B & D facility, was Herbert Wilcox's frothy *London Melody*, with Anna Neagle and Tullio Carminati. The first picture to be made in its entirety at the studios – of the 47 completed before war curtailed activity – was Carol Reed's thriller *Talk of the Devil*, with American imports Sally Eilers and Ricardo Cortez (and Margaret Rutherford, a long way down the credits). This was followed by a series of pretty undistinguished titles, punctuated with the odd Jessie Matthews musical, *Young and Innocent* (one of Hitchcock's last British films before going to Hollywood) and, of course, Pascal's *Pygmalion*.

Pinewood technicians had to get used to the producer's inordinate concern with detail. On one occasion shooting was halted while Pascal organised some tiny adjustment to an extra's costume at the rear of the crowd scene.

'It's all right, Gabby,' said co-director 'Puffin' Asquith, 'it's not in the camera.'

Pascal's reply was final, as it was slightly puzzling: 'What is *not* in the camera is just as important as what *is* in the camera.'

After war had been declared Pinewood was, first, mobilised as a food store. Later the Royal Mint made copper coins there, and later still the Army, RAF and Crown Film Units moved in to make use of the studio's facilities. It was not until 1945 that Pinewood began to return to normal, and it was 1946 before feature-film production could be resumed at full capacity.

So where was Mr Rank making his movies? Of all places, at Denham, scene of Korda's former glories. When the creditors closed in on Korda and his company London Films, debts were running in excess of £1 million. Denham had to go, and Rank, on the other side of the A40, as it were, took over the complex, bringing it under a new 'umbrella', D & P Studios Ltd, encompassing it and Pinewood.

Pascal, and his mentor Shaw, followed Rank to Denham, first with *Major Barbara*, which totally failed to repeat the success of *Pygmalion*, and then, after abortive attempts to set up both *Arms and the Man* and *St Joan*, *Caesar and Cleopatra*, which was to be Britain's most expensive film to date and, for Rank, a costly fiasco.

When Peter Noble, a promising young stage actor (today a distinguished show-business columnist), was summoned to Denham to be considered by Pascal for a role in the film, he jumped at the chance.

'Costs,' says Noble, 'had mounted alarmingly for Pascal had insisted on engaging every well-known player on the British stage to act the small parts (Claude Rains was Caesar, Vivien Leigh Cleopatra). Several famous actors had been paid huge sums just for standing by. One day one of them, Francis Sullivan, remonstrated with Pascal, "I hate to admit it, Gabby, but you are paying me hundreds of pounds for being little more than a film extra."

' "Money. Money. What does money matter?" replied the ebullient Hungarian. "So it means Mr Rank will just have to sell a few more sacks of *flour*." '

Claude Rains, who knew that Noble also wrote a weekly column, later drew him to one side and said, with a glare at Pascal: 'You have my permission to print that I will never work with this madman again.'

After a year of production, that had begun shortly before D-Day 1944, the budget of *Caesar and Cleopatra*, being both produced *and* directed by Pascal, had stretched to a little under £1.3 million. There were newspaper attacks and even questions in the House of Commons about such extravagance during wartime. The film was described as 'a disastrous loss' by Rank, who cancelled a contract with Pascal for another picture. Strangely enough, a less literate version of those Egypto-Roman events would haunt the other bastion of Rank's film-making, Pinewood, a little less than 20 years on (see Chapter 7).

Deborah Kerr, as Sister Clodagh, lectures Kanchi (Jean Simmons) in *Black Narcissus*, Powell and Pressburger's tale of simmering sexuality behind convent walls.

The film-maker was censured by the

general council of technicians' union, ACT, and forbidden to function again, except under severe restrictions, on the floor of any British studio. Not surprisingly, he left England. Shortly before his death in 1954, he interested the song-writing partnership of Lerner and Loewe in the idea of a musical version of *Pygmalion*.

Meanwhile, as film-making resumed at Pinewood, with Launder and Gilliat's excellent thriller *Green for Danger*, starring Trevor Howard and Alastair Sim, 1946 also saw the Himalayas being constructed on the back lot.

John Mortimer recalls: 'One day at Pinewood studios I saw something other than the usual crowd of chippies, prop-men, directors, electricians and members of the Army and Air Force film units. There were not only the Boulting brothers in khaki and Richard Attenborough and Jack Clayton strangely dressed in air-force blue, and even Garson Kanin in American officer's uniform, but a number of visitors who looked even more remarkable. The canteen was full of nuns.

'As I queued up behind one particularly devout-looking sister for my plate of beans and bacon, she turned round and whispered, through a delicate cupid's bow of a mouth. "It's being a virgin that makes you so bloody hungry!" '

The nuns were extras in Powell and Pressburger's film of Rumer Godden's

Black Narcissus, which was set in India.

There was more spectacular construction for David Lean's *Oliver Twist* in 1947, the director's second successive adaptation of a Dickens novel following his successful *Great Expectations* a year earlier. Using much the same team of technicians, Lean decided to go ahead and shoot the opening sequences despite the fact that he had not secured his entire cast by the film's start-of-production date.

A country road and surrounding moorlands were recreated on Pinewood's biggest sound stage for the film's famous opening, in which Oliver's mother, babe in arms, struggles across the lowering landscape to the grim stone workhouse. Five thousand turves were used to help construct the site within a week.

One of the biggest headaches was the reconstruction of the workhouse itself. Production designer John Bryan was able to find little record of such structures – presumably because so many had been torn down as an unwelcome reminder of a darker age. However, many institutions were based on old army barracks, some converted from those used by Wellington's veterans, and so Bryan used these as his blueprint.

Below: confrontation between Bill Sikes (Robert Newton) and Fagin (Alec Guinness) in *Oliver Twist*. Anthony Newley, left, as the Artful Dodger, looks on. The film had its American release delayed by three years because of alleged anti-semitism and had to undergo some cuts.

The camera crew, led by cinematographer Guy Green, had a particularly tricky time as it aimed for some unusual angles. Using steep ladders and swaying gangways, the crew also moved about on catwalks suspended from the roof by 40-foot chains.

Space was further limited when, to provide greater apparent solidity, John Bryan installed ceilings on the rooms, so cramping the efforts of the cameramen. Every inch was valuable and lamps had to be supported on mantelpieces and chairs.

As *Oliver Twist* was filmed shortly after the war, many commodities, especially coal, were almost impossible to obtain, so the special effects department constructed a 30-foot wall behind which rice paper and smoke bombs were burned to make white and black smoke in a simulation of eight chimneys.

Unlike *Great Expectations*, which was weighed down with awards, including two Oscars (for Guy Green and John Bryan) from five nominations, *Oliver Twist* was merely a popular success. Its lack of trophies may have been a reflection of the problems the film had in getting an American showing. The censor there had alleged anti-semitism and it took three-and-a-half years and seven minutes of cuts (of 'offending' profiles and close-ups) before the film was screened in the USA.

When two Pinewood stalwarts, Cyril Howard – 45 years with Rank and current managing director of the studios – and Jerry Juroe, publicity chief for the *Bond* films, were recently asked, separately, to name one of their great early studio memories, both answered: 'Marilyn Monroe'.

Top left: Jean Simmons (Young Estella), Martita Hunt (Miss Havisham) and Anthony Wager (Young Pip) in *Great Expectations*; (far left), Kathleen Ryan and James Mason in *Odd Man Out*, Carol Reed's film of an IRA man on the run; (left), Kenneth More as Douglas Bader in *Reach for the Sky*.

Two examples of Rank 'issue' thrillers: a tender moment between Claire Bloom and Richard Johnson before they resume fighting a smallpox epidemic in *80,000 Suspects*; Dirk Bogarde and Donald Churchill in a key early scene from *Victim*, which bravely, for its time, tackled a homosexuality theme. Right: Marilyn Monroe, a vision of beauty in Laurence Olivier's *The Prince and the Showgirl*.

Howard: 'It was 1956, and Monroe and Olivier were making *The Prince and the Showgirl*. A pal and I had just come out of the cafeteria and were making our way along the long corridor when this beautiful creature started coming towards us. She was the sexiest lady I had ever seen. Marilyn gave us a big, beaming smile and my pal was so overcome he disappeared into the ladies' lavatory.'

Juroe was tramping round the back lot when he came across the facade of a building from which he saw Monroe leaning out across a balcony talking down to someone at street level below. The sight, he recalls, mobilised about 95 per cent of the studio workforce to muster around this particular set.

If, a critic once wrote, 'the British cinema had an immediately identifiable image, it would have been a shot of Kenneth More, jaw boldly jutting, on the bridge of a destroyer'. More was rather a latecomer to the Rank contract, having been snapped by Korda first for five years. During his Korda

The Ruislip Lido makes a convincing night-time double for the Atlantic in *A Night to Remember*.

years, however, he made Rank films, none to greater acclaim than *Reach for the Sky* (1956), in which he was second choice, after Richard Burton, to play the Second World War fighter pilot Douglas Bader.

Soon after this film, which was the top moneymaker of 1956 and also earned More the prestigious Picturegoer top-star-of-the-year award, the actor did indeed sign up for Rank, to make seven films in five years at £40,000 a picture.

First, and probably best, in the sequence was *A Night to Remember* (1958), Roy Baker's film of Walter Lord's bestseller about the sinking of the *Titanic*. More played Second Officer Lightoller, an heroic figure amid the catastrophe of the downfall of the 'unsinkable' liner.

Part of the *Titanic* was built in a field near Pinewood – about 300 feet long, and about half the size of a real ship. More, during filming, noted how this mock vessel, in the middle of the countryside, seemed to attract seagulls which, day in day out, would wheel endlessly around the 40-foot-high superstructure with its funnels and masts.

There was, however, no tank at Pinewood large enough to show survivors in the sea trying to climb on lifeboats. So cast, crew and extras adjourned to nearby Ruislip Lido for a 'night call' at 2 a.m. in mid-November. The producer, Bill MacQuitty, concerned about overtime and other costs, urged everyone into the murky waters. More was first 'overboard', and quickly wished he hadn't been. The bitter cold and the dirt almost overwhelmed him. But before he could halt the lemming-like rush, 'the rest were in swimming around me, shouting and cursing with the agony of coldness. We struck out for the boats as though we were really shipwrecked, struggling and kicking anyone who got in our way. We weren't acting. We were desperate to be rescued. There were eight lifeboats, which would carry about 64 each. This meant that more than 500 men and women in overcoats and fur coats were thrashing about in the lido for quite a long time before they could haul themselves aboard the boats.'

So much for the 'magic' of the movies . . . reality has a way of intruding upon it from time to time.

The Gong Men

The famous trademark of a muscle-bound man banging a gong at the beginning of every Rank film was originally dreamed up by the publicity manageress of General Film Distributors (GFD) in 1935. C.M. Woolf, who had started the company when he broke away from Gaumont-British, first thought, not surprisingly, of having a wolf as his logo, rather in the manner of the MGM lion. A photographer was despatched to London Zoo to audition one contender, but the vulpine subject looked so mangy that Woolf rapidly went off the idea.

Enter Bombadier Billy Wells, or 'Beautiful Billy', as he was known to an adoring British public. Wells was a sporting idol who had become boxing's British heavyweight champion in 1911 when he beat Iron Hague. He reigned until 1919, when eventually he lost to Joe Beckett. Wells learnt to box in the army, where he beat five men within the distance. He had a magnificent physique and charm to match. Often middle-class ladies, clad in their splendid evening gowns, would be found sitting at ringside. They had no idea about the Noble Art; they came merely to ogle 'Beautiful Billy'.

He was also a schoolboy hero and used to preach to the youth, 'the best men are always the best-behaved'. They would follow his fortunes in the papers and cram the packed auditoria wherever Wells fought. When the perceptive GFD employee had her brainwave, Wells was the natural candidate. He was filmed for posterity at Walton Hall Studios in Isleworth.

A year after he started beating the gong for the film company, Wells began his own career in front of the camera appearing, briefly, in such films as *Can You Hear Me, Mother?*, *Beloved Impostor*, *Find the Lady*, *Melody in My Heart*, *Double Alibi*, *Concerning Mr Martin*, *Make-Up*, *The Day Will Dawn*, *Happidrome*, *Old Mother Riley* and *The Beggar's Opera*. His boxing fortunes were to be more mixed. Journalists wrote of him, 'He was the Henry Irving of the ring who rarely made us laugh but frequently made us sob.'

After the Second World War, it was felt that Wells, standing for the symbol which now appeared on all Rank films, should be replaced. After deliberation worthy of selecting a successor for Pope, the powers-that-be settled on hunky Phil Nieman, who stayed 'in office' until 1955 and helped to usher in the era of widescreen and Technicolor. His moment of history was recorded at Gainsborough Studios, Shepherd's Bush.

Nieman's replacement was another fine athlete, Ken Richmond. Richmond, who had competed in the 1952 Olympic Games in Helsinki (where he won a wrestling bronze) and the Empire (now Common-

Former Olympic athlete Ken Richmond is still seen today as the Man with the Gong.

wealth) Games, has now enjoyed more than 30 years as Rank's 'front man', following his successful screen test at Pinewood in the mid-'fifties. There might have been a fourth member of this illustrious group. When Rank briefly revived its film production 'arm' in 1978, it was decided that a new torso should be selected for the logo. Blond, bronzed Martin Grace, one of filmland's most courageous stuntmen – he doubled for Roger Moore in the *Bond* films as well as negotiating the trickier situations in those hair-raising *Milk Tray* advertisements on television – was the choice and was, apparently, filmed. However, it seems that he is just another face on the cutting-room floor.

In reality, none of this male pulchritude and strength were ever needed to beat the gong, because it is actually made of plaster and paper. To create the illusion, Rank employed the services of the leading percussionist James Blades, who utilised a Chinese tam-tam to provide the reverberations. Blades used the same instrument to record the sounds from 1935 to 1978, in which year he renewed the three-foot-diameter instrument after a mere 43 years of use.

Rank's colourful years 1

An unusual angle on a spectacular duelling scene from Powell and Pressburger's *The Life and Death of Colonel Blimp*.

'Cry God for Harry . . .' Laurence Olivier leads from the front as Shakespeare's Henry V.

A great ballerina in action: Moira Shearer performs in Powell and Pressburger's *The Red Shoes*.

Wilfrid Hyde-White, Ronald Squire, Jane Griffiths and Gregory Peck in *The Million Pound Note*.

Joan Greenwood, Michael Redgrave, Dorothy Tutin and Michael Denison are observed imperiously by Edith Evans as Lady Bracknell in *The Importance of Being Earnest*.

MISTRESS OF THE MANOR . . .
BUT LOVER OF THE RAGGED GYPSY
THE RANK ORGANISATION PRESENTS
MELINA MERCOURI
KEITH MICHELL
FLORA ROBSON
The GYPSY and the GENTLEMAN
A
Also Starring
PATRICK McGOOHAN
JUNE LAVERICK
in EASTMAN COLOUR
LYNDON BROOK
Screenplay by JANET GREEN
Produced by MAURICE COWAN
Directed by JOSEPH LOSEY

TO KISS OR TO KILL?
JOHN MILLS · JOHN McCALLUM
ELIZABETH SELLARS · EVA BERGH
The LONG MEMORY
A
From the Novel by HOWARD CLEWES
Screenplay by ROBERT HAMER & FRANK HARVEY
Directed by ROBERT HAMER Produced by HUGH STEWART
A EUROPA FILM
GFD

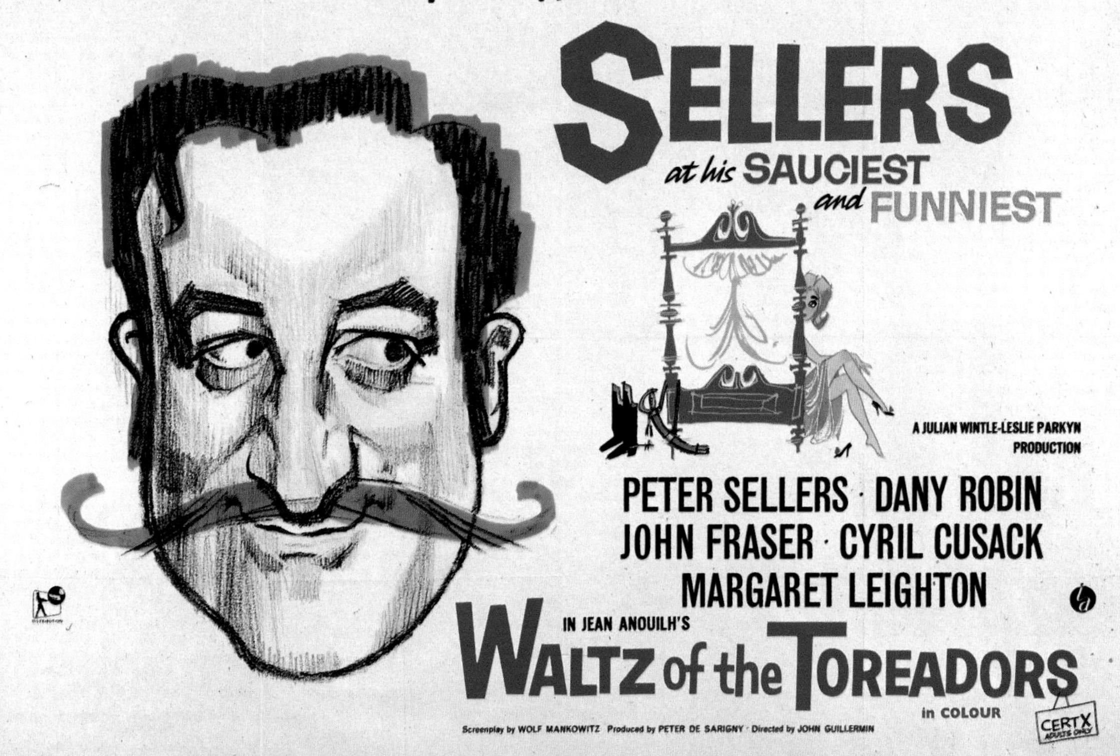
"Goodness Gracious they've slapped an 'X' certificate on me memoirs!"
SELLERS
at his SAUCIEST
and FUNNIEST
A JULIAN WINTLE-LESLIE PARKYN PRODUCTION
PETER SELLERS · DANY ROBIN
JOHN FRASER · CYRIL CUSACK
MARGARET LEIGHTON
IN JEAN ANOUILH'S
WALTZ of the TOREADORS
in COLOUR
Screenplay by WOLF MANKOWITZ Produced by PETER DE SARIGNY · Directed by JOHN GUILLERMIN
CERT X
ADULTS ONLY

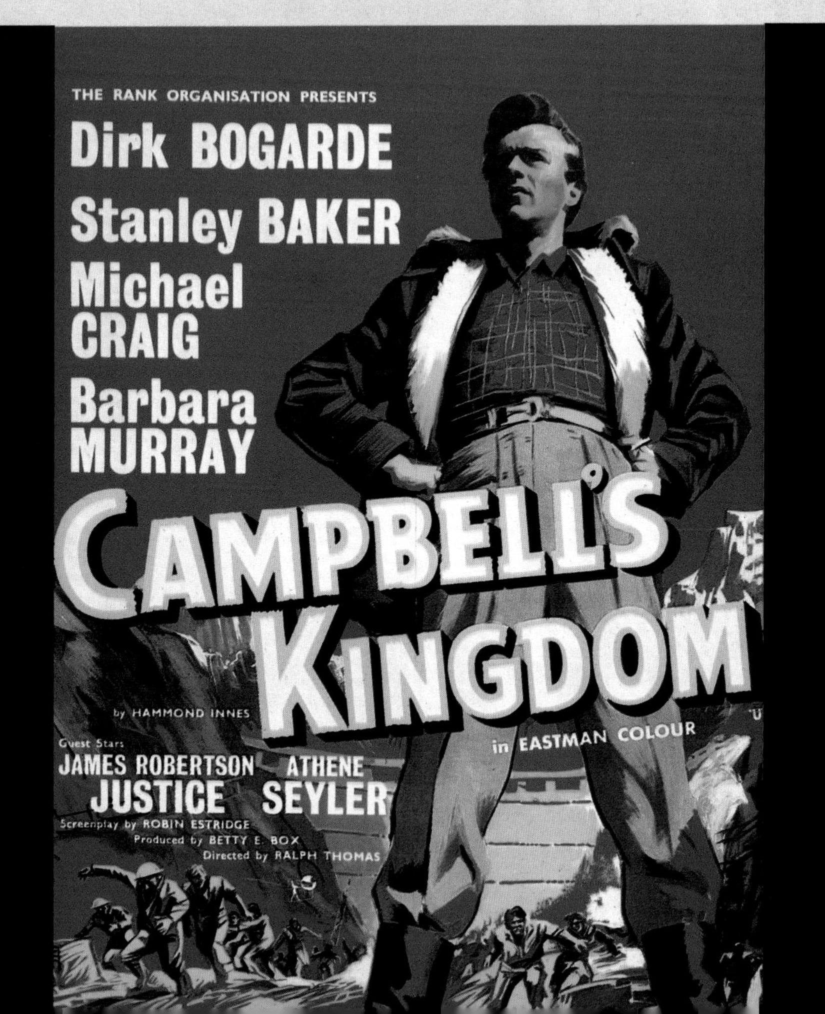
THE RANK ORGANISATION PRESENTS
Dirk BOGARDE
Stanley BAKER
Michael CRAIG
Barbara MURRAY
CAMPBELL'S KINGDOM
by HAMMOND INNES
in EASTMAN COLOUR
Guest Stars
JAMES ROBERTSON JUSTICE
ATHENE SEYLER
Screenplay by ROBIN ESTRIDGE
Produced by BETTY E. BOX
Directed by RALPH THOMAS

Shirley Eaton, as Milly Groaker, captures the attention of medical student Simon Sparrow, played by Dirk Bogarde, in *Doctor in the House*.

Dirk Bogarde and Yoko Tani in a romantic interlude from *The Wind Cannot Read*.

John Gregson, as Captain Bell, helps lead the assault on the German pocket battleship *Graf Spee* in Powell and Pressburger's *The Battle of the River Plate*.

A tempestuous scene from *The Gypsy and the Gentleman* with Patrick McGoohan and Melina Mercouri.

Far-Eastern confrontation (in *Ferry to Hong Kong*) between Noel Purcell, Curt Jurgens and (right) Orson Welles.

Hayley Mills was 14 and already an established cinema star by the time she was pictured here, with woolly friend, in *Whistle Down the Wind*.

Stealing the thunder in *North West Frontier* from more established stars such as Kenneth More and Lauren Bacall was this glorious turn-of-the-century locomotive.

1 2 3 4 5 6 7 8 9 10 11 12

13

14 15

Directors from the 'fifties:
1 Julian Amyes
2 Ken Annakin
3 Anthony Asquith
4 Roy Baker
5 John Paddy Carstairs
6 Basil Dearden
7 Clive Donner
8 Cy Endfield
9 Lewis Gilbert
10 Brian Desmond Hurst
11 Philip Leacock
12 Jack Lee
13 Joseph Losey
14 Ronald Neame
15 Ralph Thomas

CHAPTER 3

King Gong

The Archers' Target

By the early 1940s, Mr Rank was pretty much master of all he surveyed on the film horizon. He owned two of the main cinema circuits, a principal distribution company and a clutch of studios. All he needed now was a flow of quality product – but at a time when gathering war clouds were casting enormous uncertainty over Britain's future.

Michael Balcon, who had arrived at Ealing studios in 1938 via Gaumont-British and MGM, was trying to provide some continuity of film-making, and there were the odd pockets of resistance at Shepherd's Bush and Welwyn. Rank, with the profits of *Pygmalion* still tinkling pleasantly, was determined to make an all-out assault on British film production.

Under J. Arthur Rank was to evolve, according to Alan Wood, 'a system of film-making which was completely novel at the time. He gave a free hand to the men who knew how to make films and allowed producers and directors to make them as they liked. This, surprisingly enough, was something which had not been done in Britain for many years.

'As a general rule films were being made not according to the wishes of creative artists, but according to the wishes of the middle-men of Wardour Street – the big distributors who earn the highest possible salaries by taking the lowest possible view of the public's intelligence and taste; who lunch at Claridges or the Dorchester, go back to their offices smoking big cigars and then proceed to lay down the law about what the man in the one-and-sixpenny seats wants.'

The trailblazer for this new initiative was another extraordinary foreigner – as Pascal had been – called Filippo Del Giudice, fondly known as 'Del' by all those who came to know the Italian lawyer, a refugee from Mussolini's fascism who had ended up in London teaching their native tongue to

Previous page: Trevor Howard and Celia Johnson in an atmospheric scene from *Brief Encounter*.

the English-speaking sons of Soho's Italian waiters.

'Del' started up Two Cities Films in 1937 and, with backing jointly from friends and Paramount, produced *French Without Tears*, with Ray Milland, which was directed by 'Puffin' Asquith. After war was declared, the producer was interned and when, four months later, he came back to civilisation, his film company was defunct. Yet, a year on, he had not only revived Two Cities but also managed to persuade the ever-popular Noel Coward to make a film for him based on the wartime experiences of the Master's great chum, Lord Louis Mountbatten.

In Which We Serve (1942) was not only written, produced, co-directed and scored – all conditions laid down by the Master – but also starred Coward himself in a thinly disguised impersonation of Mountbatten. Most of *Spotlight* were in it too, from the dependable John Mills and Bernard Miles to young Richard Attenborough, making

Above: inspired by the story of Lord Louis Mountbatten's wartime naval exploits in HMS *Kelly*, *In Which We Serve* was the tale of a destroyer from its building to its torpedoing. Noel Coward, writer and co-director, can be seen far right. Richard Attenborough (left) made his film début as a cowardly stoker.

his film-acting début as the cowardly stoker.

Coward's co-director, also making his top-flight bow, was David Lean, former clapper boy, cutting-room assistant and editor, who together with the associate producer, Anthony Havelock-Allan, and cinematographer Ronald Neame would form his own company directly sponsored by Rank, Cineguild, following a couple more Coward-Two Cities collaborations, *This Happy Breed* and *Blithe Spirit*.

Although *In Which We Serve* was filmed at Denham, it was not financed by Rank, owing to earlier reservations expressed by C.M. Woolf about the project's rising budget. At £180,000, he was unsure it could recoup and passed. Rank rivals British Lion took the film on, belatedly, for distribution. Woolf's concern was probably justified, as the film ended up costing £240,000. Fortunately, it proved a popular hit both in Britain and America and the story ended happily for Rank with GFD securing a deal with Two Cities to finance its future production programme, and later taking over the distribution and ownership of *In Which We Serve*.

If *In Which We Serve* stirred audiences in the grim, backs-to-the-wall, early days of the war, Shakespeare's *Henry V* proved just what was needed to revive the flagging morale of a nation moving into the fourth year of hostilities with no apparent end in sight.

Backed by 'Del' and Two Cities/Rank, *Henry V* seemed a singular triumph for Laurence Olivier, who not only – like Coward – produced, directed and co-adapted the piece, but also starred as the warrior king. In fact, Olivier was only his own fourth choice for director, having failed to woo William Wyler, Terence Young and Carol Reed.

Apart from its great propaganda value – the stirring speeches were wonderfully timely – the film's major creative triumph was the manner in which it 'opened out' a stage-bound play. With Denham studios doubling as Elizabethan London, the action starts first in the Globe Theatre for what seems to be a contemporary performance of the play. Suddenly, in a magical transformation, the camera passes through the proscenium, into the heart of the very sets themselves and then out to real exteriors.

When a thousand arrows flash high over the field of 'Agincourt', the scene is in fact far distant from Denham – we actually see the fields of Lord Powerscourt's estate at Enniskerry, near Dublin, where legions of neutral Irishmen did stout service as period extras.

While Two Cities smacked of something rather international, certainly continental, Gainsborough could not have been anything but solidly British, with its connotations of

old houses and portraiture. Before the war Gainsborough Pictures, part of Gaumont-British, with studios at Shepherd's Bush and Islington, was most associated with the Aldwych film farces, starring Tom Walls, Ralph Lynn and Robertson Hare, and Will Hay comedies such as *Oh, Mr Porter*, *Convict 99* and *Old Bones of the River*. Hitchcock's *The Lady Vanishes* and Carol Reed's *Bank Holiday* were rare, if classic, exceptions to this comic rule.

Under the continuing guidance of Edward Black, from the showbusiness family that also spawned the entrepreneurs George and Alfred Black, Gainsborough kept the wartime mixture pretty much as before – comedy from Arthur Askey, Tommy Handley and the Crazy Gang, and topical dramas like *Cottage to Let*, *Uncensored* and *We Dive at Dawn*, all of which were directed by the versatile 'Puffin' Asquith.

Gainsborough (which came under Rank's

Three glimpses of Gainsborough costume melodrama: (far left), Stewart Granger intervenes as wicked James Mason threatens Phyllis Calvert in *Fanny by Gaslight*; (left), Felix Aylmer and Margaret Lockwood in a peaceful moment from the otherwise roistering *The Wicked Lady*; (above), James Mason as *The Man in Grey*,

aegis with the acquisition of Gaumont-British) then made, in 1943, a box-office blockbuster most appropriate to the resonances of the company name, *The Man in Grey*, a Regency-set melodrama which starred Margaret Lockwood, James Mason, Stewart Granger and Phyllis Calvert, whose star status was confirmed in this and subsequent costume romps such as *Hungry Hill*, *Jassy* and, most notoriously, *The Wicked Lady*.

Of *The Man in Grey*, which also contained a rather strange present-day linking device, a prologue and epilogue featuring a Jamaican pilot and a Wren, *Time* wrote that it had 'all the time-tested materials: gypsy fortune-teller; scowling, black-browed villain; gushy diary kept by a doe-eyed girl who munches candied violets; fire-breathing adventuress who dotes on discord and low-cut-gowns . . .'

Décolletage was also the order of the day

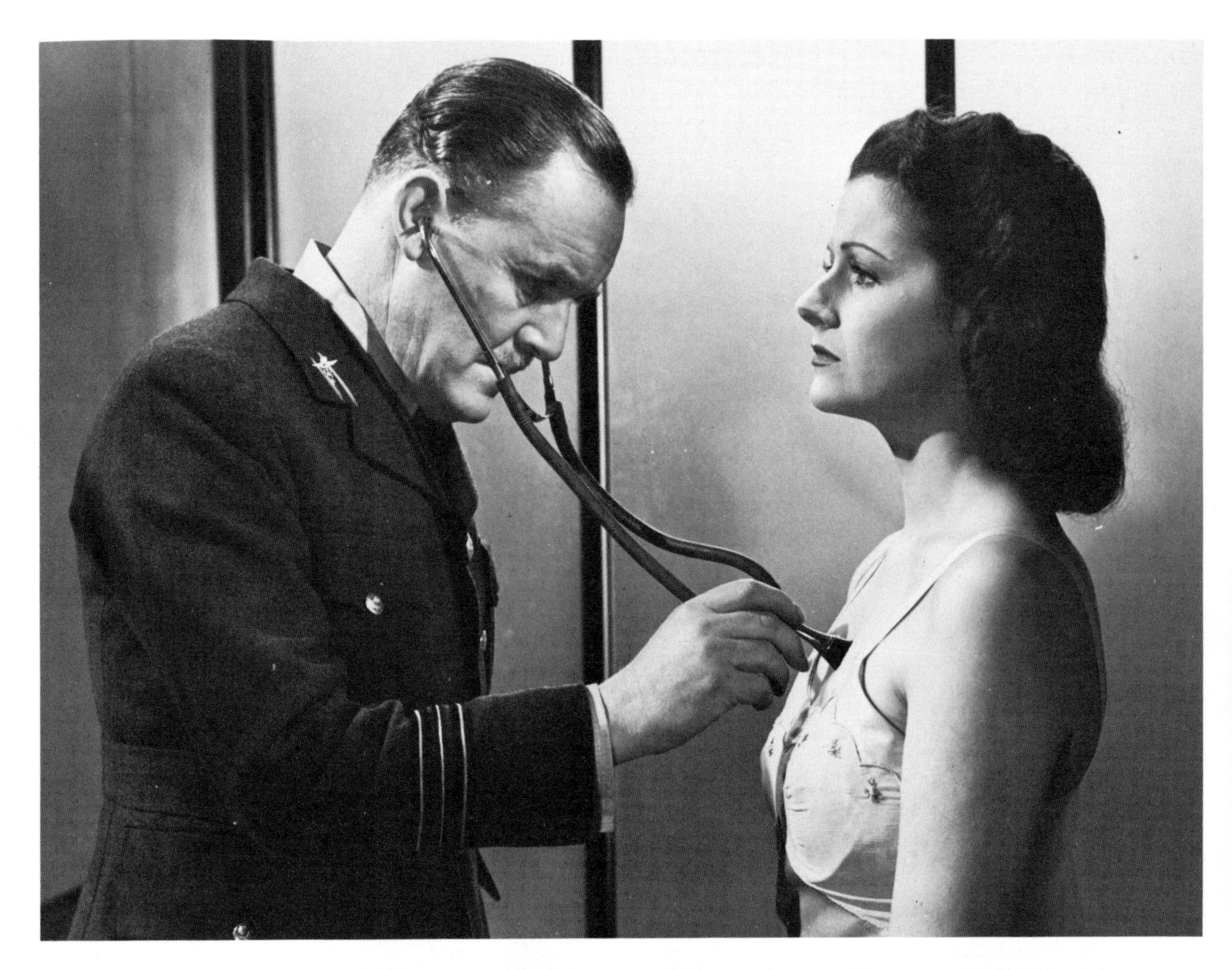

Above: Margaret Lockwood tries to put a brave face on bad news from the doctor in *Love Story*; (right), there's life after work in a munitions factory as Patricia Roc prepares to go out in *Millions Like Us*.

in *The Wicked Lady*. Miss Lockwood, a murderous husband-stealer in the first film, now became a highwaywoman, with a neckline as low as her morals: so low, in fact, that a good deal of it had to be re-shot for sensitive American audiences.

In 1946, the year she signed a new seven-year contract for Rank, Miss Lockwood replaced Greer Garson as Britain's favourite female star. That same year, the critic Milton Shulman, writing in the *Evening Standard*, cited Lockwood, Phyllis Calvert, Patricia Roc and Jean Kent – who had claimed all the major female roles between them – and declared he could find five girls as pretty and talented by watching the secretaries get off the escalators at Leicester Square Underground station.

Perhaps it was their very down-to-earthness, stranded in plots wilder than those of any Mills & Boon novel, which gave these actresses such a popular following. The presence of the likes of James Mason, Stewart Granger and Dennis Price was, however, never questioned and certainly did not hurt the box office.

When criticism came, its source was none other than Mason, who after all his wartime hits left for the States with a broadside at Rank himself, saying, 'He is the worst thing that has happened to the British picture industry. Rank has so much money from his flour-milling business that he has been able to move in and absorb the whole industry.

'He makes the mistake of buying markets to expand his empire and he does not seem to care how much it costs. He has no apparent talent for cinema or showmanship. He surrounds himself with a lot of quaint folk who know nothing about the creative side of film-making.'

Sidney Gilliat, son of a Fleet Street editor, first came across his future partner, Frank Launder, writing titles for a silent film of Launder's novel *Under the Greenwood Tree*. Later they met and collaborated as scriptwriters at Gainsborough where, under Edward Black, they wrote *The Lady Vanishes* and *Night Train to Munich*.

After joining forces to write and direct *Millions Like Us* – well, like Patricia Roc, Gordon Jackson and Eric Portman, to name but three – Launder and Gilliat alternated on writer-director assignments, with *Two Thousand Women* (Launder), about the inmates of a concentration camp, and *Waterloo Road* (Gilliat), which pitched gutsy John Mills against bounder Stewart Granger on the home front.

The duo then, logically, and with their own outfit Individual, slid in under the banner of a newly established company, Independent Producers Ltd. which seemed to encapsulate all of Rank's creative 'free-hand' ideals. At IP they joined Michael Powell and Emeric Pressburger (see page 52) and were joined by the aforementioned Cineguild and Wessex (Ian Dalrymple). It was a powerful, prestigious and, above all, money-making line-up of talents.

It also gained the indirect adjunct of Michael Balcon's Ealing Films. To survive after the war, Balcon needed a proper distribution/exhibition outlet. He had tried his own operation without much success and so, swallowing his pride – Balcon had been noisily critical of Rank's massive film influence – he made a deal with the big boys.

In fact, it was a good arrangement for Balcon. Rank gave him a guaranteed outlet and also financed 75 per cent of the cost of each film. Balcon even kept total autonomy, as well as having a seat on the Rank board. There would be 56 films under the tie-up and although it was not to prove, in the long term, a financial success for Rank – indeed, quite substantial losses were accumulated – some of Britain's best post-war pictures resulted, among them *The Blue Lamp*, *The Cruel Sea*, *Hue and Cry*, *Kind Hearts and*

Coronets, *The Lavender Hill Mob* and *The Ladykillers*.

Just as, towards the end of the 'forties, everything was looking rather rosy for Rank, the blow fell. It came in the wake of an *ad valorem* duty imposed by the Labour government on the export of American films to Britain, apparently devised to deal with the hard currency shortage, which limited the profit revenue that could go to America. The Americans retaliated with a complete embargo on their films to Britain.

With thousands of cinemas housing blank screens – American films were then as now the staple diet of British exhibition – Rank was urged to pour millions more into production 'in the national interest'. Then, having persuaded Rank to spend a fortune, the government double-crossed the industry and made a deal with the Americans. The upshot was that a six-month backlog of American films poured on to the market just as Rank's 'sausage machine' was beginning to turn.

It was a financial catastrophe for Rank – one which opened the door for an important new name in the company story, that of John Davis.

A London-based accountant, Davis had come into the fold via Odeon Theatres and for a while remained solely on the cinemas side. His worth as a single-minded money-man swiftly impressed Rank and soon Davis started having a say in production. At this time of crisis, Davis was managing director and, ever a critic of what he saw as extravagance and waste, had *carte blanche* to pare down the company in its struggle against possible ruin.

The film-maker teams were the first to go, followed by the sale of Lime Grove studios to the BBC; Highbury was shut and two more recent experiments, *This Modern Age* (an attempt to produce a British version of America's famous *March of Time* documentaries) and GB Animation (training

a new bedrock of British animators), were aborted. There were the inevitable redundancies and even a compulsory executive salary cut.

As well as fashioning a new, streamlined Rank for the post-war austerity (the all-embracing company name of the Rank Organisation appeared in 1953), Davis, amid a torrent of opposition and critical flak, also masterminded the combining of the Gaumont and Odeon cinema circuits into one mighty chain.

Left: Rank imported American director Wesley Ruggles to try to take on Hollywood at its own musical game with *London Town*, starring Sid Field, Greta Gynt and Petula Clark. It was a resounding flop. Above: Mr Rank on the set of *The History of Mr Polly* with producer-star John Mills.

Always elegant, with carnation in buttonhole, Davis, later Sir John (Rank himself was finally ennobled in 1957 and died in 1972), seemed to have created an atmosphere of fear and loathing as he revived the fortunes of the Organisation. Arrogant, ruthless, often plain rude, he used to live at the Dorchester Hotel during the week and, after lunch on Fridays, would make what became a dreaded sortie back into the office before leaving for the weekend.

Employees and colleagues summoned to his presence had to walk all of 40 paces to his desk as he railed about some alleged ineptitude, and nobody got the last word with Davis.

Michael Balcon, who finally had to sell his precious studios to the BBC in 1955, resisted Davis's suggestion to move into Pinewood (where all Rank production was now based). He regarded Davis as an upstart – or, according to one insider, 'an accounts clerk who had been in the right place at the right time'.

The Archers' Target

A stairway reaching across the universe from Heaven to Earth . . . two nuns locked in a terrifying struggle on the edge of a precipice high in the Himalayas . . . an hysterical dancer carried to her death by her red ballet shoes. All these images stay with filmgoers long after they have seen the films in question.

Yet, perhaps the single most enduring image of the Michael Powell and Emeric Pressburger partnership is the emblem of their production company, the Archers: an arrow thudding into a red, white and blue target, which appeared at the start of their films.

It was an emblem which promised real film magic, something these two men delivered in movie after movie during their 18-year collaboration.

First brought together by Korda on *The Spy in Black* in 1938, Powell, Kent-born but film-educated in France during the 'twenties, and Pressburger, a Hungarian who had written scripts for the German studio UFA, immediately gelled as a team.

After stepping in to save the wartime propaganda film *49th Parallel* when Ministry of Information money ran short of completion, Rank went on to back Powell and Pressburger's next film, *One of Our Aircraft Is Missing*. When it was completed, Rank met with them and made a remarkable offer: he would provide finance through a new company, Independent Producers, and guarantee distribution, while allowing them complete creative control over their productions.

The arrangement, an extraordinary one for the time, reflects great credit on Rank for providing security and creative freedom for two gifted film-makers. It would also result in a group of the most imaginative films ever to be produced in Britain.

First out was *The Life and Death of Colonel Blimp*, with Anton Walbrook, Deborah Kerr and Roger Livesey. The message of the film was that the Second World War simply could not be fought according to 'the rules' and that 'Blimps' were out of touch.

It was heavily cut at the time of its initial release and also the subject of considerable controversy when Churchill tried to have it banned (he'd tried originally to stop its production) on the grounds that it revived the whole idea of a Blimpish army officer.

The sympathetic – and undoubtedly realistic – presentation of the main German character also contributed to government doubts about the movie. But the furore surrounding it only made it more intriguing to the public, who were enticed by cinemas to 'see the banned film'.

The film also marked the appearance of that famous Archers' credit line, 'written, produced and directed by Michael Powell and Emeric Pressburger'. Traditional distinctions between the various duties seemed meaningless in their case because of the closeness of the teamwork.

Mysticism and a weird and wonderful feeling for English and Scottish landscapes suffused their next two films – *A Canterbury Tale* and *I Know Where I'm Going* – but it was *A Matter of Life and Death* (1946) which, for many, marked the zenith of their technical achievement.

Originally inspired by a government request for a film to improve Anglo-American relations, it starred David Niven, Kim Hunter and Roger Livesey in a fantasy about a bomber pilot who falls out of a burning plane and miraculously survives.

Alternating, daringly, between black and white and colour, the story takes the airman to Heaven itself, up the famous stairway, where he stands trial to put his case for life. The film was chosen as the first-ever Royal Film Performance.

In *Black Narcissus*, a film about repressed nuns, the Himalayas had to be reconstructed on Pinewood's back lot. A trip had to be made to Kew Gardens, too, for the exotic scenery at the end of the picture. The film also marked the Archers' first connection with the gifted composer Brian Easdale, who wrote music for the climactic scenes *before* they were shot. The film-makers then choreographed the action to fit the mounting hysteria of the music.

Ask many famous dancers what influenced them most in choosing their art, and they will answer, '*The Red Shoes*', which mixed a heady brew of fantasy and reality in its tale of a young ballerina (Moira Shearer) torn between two men (Anton Walbrook and Marius Goring).

The film was a powerful fusion of many talents and also proved to be extremely expensive with locations in France and sets, such as one for Covent Garden Opera House, built at Pinewood. The original budget had doubled by the end of shooting and Rank's accountants were horrified.

When the film was first screened for Rank himself, and John Davis, both were convinced they had 'lost their shirts'. Indeed, the film was a flop on its first short release.

But in the true tradition of a fairy tale, *The Red Shoes* ultimately turned out to be

Michael Powell and Emeric Pressburger at work in their heyday; (bottom), Anton Walbrook, Deborah Kerr and Roger Livesey in *The Life and Death of Colonel Blimp*.

one of Rank's greatest commercial successes all round the world.

Sadly, the gulf between Rank's perception of the film and the intentions of Powell and Pressburger inevitably led to a parting of the ways, though there was a return to the company in the mid-'fifties for the last of the Archers' true collaborations, *The Battle of the River Plate* (with Anthony Quayle, Ian Hunter and, in a typically unclichéd portrayal of a German officer, Peter Finch as captain of the doomed *Graf Spee*), and another, rather dull, war story, *Ill Met by Moonlight*, with Dirk Bogarde.

For reasons that have never been made clear, Powell and Pressburger decided to separate after the last film. Powell went on to make the much-reviled *Peeping Tom*, which effectively finished his career in Britain. Pressburger wrote some scripts and novels, but his work never rose to its previous heights.

There have, however, been a series of touching postscripts to their fertile career together. Powell has become a much-revered figure to a younger generation of American film-makers, including Francis Ford Coppola and Martin Scorsese, while the two of them have been regularly accorded worldwide industry honours and tributes.

The Archers clearly found their target.

Three examples of the Archers' art: (left), Marius Goring, Moira Shearer and Anton Walbrook in *The Red Shoes*; (top), John Chandos, Leslie Howard and Eric Portman in *49th Parallel*; (above), Roger Livesey addresses a heavenly court in *A Matter of Life and Death*.

Five of the most popular Ealing films: (top), Christopher Lee, James Robertson Justice, John Gregson and Kenneth More are the most familiar faces in this scene from *Scott of the Antarctic*; (above), Peter Sellers and Danny Green placate Katie Johnson, with Alex Guinness hovering out of sight in *The Ladykillers*; (top right), Frederick Piper, Raymond Huntley, John Slater, Barbara Murray and Stanley Holloway in *Passport to Pimlico*; (middle right), six guises of Alec Guinness in *Kind Hearts and Coronets*; (right), Stanley Holloway, Alec Guinness, Alfie Bass and Sid James come up with solid gold Eiffel Towers in *The Lavender Hill Mob*.

CHAPTER 4

Charm School

The Image Maker

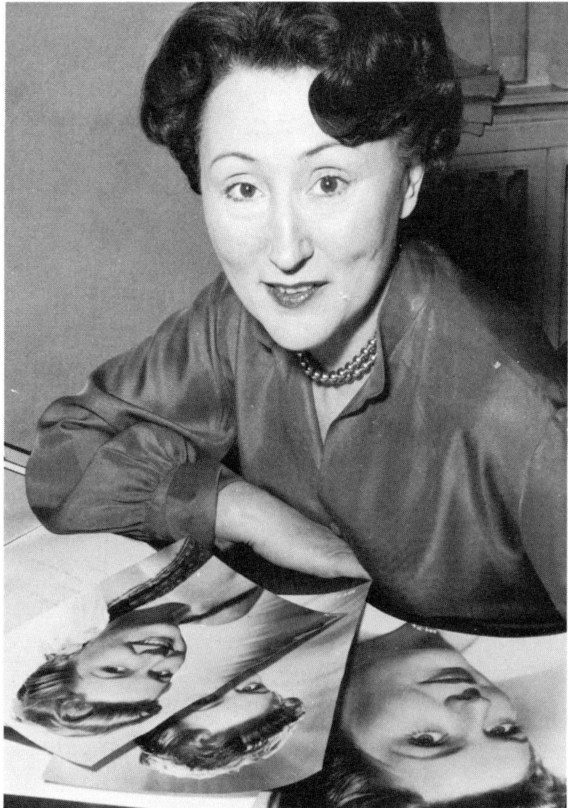

Previous page: Virginia McKenna and Dirk Bogarde in a Mau-Mau drama, *Simba*; (top), Rank charmers Susan Beaumont, Donald Sinden and Belinda Lee arrive for a West End première; (left), Olive Dodds, with stills of Susan Beaumont, in her time as director of artists; (above), Belinda Lee and a very young Richard O'Sullivan in *Dangerous Exile*.

A page full of Rank contract artists' snapshots in Pinewood Studios' glossy 21st-anniversary brochure, dated 30 September 1957, provides readers with a fascinating cross-section of the British film industry.

The men, invariably with that Brylcreemed look, are either pretty, like Dirk Bogarde, David McCallum, Keith Michell, David Knight and Ronald Lewis; macho, in the manner of Stanley Baker, Patrick McGoohan, Tony Wright and Peter Finch; or simply solid, such as John Gregson, Kenneth More and Eric Portman.

The women are sensuous, like Diana Dors, Belinda Lee, Maureen Swanson, Anne Heywood and Kay Kendall; or gamine (Jean Carson or Virginia McKenna); others were plain homely, like Susan Beaumont, June Laverick and Muriel Pavlow. There are more than 30 faces in all (many of their owners now sadly dead), from the still-active (Donald Sinden) to the who-she? (Beth Rogan).

In the fifteen years between the end of the Second World War and the late 'fifties, when the system was finally wound down, Rank kept a 'star' roster of (at its zenith) some 70 contracted artists: a veritable A–Z, from Jill Adams to Mai Zetterling.

David Henley, a former general secretary of Equity and, later, agent with the mighty Myron Selznick office, was taken on by Rank in the mid-1940s to be director of artists – with particular responsibility for finding new acting talent. The Organisation wanted to put artists under contract in the Hollywood manner.

The newcomers would be in the Rank 'family', part of a prized Company of Youth, a set-up which the fascinated press swiftly dubbed the 'Charm School'.

And there *was* a 'school', as such, established at Rank's experimental Highbury studio. Run by drama coach Molly Terraine, with expert assistance from Helen Goss, it trained its pupils in everything from voice production to fencing.

In 1945 Olive Dodds, later to become director of artists herself, joined Henley as his assistant. On her own admission, she did not know much about films, but came into the business on the insistence of Bernard Miles, to whom she had given invaluable help during the making of his *Tawny Pipit* (1944) while she was working in PR for the Ministry of Agriculture.

At this time, domestic cinema-going was enjoying an all-time high (more than 30 million admissions a *week*) and British artists were enormous crowd-pullers. The great Gainsborough names – Margaret Lockwood, Stewart Granger, James Mason, Phyllis Calvert, Patricia Roc and Dennis Price – virtually guaranteed box office.

Mrs Dodds recalls: 'Rank's design was, I think, to harness as many of the confirmed star players as would fit into the spread of filmscripts then either waiting to be made or being discussed and developed; and, in addition, to look for new young players or personalities who could be helped to develop into a new, additional line-up of box-office, or at least well-known supporting, artists. In those days, all box-office draws were either romantic leads or star comedians. Very rarely did character actors prove to be box office at that time.

'There were very few drama schools and there were certainly no local government grants to help promising youngsters with the fees. Hence the idea of the Company of Youth.'

One of its earliest 'pupils' was 16-year-old Diana Dors (née Fluck), platinum-blonde, buxom and a sight for sore eyes as she swung down Knightsbridge clad in the late-1940s equivalent of hot pants and a revealing off-the-shoulder blouse. Mrs Dodds, driving by in a taxi, was horrified to see the teenager carrying a brown paper bag full of cherries, the stones of which she was casu-

ally spitting into the street. This wasn't at all good for the image. Young ladies of the Charm School didn't do that sort of thing. A gentle reprimand followed.

Mrs Dodds, described by Dirk Bogarde, who was contracted as a star from his very first film, *Esther Waters*, in 1947, as 'a bright-eyed, slender little woman . . . who looked rather like a blackbird with a hat and veil', was also characterised by the actor as a person who 'would part the thorns and brambles and strangling vines, suggest new tracks, new directions, when to move, when to lie low'.

Today, still bright-eyed if not as dark-haired as a 'blackbird', Mrs Dodds describes how she had to combine being an 'agony aunt' with 'a hot number at contracts'. The latter were, undoubtedly, 'slave' contracts, though, as Mrs Dodds points out, 'No one put a gun at your back. In those early days, people used to beat a path to the door to get one.

'The minimum fee was £20 a week for 52 weeks a year whether you worked or not: seven-year contracts with options every year renewable on the company's side only. There were extras too, like having your hair done and teeth straightened.

'If you brought the Organisation into

Far left: Kenneth More, who signed for Rank after a Korda contract, has villain Herbert Lom at his mercy in *North West Frontier*; (above), Lord and Lady Rank with Anne Heywood at the première of the actress's *Violent Playground*.

disrepute, it could suspend the contract and you'd not be allowed to work. In fact, we very rarely suspended people. Things like illness and babies were different. The company was surprisingly sentimental about babies.

'Then there was the "loan-out" system. Another company might ring up and ask if one of our artists was free. If we hadn't a film for them, I could go to the board – which then consisted of John Davis, Sydney Box, Michael Balcon, Earl St John and Rank himself – and get its permission. We were entitled to 50 per cent of the profits on a sub-let, but, quite often, the board wouldn't let an artist go. We also had arrangements with theatre companies at Worthing, Bromley and Tunbridge Wells so that some of the younger actors could get proper experience.'

Joan Collins, 'Britain's Bad Girl' as she was quickly dubbed by the press, was a sultry 20-year-old when signed up by Rank after a £30-a-week stint, and one film (*I Believe in You*), at Ealing. She began her seven-year contract on the grander sum of £50 a week but then proceeded to be loaned out much more often than being used in-house.

When the chance arose of her starring as Juliet opposite Laurence Harvey in a Rank Italian co-production of *Romeo and Juliet*, Joan found that her looks were fatally against her. 'You will havva the nose job,' the director, Renato Castellani, told her. 'Julietta she hassa the Roman nose – you havva the nose it goes up – is not aristocratic.' She declined surgery, even in the cause of the Bard.

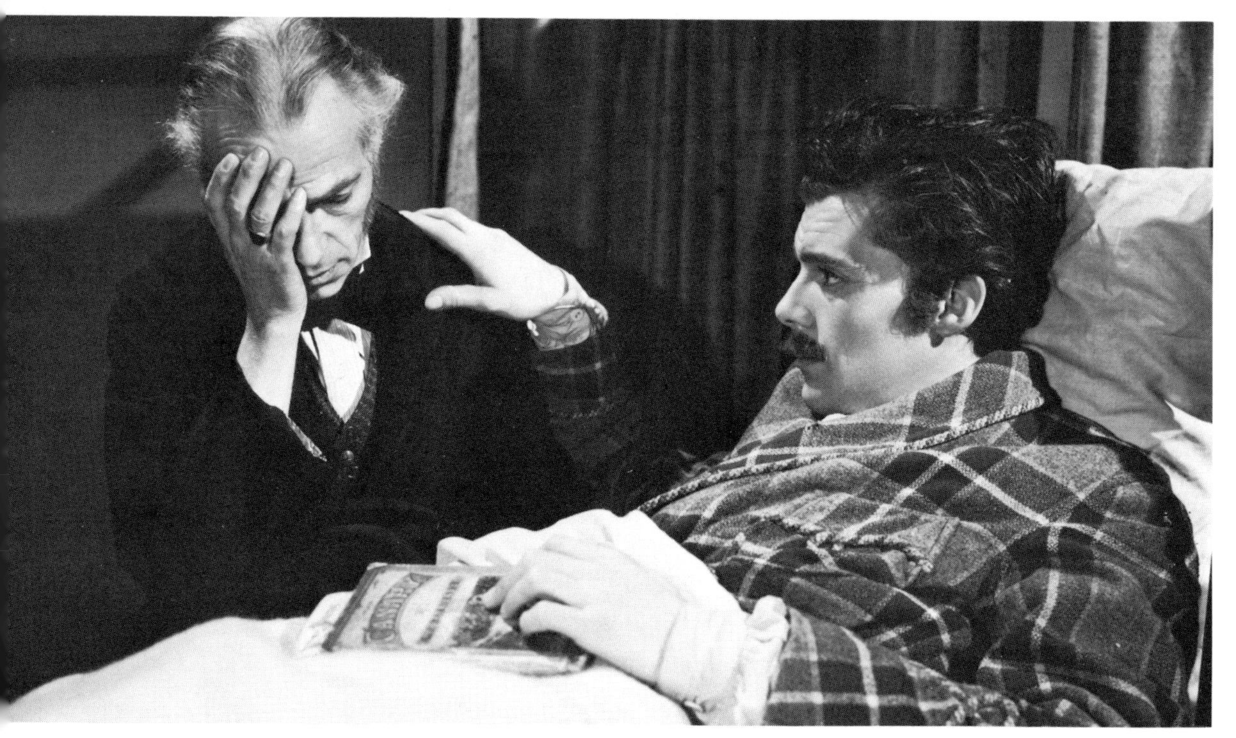

Dirk Bogarde was a Rank star from the moment he signed a film contract following West End theatre success. Here he is in three very different movie guises: (far left), with little Jon Whiteley, in *Hunted*; (top), as Borstal inmate, along with John McCallum, Jimmy Hanley, Richard Attenborough, John Blythe, Michael Medwin and Alfie Bass in *Boys in Brown* (the concerned governor is Jack Warner); (above), Bogarde's starring début in *Esther Waters*, with Ivor Barnard.

Anthony Steel, of the dimpled chin and almost impossibly good looks, was put under contract more or less direct from service as a major in the Army.

Although completely inexperienced, he loathed having to go to the School and being made to walk round the room with a book on his head while Molly Terraine clapped her hands to keep time.

Olive Dodds remembers: 'Although he used to plead with me to take him away, he had the guts to stick it out until he started to get small parts and later, of course, leads – quite quickly considering his previous lack of experience. He was one of the few really wild ones. Whenever the roundabout on the road from Pinewood to London had been run through, we used to say, only *partly* joking, that Tony must be working at Pinewood.'

Like Bogarde, the top echelon of stars – Margaret Lockwood, Jack Hawkins, Kenneth More – would be contracted on a so-many-films-a-year basis for which payment was guaranteed whether they made them or not.

Designing a contract for Hawkins, however, took almost a year of protracted negotiation. His agent demanded, successfully, that the actor should have first star billing at all times. Rank's proviso was that an exception would be in the case of a teaming with a truly major international star name. One of Hawkins' first pictures after signing the contract had as its leading lady another client of the same agent. The actress, Margaret Johnson, also happened to be the agent's wife. The agent was on to Mrs Dodds in a flash saying, 'Of course Jack would waive his billing position for Maggie.' The tart reply was that the Organisation would *never* consider subjecting its

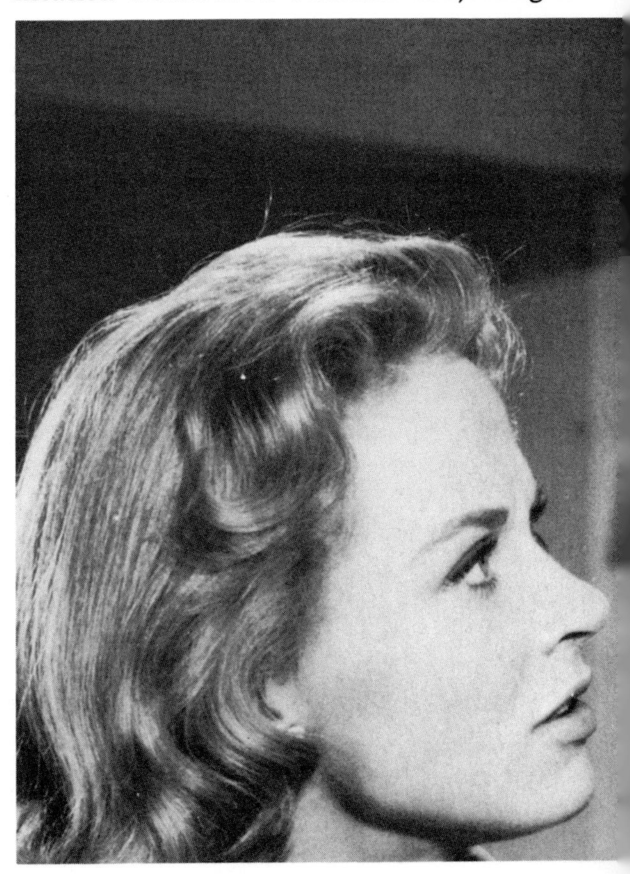

Above: teenage delinquent David McCallum, with Anne Heywood and Stanley Baker, in *Violent Playground*; (right), Julia Arnall and David Knight are the concerned couple whose child has been snatched in *Lost*.

new major contract star to such a put-down.

According to Mrs Dodds, Dirk Bogarde liked being under contract, 'whatever he might say. He liked the security and the lifestyle it afforded him. When options were due for renewal, the board would discuss it about three months before the end of a particular contract.

'If business was generally on the slide, the company would take the opportunity to shed a few people. I would remind Dirk that the option was coming up, adding that there was this or that film in the pipeline. He'd generally say at first he didn't want to do it. I'd then remind him that if he was actually working when the option was being discussed, they would never drop it, thinking that maybe a great new success was in the offing.'

If Rank planned to drop a contract-player, it would try to give as long a notice as possible. A few asked to be released because they felt they were not getting enough actual work. Sandra Dorne, for example, felt that she clashed with Diana Dors, who in any case had a long head start. Claire Bloom, in her early years, wanted to concentrate on theatre work and, indeed, it was agreed she should be allowed to do so.

When Mrs Dodds first saw Stephen Boyd, she contacted his agent to say how much she liked his work and that she wished to offer him a contract. There was, however, one problem: Boyd had a slight sibilance in his voice which sounded a bit 'sissy'. Could the agent suggest he had a few lessons to iron out the impediment? When the contract came to be negotiated, Boyd declared he wouldn't work for any organisation that employed Olive Dodds.

'It's the only time I've been personally blacked,' she observes.

From her early teens, Petula Clark was a welcome young face in Rank films: (top), aged 17 in *Vote for Huggett*; her first straight acting role is in the hospital drama *White Corridors*; (above), with Jimmy Hanley in *Don't Ever Leave Me*; (right), watched by Natasha Parry and Diana Dors, Pet succumbs to the charms of Douglas Barr in *Dance Hall*.

Diana Dors was Britain's first post-war sex siren: (top left), in *Diamond City* and (top right) in *A Boy, a Girl and a Bike*; (above), the archetypal platinum blonde in *Value for Money*; (left), several years on, and a fine character actress, in *Nothing But the Night*.

'Britain's Bad Girl', Joan Collins (top), applies a little eyebrow make-up before filming *Turn the Key Softly*; (above), pictured in a provocative publicity shot; (right), more mature but sexier than ever, in *Revenge*; (far right), back to the Rank fold, and suitably soapy considering her *Dynasty* status, in *Nutcracker*.

Far left: Virginia McKenna and Paul Scofield in *Carve Her Name with Pride*; (left), Melina Mercouri, Keith Michell and Patrick McGoohan in *The Gypsy and the Gentleman*; (middle left), David Tomlinson and Petula Clark live happily ever after with the Great Dunmow Flitch in *Made in Heaven*; (bottom left), Hardy Kruger as the titular hero of *The One that Got Away*.

Peter Finch succumbed to a Rank contract but seemed to regret it from the word go, describing the Organisation's films as 'very British stiff-upper-lip, unimaginative and pandering to popular taste at an unnecessarily low level'. Yet two of his three British Film Academy awards for best actor came in very different, and imaginative, Rank films – *A Town Like Alice* and *No Love for Johnnie*.

Pencilled in for the lead role in 1958's *Ferry to Hong Kong*, aimed squarely at the international market, Finch was dropped at the last minute in favour of Curt Jurgens, who, it was felt, was a bigger box-office name and better 'insurance'. This must have been almost the final straw for Peter Finch.

Kay Kendall's problem was money. Mrs Dodds reveals: 'I used to lend her quite a lot of money, but as long as she had it, she spent it. At the time she was living in a very smart Belgravia flat and when one day she asked me again if I'd lend her money, I said no. I told her she'd already hocked her salary forever and a day and, apart from anything else, she must move as her flat was far too expensive. About a fortnight later she rang me and said she'd done what I suggested and moved. "What's your new address?" I asked. "The Connaught Hotel." '

Part of the 'system' was the inevitable hoopla – the publicity, the pictures, the parties and the premières. Patrick McGoohan, who hated being under contract, was summoned by director Joseph Losey to appear with his *The Gypsy and the Gentleman* co-star Keith Michell at a party he was throwing at his home for their other co-star, the Greek actress Melina Mercouri, as well as some 'important' industry types.

McGoohan arrived and proceeded to sit in a far corner of the main room with the gramophone records. Michell was charm itself and circulated madly. The ubiquitous Mrs Dodds asked Michell if he'd go and talk to McGoohan as the actor seemed to be 'all alone. Keith said to me, "You're mad. Who do you think they're all talking about? Patrick, in the corner, doing bugger all, while I'm working my pants off." '

Fan magazines and cinema books proliferated in the 'fifties, and none would have been complete without glowing references to Rank's 'young stars'.

F. Maurice Speed's *Film Review 1956–57* profiles newcomer Julia Arnall with such riveting information as: 'One of her assets is the ability to cry when needed, without resort to glycerine or anything like that. Once asked what she thought about to bring on these tears, she replied with a smile: "Please, *please*, don't ask. If I told anybody, it would not work any more!" '; of Tony Wright, another new face, it says: 'Tall, blond . . . sailed all over the world – "and I was sea-sick the whole time" . . . it was only due to the publicity consequent upon his saving a woman from drowning in the Seine that he received an offer of a starring role in a Slim Callaghan picture and, eventually, the offer of a Rank contract.'

If such mind-boggling banality were not enough, readers of the same year's *Preview* (Eric Warman) were treated to an essay on film festivals by Donald Sinden, who was perhaps honing his style for two much later volumes of autobiography. He wrote: 'I like being a star. And to attend a film festival as a star is an exciting business. This may sound egotistical. But at least it's sincere. Anyway, if one has achieved some measure of success in one's chosen job, well, what's wrong with being proud of the fact?

'And being a *British* star gives me particular pleasure. At these film festivals one is able to do one's bit – even if it is only a bit – for the old country. I mean by being a sort of ambassador representing British films and the British way of life.'

Bearing in mind that, even with growing competition from television, cinema admissions were still running in excess of 17 million a week, there was a huge appetite for startling Sinden observations such as, 'When I find myself compelled to look into a mirror, I often wonder what people see in me. But that Tony Steel! Now there's what I believe our American cousins call "A hunk of a man".'

The setting may be mundane – a roadside café – but the action is resolutely macho in *Hell Drivers* with Sean Connery, Sid James, Patrick McGoohan and Stanley Baker.

Mrs Dodds believes the Rank 'system' had both its up and its down side.

'One of the advantages of having been under contract, for even quite small fry, was the plugging of their names and faces so that, at least in the business, they were known. This enabled many to continue a career after perhaps only a brief period under contract.

'Where the system failed was in not going along with the Hollywood idea of telling directors they *must* use people under contract. We never forced anyone to use one of our actors or actresses. So often,' she remembers, 'you'd find our people hanging around for great periods of time without work.'

Then, of course, there were the stars who got away. Sean Connery, for one, would not come under contract. Another bright young actor, who had had a great stage success, was approached but gently rejected the notion, saying: 'You see, this may well be just a flash in the pan. I come from a large mining family. I'm going to give this business two years and if I'm still making the grade then, I'll stay in it. If not, I'll go back to the mines.'

Richard Burton did make the grade, but the Charm School lost a new student.

The Cornel Lucas photo folio: (left), Lucas, in his 2,500th camera session, settles newcomer Shirley Eaton as she undertakes her first; (top), Anthony Steel; (above), Christmas special with starlet Susan Beaumont.

The Image Maker

By definition, the boys and girls who signed up for the Charm School had to be photogenic. But photogenic and, for that matter, plain charming was not necessarily enough. There had to be an image too, almost an aura.

Cornel Lucas was Rank's supreme image-maker of the 'fifties, the studio photographer whose star portraits not only graced the foyers and stairways of Odeon and Gaumont theatres but also adorned the pages of a proliferation of fanzines and cinema books.

At his exotic Pool Studio at Pinewood Lucas's staff, including a permanent electrician, prop man, hairdresser, make-up artist and manager, welcomed both eager newcomers and oldtimers.

The brief was 'an international look'. 'We were all greatly influenced by the general move into the international market,' Lucas recalls, 'and we had to incorporate that into our work.

'British films made in the 'thirties and 'forties were moderately English in feeling. Suddenly they were becoming more transatlantic and our pictures had to reflect the same thing. There was, for instance, a great deal more glamour than there had been in the past.'

Lucas, as handsome as some of the actors he photographed (and married to the beautiful Belinda Lee, who was to die so tragically young, aged 24, in a car crash), settled on portraiture after first considering a career in cinematography.

'I finally rejected that because a camera team was too large and too rigid in the way it worked. As a photographer, I could be my own director, producer and team.

'However, I didn't like production work either. As a stillsman, it was always a case of grubbing for pictures and not being able to concentrate properly on people.'

His first star session was with the legendary Marlene Dietrich, who had asked to see his work and agreed to give him a go; but the assignment, in the carefully prepared corner of a Denham stage, got off to a less-than-propitious start.

Lucas had set everything up and decided to have some music playing. He failed to notice the arrival, in a shaft of light, of Dietrich and an eight-strong entourage, who walked in to the strains of 'Colonel Bogey' coming from his radio.

'She must have thought I was a bit of a joker. She turned off the radio with a twinkle in her eye and in fact it helped break the ice.' To his astonishment, Dietrich subsequently passed every shot he'd done.

'This really decided me on it. Portraiture was *the* thing for me.'

Lucas's image-building years at Pinewood must have seen some strange contrasts. There were the new, young actresses who, on £20 a week, could never remotely have afforded the furs and jewels they were asked to wear for photographs.

Then there were stars to whom a portrait session was rather akin to pulling teeth. Kay Kendall told Lucas she would rather do two pictures than one stills session and even, on occasion, tried climbing out of the dressing-room window to avoid the probing of his plate camera.

Robert Newton would succumb only if Lucas was prepared to read a script with him.

Various forms of censorship also posed a few photographic headaches. The belly-button simply could not be displayed in pictures at that time; mysteriously, zips on the back of trousers and skirts were taboo in Italy, while cleavage was a continual problem everywhere.

Lucas, who finally quit to go into advertising when the 'contract' system was being run down, has his own version of the story of Rank, Richard Burton and the contract that never was.

Before an artist was given a film test, Lucas would generally do a session and then be asked his opinion about the facial qualities of the subject.

He recalls that one day he had been asked to photograph Burton when suddenly the session was cancelled without an explanation. On a later occasion, Lucas enquired why this had happened. Because, he was told, the actor's face was too pitted from acne. It would never photograph well for the screen.

From the Lucas folio: (far left), Jill Ireland; (above left), Dinah Sheridan. Above: stars of today and tomorrow gather for a laugh and a snap. The men: Lyndon Brook, Peter Finch, Terence Morgan, Jack Hawkins, Michael Craig, George Baker, John Gregson and Donald Sinden. The women: Diane Cilento, Eunice Gayson, Diana Dors, Susan Stephen, Sarah Lawson, Belinda Lee and Jill Adams; (right), Barbara Murray and Dirk Bogarde.

CHAPTER 5

Box of Delights

Four of the Best

They were never fashionable, which is presumably why a number of volumes purporting to be major encyclopaedias of the cinema completely ignore them. Yet between them, in collaboration and separately, Sydney, Muriel and Betty Box made more than 70 British films over a 25-year period from the end of the war. Many, and most successfully, were for Rank.

There were even a couple of years, 1947 and 1949, when the Boxes were directly responsible for six films a year. 1954 saw five and even as late as 1959 there were four, including two directed by the redoubtable Muriel.

Theirs was bread-and-butter film-making, unlikely to make critics' Top Ten lists but often among the top money-makers and, from time to time, award charts. The achievement was all the more remarkable because women as producers and directors, not to mention running studios, were, and are, extremely rare in this male-dominated industry.

Muriel started out as a script girl for Anthony Asquith and in 1935, the year they wrote their first script together, she and Sydney, who had started in journalism, were married. The 53-minute thriller, *Alibi Inn*, featured Wilfrid Hyde-White a long way down the credits. As a team, Muriel and Sydney proceeded to write dozens of one-act plays.

In 1939 Sydney set up a company to make training films for the army, supervising some 200 documentaries in all.

He also produced other films – from the six-minute *Telefootlers*, a warning about how telephone gossip could give information to the enemy, to the full-length feature *The Flemish Farm*, a stirring piece with Clive Brook and Clifford Evans about a Belgian airman who returns to his Occupied

Previous page: Peter Finch, in British Academy Award-winning form, as Labour MP Johnnie Byrne in *No Love for Johnnie*; (far left), Ann Todd and James Mason in *The Seventh Veil*; (left), Michael Denison and Claire Bloom in *The Blind Goddess*; (below), Sir Patrick Hastings, author of the stage play *The Blind Goddess*, and Lady Hastings with producer Betty Box on the set at Islington Studios.

country to retrieve a flag that has been buried there. Sydney's tea girl was his younger sister, Betty.

The real breakthrough for the Box trio came towards the end of 1945 with the release of *The Seventh Veil*. To call this frankly lurid melodrama a success would be an understatement. In the year of *Brief Encounter*, *The Way to the Stars*, *Dead of Night* and *I Know Where I'm Going* – an outstanding quartet in any year – *The Seventh Veil*, which cost only £100,000 to make, was the runaway top earner in Britain.

Ann Todd plays a beautiful young pianist who escapes her tyrannical guardian (limping James Mason) but cannot then choose between two other boyfriends until a friendly psychiatrist steps in and gives her some extremely perverse guidance. The lush music, supervised by Benjamin Frankel, was performed by wartime favourite Eileen Joyce. The blend was described by one critic as 'a rich, portentous mixture of Beethoven, Chopin, Kitsch and Freud.'

Sydney co-produced the film, with John Sutro, and co-wrote the screenplay, exotic but novelettish, with Muriel. Their efforts even brought them a Hollywood Oscar. The film was made independently at the small Riverside Studios at Hammersmith, but with a Rank distribution contract. Betty remembers that at a small reception, designed to spread good word about their film, she was particularly asked to impress a young man from the trade press called Peter Rogers.

After giving him the treatment, she found out that he also worked for Rank, as a writer on the company's religious film side (see Chapter 8). The couple later married.

Betty continued as her brother's assistant at Riverside on a series of films, including *The Years Between* and *A Girl in a Million*, before Rank, principally on the strength of *The Seventh Veil*, offered her the command of his Islington studios, to make seven films a year. Sydney, meanwhile, was appointed to run Gainsborough at Shepherd's Bush with a production slate of no less than 25 films a year.

Betty's elevation, at the tender age of 27, delighted a chauvinistic press.

Kerr Logan, a noted showbusiness writer of his time, wrote: 'One of the studio hands said: "Send for the boss." The boss came, and the problem was solved. She had passed me unobtrusively a little earlier in one of the studio passages. She was a fair-haired, smallish, quietly dressed woman, in appearance a private secretary but in fact a film executive – Britain's first woman producer.'

In Logan's article, 'The Girl with £500,000 to Spend', Betty had to explain how she would tactfully deal with men at the script conferences. During her two years at Islington, she produced a host of popular pictures – the *Huggetts* series with Jack Warner, Kathleen Harrison and Petula Clark; *Miranda*, about pretty mermaid Glynis Johns; and *Dear Murderer* (genteel sex and violence) among them.

Logan went on with relish about Betty's having told him that on *Dear Murderer* she had to send starlet Hazel Court back to wardrobe to have her stockings changed. They were sheer fully-fashioneds, but not sheer enough.

'You have to be a film producer to discriminate like that, girls,' commented Logan.

A number of the films were directed by newcomer Ken Annakin, who after being invalided out of the RAF with amnesia had become an assistant cameraman. One of his was *Miranda*, on which Betty recalls particular problems:

'Altogether we had six different tails made for Glynis to swim in before we found the right one. The first few we tried dragged her down and somebody was always jumping in to rescue her. Eventually we summoned the experts who designed the apparatus for the frogmen in the war and they produced a tail of very light, plastic rubber, filled with water. Then we discovered that it looked clumsy when she was sitting on a rock, so we had a second tail made in a curve for her to wear in the cove scene.' The credit at the end of the film read: 'Tail by Dunlop.'

In 1954 Betty made a sequel to *Miranda* called *Mad About Men*. For this, her by now regular collaborator was director Ralph Thomas, whom she had met on the original film when he was doing trailers for Rank and found full of helpful advice. By now Glynis Johns had perfected her fishy act (not so co-star Dora Bryan, who, after leaping into the tank, was completely upended by her tail).

Betty and Ralph Thomas's most prolific 'star' relationship was with Rank-contracted Dirk Bogarde. Together they made ten films, from *So Long at the Fair* in 1950 to *The High Bright Sun* in 1964, via four *Doctor* films (see Chapter 6), *Campbell's Kingdom* and, among others, one that coincided with Pinewood Studios' 21st anniversary, *A Tale of Two Cities*.

The plan had been to shoot some scenes for *Tale* in Avignon, until it was realised that the schedule was smack in the middle of the tourist season. So the team settled on Bourges instead, an unexciting town despite its beautiful cathedral. It was empty, too, because it was harvest time and the locals were out in the fields all day.

Betty badly needed French peasants for the crowded guillotine scenes. Nearby was

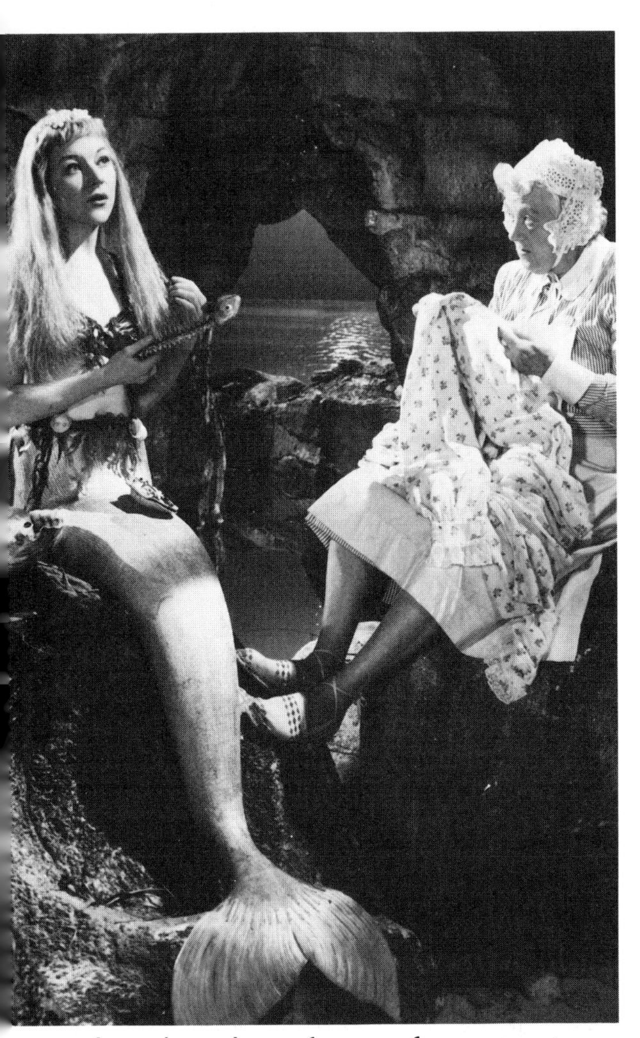

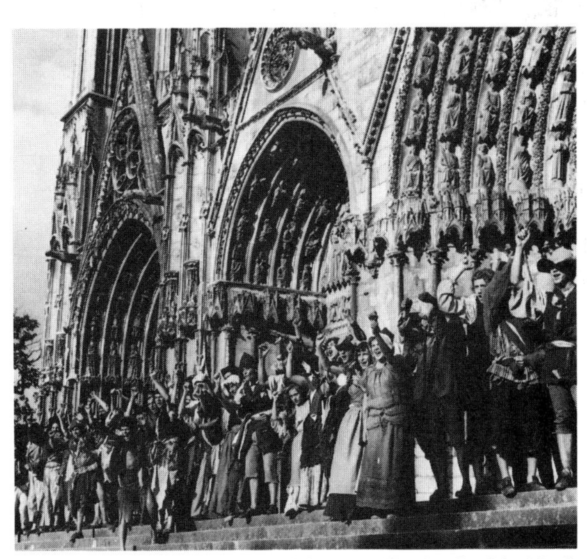

Above left: Dora Bryan and Margaret Rutherford in *Mad About Men*; (top), Griffith Jones and Glynis Johns in *Miranda*; 'Hang the bums!' cry the crowd artists in *A Tale of Two Cities* (above).

an American Army base and a contract was drawn up for US servicemen to be extras, the proviso being that they would be allowed to bring their own water. The main problem was that this bunch of six-footers would have to cram themselves into 5-feet 8-inch peasant outfits.

Orders were issued (as were tomatoes for throwing) for them to 'shake your fists and cry, "Death to the aristocrats!" '. On the first take, the cry went out, 'Hang the bum.' When the scene cut, the apologetic extra who had shouted this explained that he had got carried away because he came from a hanging state.

The unit returned to Pinewood to finish off the film, including a crucial Bastille sequence. On the very day of the anniversary, the rain poured down and the set completely dissolved.

Earlier in the 'fifties, a couple of the Box-Thomas output were produced under the auspices of a Rank-National Film Finance Corporation (the NFFC, a government-sponsored film 'merchant

TIRANO
FRONTIERA

Far top left: Stanley Baker menaces Anthony Steel in *Checkpoint*.

Far bottom left: Kay Kendall and Peter Finch flank their television son in *Simon and Laura*.

Bottom left: a motley collection of crooks in *The League of Gentlemen* – Jack Hawkins, Roger Livesey, Bryan Forbes, Terence Alexander, Norman Bird, Kieron Moore, Richard Attenborough and Nigel Patrick.

Left: Elke Sommer shapes up for duty in *Deadlier than the Male*.

bank', had been set up in 1949) grouping called British Film Makers, which, after fourteen titles, was succeeded by Group Film Productions, a wholly-owned Rank company. It, in turn, changed its name eventually to Rank Organisation Film Productions, turning out no less than 96 films between 1953 and 1967.

At the end of the 'fifties, Rank sponsored another adjunct, Allied Film Makers, set up by Bryan Forbes, Richard Attenborough, Basil Dearden and Michael Relph (who had made some fine Ealing films), Jack Hawkins and Guy Green.

Bogarde, heroic and flawless in Betty's films, bravely tackled the controversial subject of homosexuality in Allied's *Victim*. Under AFM Relph and Dearden also made a splendid tongue-in-cheek thriller, *The League of Gentlemen*, as well as *Man in the Moon* and *Life for Ruth*.

Allied gave Forbes the chance to direct his first film, *Whistle Down the Wind*, a big success, and *Seance on a Wet Afternoon*, a courageous flop.

Betty's last film for Rank was *Doctor in Trouble* in 1970, while husband Peter's *Carry On* sequence continued.

Meanwhile the other duo, Sydney and Muriel, were working together as Muriel began her own directing career on films such as *Street Corner*, *Simon and Laura* and *Eyewitness*. Their collaboration ended in 1958, when Sydney became a television executive, and a little over ten years after that they were divorced.

Four of the Best

If the British film industry can be said to boast technical expertise equal to, and often better than, that of anywhere else in the world, there is one quartet that epitomises that excellence: Charles Staffell, Andy Knapman, Geoff Labram and Paddy Bennett are all masters of their various crafts, and between them they have put in something like a total of 160 years at Pinewood.

You would know Andy's work from a detailed House of Commons re-creation in *No Love for Johnnie*, Oliver Reed's grotesquely burning body in *The Devils* or the volcano in *You Only Live Twice*.

He is a master plasterer and for the past ten years has been head of the studio's 90-strong plasterwork and plastics department. With his father a plasterer before him, Andy started his apprenticeship at the old Lime Grove studios. Working on the epic *Christopher Columbus*, helping to fashion the navigator's ship, he moved to Pinewood when the film itself transferred from Shepherd's Bush to rural Bucks. . . and stayed.

'All the difficult jobs come to me,' he jokes. One of the most difficult, perhaps the most demanding, was his 75-foot-high volcano on the 1966 Bond film. Built at the back of the lot, it was the biggest single-span piece of girder work in the whole of Europe at that time. 'We cracked that in about three months,' he says.

The technology of his craft is constantly evolving: 'In the early days there were no such things as plastics or fibre-glass. Bottles, to crash over people's heads, used to be sugar, then became plastic and are now chemical. Latex rubber took the place of papier mâché.

'The great thing about this job – and our work, remember, is the seen stuff – is that you come in around 8 or 8.30 each morning and you literally never know what you're going to be asked to do next.'

Head of technical services ('a term I invented for myself'), Geoff Labram works mainly in a medium that is heard rather than seen. Though in overall charge of sound, camera *and* cutting rooms, Geoff has been steeped in the aural side of things ever since leaving school to work for a radio valve company.

When he started at Pinewood after the war, he was the 'lowest of the low'; then he graduated up the sound ladder, working on many film locations. Finally he opted to stay 'indoors' with a studio-based job.

Geoff believes that much of today's sound quality 'leaves much to be desired. Not that the equipment hasn't got better, it's just that the man doing the recording is often asked to do the impossible – working, for instance, at great distances with personal microphones, with the chance of sound becoming easily muffled.

'Take a film like Ridley Scott's *Legend*, which was made here. There wasn't a single foot of usable sound on the whole film. The whole thing had to be re-recorded.' Geoff, whose department has scooped many awards including an Oscar for the sound recording of Norman Jewison's *Fiddler on the Roof* (filmed at Pinewood in 1970), admits he is a little nostalgic about times past at the studio.

'In the days of a lot of studio production, there were so many more characters around. There was almost a holiday camp atmosphere about the place. Now, it's more of a film factory.'

Call for Paddy Bennett, and you might not get a response. Call 'Paddy Props', and a cheerful Irishman would bring you anything you required for a scene – from a packet of 20 (period) Player's, in *The Battle of Britain*, to a complete circus, for *Octopussy*.

The volcano constructed for *You Only Live Twice* was a triumph in craftsmanship for the Pinewood plasterwork department.

A former steeplechase jockey, Paddy arrived at Pinewood in 1946 for a six-week stint handling horses on *Captain Boycott*. Forty years later, he has just retired, having been head of the props department for the past seven.

Food sequences have tended to cause him the greatest headaches, requiring, as they do, very close liaison with continuity. A piece of meat may have to be eaten over and over again but it must always seem to be the same piece and at the same point of munch.

On *The Magnificent Two*, with Morecambe and Wise, Paddy had arranged for some corn-on-the-cob bubbling away in a pan. Nearby a painter was coming down a ladder when a blob of emulsion paint from his can dropped into the pan below just as the director was calling 'Action'. Paddy said he kept his fingers crossed that the player due to eat it would not be taken ill as a result.

When, in the first *Superman* movie, Superman flies off Lois Lane's balcony, the camera follows Lois across the room and she opens the door to Clark Kent (Superman's *alter ego*). The action is seen in a single shot without cutting.

The effect, executed by veteran Charles Staffell, is described as 'a double front projection shot'. That is, the first part of the shot, with Superman flying off the balcony, was done in one pass on the front projection system. It was then re-projected and the camera moved round to the real set and followed Lois to the door.

Such magic is the hallmark of the work of Staffell and his special process department which, in the late 'sixties, won a Hollywood Oscar, the first such general technical award made by the Academy of Motion Picture Arts and Sciences to Britain.

A pioneer of front projection, Staffell first became fascinated in the movies as a young cinema house manager in West London. Working at Denham in the late 'thirties with Korda, and particularly the special-effects wizard Larry Butler, provided him with some of his most enduring memories – of *The Thief of Baghdad*, in particular, still regarded, despite its age, as one of the most sophisticated effects films of all time.

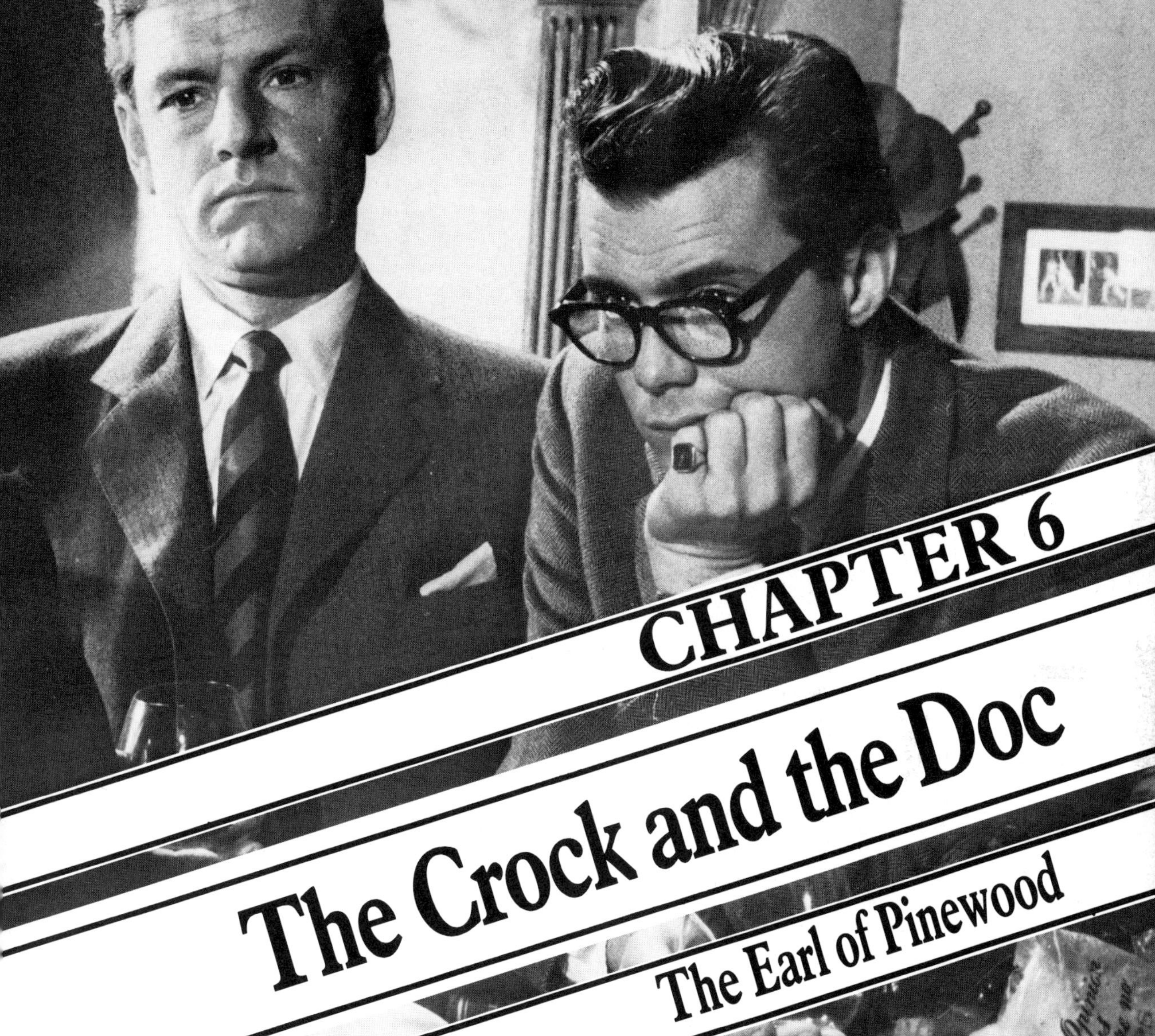

CHAPTER 6

The Crock and the Doc

The Earl of Pinewood

Previous page: Donald Houston, Donald Sinden, Kenneth More and Dirk Bogarde are the aspiring medics finding liquid respite in *Doctor in the House*; (right), Kenneth More and Kay Kendall with the Spyker at Brighton in *Genevieve*.

Motorists negotiating country lanes near Moor Park Golf Club in Hertfordshire, *north* of London, must have been astonished suddenly to find signposts proclaiming '*Brighton: 6 miles*'. A local copper was positively bewildered when, glancing out of his bedroom window one morning, he saw another sign, '*Beware: Cattle Crossing*', which seemed to have sprung up mysteriously overnight. It was in the gathering winter of 1952–3, and one of Rank's most successful, and enduring, films had begun shooting.

That *Genevieve* even made it before the cameras was a triumph for the persistent 39-year-old producer-director Henry Cornelius. South African-born and Sorbonne-educated, 'Corny', as he was known, first learned his craft as an assistant to the great French director, René Clair. As director, he had made the popular Ealing comedy *Passport to Pimlico* (1949).

Armed with a script by William Rose, an American, Corny went out to Pinewood Studios to persuade Earl St John to back the film on behalf of Rank. St John, confronted with this whimsical comedy about two young couples who plan to race their old crocks home from the London-Brighton Veteran Car Rally, was incredulous. 'If we made that sort of film, I'd get the sack and, frankly, I can't afford to lose my job,' he told Corny.

But the film-maker just would not take no for an answer and returned two or three more times to work on St John.

Finally the Organisation's executive producer asked what the budget would be. The answer was £115,000 – not a vast amount, he admitted, but he'd still have to get board approval.

Rank eventually agreed to provide 70 per cent of the investment as long as Cornelius could find the remaining 30 per cent, which he managed thanks to the involvement of the government-sponsored 'merchant bank', the National Film Finance Corporation (NFFC).

Casting was to prove perhaps the key to the film's eventual success.

Kenneth More was, at the time, wowing West End theatre audiences in Terence Rattigan's *The Deep Blue Sea*. 'Critics hailed me almost as an overnight discovery,' he recollected, 'conveniently forgetting I was already 38 and that I'd been working in the theatre for nearly 20 years.' More had also been seen in a handful of small screen roles, including *Scott of the Antarctic* (1948).

Corny visited the actor backstage and handed him the *Genevieve* script, reminding More he had played a 'spit and a cough' in the director's *The Galloping Major* a year earlier. More was hesitant, since taking on the assignment would mean working all day in the studios and all night on stage.

'I don't think you can afford to say "no" to this,' More remembered him saying, and there was 'something in his tone of voice that impressed me.' So More signed on, for a fee of £3,500, to play the hearty advertising agent Ambrose Claverhouse. His girlfriend was to be played by vivacious Kay Kendall (born Justine McCarthy) who, though only 26, had made an earlier bid for stardom in the famous flop *London Town*. Playing the other couple, the more sober Alan and Wendy McKim, were to be John Gregson, who had already featured in some Ealing comedies, and Dinah Sheridan, the English rose of *Where No Vultures Fly* (1951).

Filming took place between October and February in miserable weather. The action was meant to occur over a sunny summer weekend, so mobile generators would travel round with the unit to provide power for the many arc lamps needed to help brighten up the images.

Genevieve may have turned out light, frothy fun, but the mood of at least two members of the cast, Kay Kendall and John Gregson, was far from cheerful, thanks to the dreary weather and the 'perfectionism' of Henry Cornelius.

More remembered: 'One day, in a drizzle, Kay and I had to drive towards the camera in our old Spyker. Cornelius was not happy with the shot, so we did it a second time. He was sorry, but a hair caught in the gate of the camera. We did it a third time, a fourth and then a fifth time. We were soaked to the skin, but because it was supposed to be a sunny day (an illusion created by the arc lights) we could not wear raincoats. Each time we shot this scene we had to drive down the road for several hundred yards, coax the old, asthmatic engine to keep running as I turned the gasping, trembling machine, and then we drove back. After the fifth time, Cornelius shook his head.

' "Just once more," he said. I was about to reverse when the whole car rocked on its antique springs. Kay had jumped out. Alongside the passenger seat was a wicker basket to carry a parasol – about the only weather protection drivers in the early 1900s had. She seized the parasol with both hands and began to beat Corny over the head with it. At first, I thought she was just joking. Then I realised she had gone hysterical with the cold and the misery of driving up and down in the rain. "You miserable little bastard!" Kay cried as she belaboured him. I knew exactly how she felt and sympathised with her.'

Olive Dodds, the Organisation's director of artists and regular confidante of her charges, said that Kay Kendall spent hours with her 'trying to persuade me to get her out of the film, which they all thought, while shooting on it, would be a disaster. The combination of the long filming, the many takes, changes in script and very, very

GENEV

One of many delays in the stop-start progress of a beautiful veteran car in the classic comedy *Genevieve*, observed with obvious concern by its rally team, John Gregson and Dinah Sheridan as Alan and Wendy McKim.

bad weather had put them all into the glooms. Of course, there was no way anybody could pull out of a film already half-made. In my view, it proved to be the one part that appeared to have been written for Kay and Kay alone.'

More continued: 'Having overcome trouble with the weather, we went into the studio – and seven-eighths of the way through the film, the company ran out of money. We were well over our budget because of Corny's insistence on repeating each shot so many times. The producer had an insurance policy against such a contingency but insurance companies never like to pay out, and under the terms of the contract they had to pay the producer what was then a large sum, about £20,000. To cut all possible costs, the insurance company had their men prowling round the studio (Pinewood) switching off any lights that were not needed.'

As if confirming the worst – apparently, the 'front office' didn't like the finished film – the opening at the Odeon, Leicester Square was, according to Keith Robertson of Rank Film Distributors (now RFD's director of administration), then still General Film Distributors, 'a non-event . . . It was, at first, very coolly received. But somehow, with the word of mouth, it took off and the results were amazing. In those days it took about 18 months for a film to go through the sequence of six-day bookings, three-day bookings, Sunday nights . . .

'We didn't let *Genevieve* go to Sunday nights, we put it out as a reissue double bill with our other big hit, *Doctor in the House*. We'd always had double-feature programmes, but it was always a first feature and a B-picture. This was the first of its kind – "The Doc and the Crock" – and it proved to be one of the most successful double programmes we ever put on.'

Full of now-classic moments like Kay Kendall's impromptu trumpet solo, the

creaking bed rocked by the chimes of the huge clock opposite, and More telling Kay to 'get out and bloody well push' the recalcitrant Spyker, not to mention wonderful cameos by Geoffrey Keen as a traffic policeman and Joyce Grenfell as a hotel proprietress, plus Larry Adler's fine harmonica score, no wonder *Genevieve* was named Best British Film of 1953. It also, perhaps surprisingly for something so quintessentially English, earned two Oscar nominations, for William Rose's deft screenplay and Muir Mathieson's music direction.

Sadly, only one of the starring quartet is still alive today: Dinah Sheridan. Kay Kendall died in 1959 (a year after Henry Cornelius), John Gregson in 1975 and Kenneth More in 1982.

Dirk Bogarde, Donald Sinden and Kenneth More learn a little anatomy in *Doctor in the House*.

As Miss Sheridan reflected recently: 'It's very sad. I'm very much the lone survivor – if you don't count Genevieve herself, who's still chugging up and down roads in Australia for tourists. She will be our epitaph.'

Producer Betty Box was touting her latest film round the provinces – a Rank thriller called *The Venetian Bird*, starring Richard Todd and Eva Bartok – when she popped into the bookshop on Cardiff station and bought a new title, *Doctor in the House* by Richard Gordon.

She thoroughly enjoyed what she read, an hilarious account of medical-student japes, and quickly made enquiries as to its film availability. The answer was that Rank's great rivals, ABPC (Associated British Picture Corporation), had bought an option. When she rang again, Betty was told that the option had in fact now expired. She quickly handed over £100 and later paid the laughable sum of just £750 for the rights (she would make Rank pay author and publisher £15,000 next time round).

To Dirk Bogarde, she sent a roughed-out script with the suggestion he play the central role of aspiring doctor Simon Sparrow. Bogarde recalls: 'I was not, I remember, immediately impressed. It all seemed a bit light, the role a bit dim-witted, and every other character had funnier things to say and do. I was to be the simple juvenile.'

Bogarde's personal manager, Tony Forwood, was altogether more positive, explaining to his charge that here was a potential comedy hit that might help lead the actor away 'from spivs and service heroes, to which [he] was obviously becoming addicted'. So Bogarde told the producer the answer was 'yes'. However, Betty had by then hit a slight problem: Earl St John was opposed to Bogarde taking the role.

According to Bogarde, 'He didn't think I could play light comedy; my metier, he said, was action stuff. I did not have the necessary charm or lightness, and he reminded her that my last effort at comedy (*The Penny Princess* with Yolande Donlan), at his own instigation, had been a complete and total catastrophe for all concerned;

especially myself. It would be disastrous to play me in such a part.'

Nevertheless, Betty and director Ralph Thomas persevered and fought to keep Bogarde – and won. As far as the actor was concerned, their successful stand resulted in his having a career in the cinema.

Signed up to play students alongside Bogarde were Kenneth More, Donald Sinden and Donald Houston – who, at respectively 33, 40, 30 and 30, were hardly youthful; not that the public seemed to notice. Muriel Pavlow and Kay Kendall were the main female interest. Essential, however, to the eventual success of the film, and its six subsequent sequels, was the casting of James Robertson Justice as the overbearing surgeon, Sir Lancelot Spratt (his character Captain Hogg, in *Doctor at Sea*, was also Spratt – in all but name).

Jimmy Justice was an extraordinary, larger-than-life character who, it is said, was first spotted in a West End bar and asked if he would like to be in films.

According to Olive Dodds: 'When he was working at Ealing (on *Fiddlers Three* and, later, *Scott of the Antarctic*) he was also running an engineering and haulage business. Believing all that hanging around between shooting wasteful, he set up a drawing board, installed a telephone and continued to run his business from the studio. He claimed to be a Communist, but was certainly the most feudal Communist I've ever come across.

'He ran an estate in Scotland as imperiously as a Regency duke, and often dressed like the modern version of one. Jimmy never agonised over a part and was great fun to be with – even if he was pretty intolerant of lesser mortals.'

The bulky, flame-bearded Justice, more personality than mere actor, was also close friends with Prince Philip and could often be seen chaperoning young Prince Charles on visits to Pinewood.

Doctor in the House opened in the spring of 1954, and by the end of the year had taken nearly £500,000 in Britain alone, almost five times its budget. It was the top money-maker of '54 and also earned Kenneth More the Best Actor award (perhaps confirming Bogarde's doubts about the substance of his own, top-starring, role).

In an end-of-the-year *Daily Sketch* fea-

'If you had a rotten part, you'd often try and cast a continental girl,' says producer Betty Box. So Brigitte Bardot, seen here in a risqué scene from *Doctor at Sea*, was a distinct plus all round. Dirk Bogarde is about to do a double-take.

ture, lauding the efforts of Betty Box as 'the biggest laugh-getter in British films', came the announcement that *Doctor at Sea* was about to go into production, hot on the heels of the first success, and teased: 'The search is proceeding for a Parisian actress to play the heroine – a stranded cabaret performer. Leastways, Miss Box wants a French star; the Rank boys, at present, don't. Well, you know who gets the last word in an argument.'

Betty's casting of continental starlet Brigitte Bardot – said to have replaced first

choice Kay Kendall, though the producer denies it – proved a Pinewood sensation. Betty had wanted her for an earlier comedy, *A Day to Remember*, about a pub darts team's day-trip to Boulogne, but Bardot was tied up with ballet training. Betty admits there was also a rather cynical reason behind the casting of girls like Bardot and, later, Mylène Demongeot: 'If you had a rotten part, you'd often try and cast a continental girl. The dialogue didn't particularly matter and it was always going to be a plus for the foreign market.'

Encouraged by her husband, Roger Vadim, the gorgeous, pouting Brigitte joined Bogarde, Justice and Brenda de Banzie for *Doctor* duty early in 1955.

On a cargo ship bound for the Tropics, Sparrow, now a qualified medic, suddenly discovers Bardot while she is taking a shower. With characteristic British modesty, filming of the actress was to take place from the other side of the shower curtain, with her naughty bits properly covered.

However, because of the way the set was lit, the camera was able to pick out the outline of the garments which, frankly, looked foolish. With a complete lack of inhibition, Bardot came to the rescue. She stripped off completely and presented herself naked before an agog crew. Word of this scrumptious starlet whizzed round the studio like wildfire and often the stage was bulging at the seams with everyone sneaking in to try to have a look at her.

No such exotica occurred in *Doctor at Large* (1957), which saw the return to a solid British setting with Muriel Pavlow and Donald Sinden back to join regulars Bogarde and Justice. The parochiality clearly did not hurt as the film proved top money-maker of the year.

The series remained number one box office on its next outing, in 1960 (*Doctor in Love*), but this time there was no Dirk Bogarde or Simon Sparrow; instead Doctors

Far left: Barbara Murray gets some unusual medical help from Dirk Bogarde in *Doctor at Large*; (below), with Shirley Anne Field around, and despite James Robertson Justice, no wonder Leslie Phillips is a 'Doctor in Clover'.

Burke and Hare (Leslie Phillips and Michael Craig) romped through adventures that were beginning to resemble *Carry Ons*.

Bogarde mustered again for *Doctor in Distress* (1963), but after that it was Leslie Phillips all the way – somewhat schizophrenically as, variously, Dr Grimsdyke and Dr Burke – in *Doctor in Clover* (1965) and, finally, *Doctor in Trouble* (1970).

Strange to relate how the long-running series might conceivably have been strangled in its infancy. Betty Box tells how Rank wanted to retitle *Doctor in the House* to something called *Campus Capers*. 'You see,' they tried to persuade her, 'films with doctors and hospitals are bad news.'

The Earl of Pinewood

When Earl St John, the man who gave film breaks to the likes of Peter Finch and Norman Wisdom, retired from the Rank Organisation in 1964, he was the longest-serving resident American in the British film industry.

Stories about his early days as a cinema executive were legion. For example, on one occasion he turned away the Prince of Wales from the box office of a half-empty theatre in order to get publicity that implied that the film was playing to full houses.

It was fatal to remark to him that it was a nice day. With an eye on the cinema queues, he would invariably reply, 'I hope it rains like blazes.'

Louisiana-born, in 1892, St John first peddled films as a teenager for his uncle. Chaplin's comedies and a classic religious silent, *From Manger to Cross*, were among the pictures he carried across Mexico in carpet-bags.

After service in the First World War, as a GI 'doughboy', he came to Britain, working first as an independent exhibitor in Manchester before coming to London as head of exploitation for Paramount. From the mid-'twenties, St John began to enlarge the Paramount circuit of cinemas, starting with the Plaza, London followed by a fairly close neighbour, the Carlton, Haymarket.

Left: Earl St John, an executive producer with the instincts of an old-style cinema showman. Above: Peter Finch, picked out for stardom by St John, and Virginia McKenna in *A Town Like Alice*.

When Odeon Theatres bought out Paramount Theatres in Britain, it took over St John's contract, and just before the Second World War he became personal assistant to the rising executive star, John Davis.

It was after he had been appointed production adviser to the Organisation and then made its Pinewood-based executive producer, from 1951, that eagle-eyed film buffs would have probably noticed the name of this grey-haired, always immaculately dressed producer. 'Earl St John, Executive Producer' was a regular fixture on the credits of films such as *Above Us the Waves*, *The Card*, *The Million Pound Note* and *The One That Got Away*.

He ate, slept and drank movies, as ardently at the end of his life as when he filmed Pancho Villa's Mexican war in his youth.

He would recall: 'We cameramen kept that war going overtime. Our film company even paid Pancho thousands of dollars to stage some live battle scenes.'

His eye for new talent (see Chapter 7) was ever-alert. While at the première of a Disney film, *Robin Hood*, he was particularly impressed by the young man who played the Sheriff of Nottingham. The name on the programme was that of Peter Finch. St John bumped into Finch on the stairs of the theatre and invited him to come and talk business at Pinewood. Next day he gave Finch what would be a pivotal role in his burgeoning career: the Australian soldier, Joe, in *A Town Like Alice*.

The Earl of Pinewood, as he was often referred to, was executive producer on no less than 131 films and was always keen to prove that, despite the austerity of the 'fifties, British studios could still turn out films to match, or even better, their Hollywood counterparts.

CHAPTER 7

Wit and Wisdom

The Cleo That Never Was

Previous page: Norman Wisdom in typical trouble during *Man of the Moment* with Belinda Lee; (above), Moira Lister, Jerry Desmonde, Megs Jenkins and Lana Morris have mixed feelings about Norman in *Trouble in Store*.

Late in 1953, cinema queues ringed Gaumont theatres every night all over the UK for an unremarkable double feature: a modest British comedy and an American crime thriller. The magnet for the queues was the star of the little British film – Norman Wisdom. During the first four weeks of its release, *Trouble in Store* broke house records almost everywhere it was shown. Described as 'the most astonishing phenomenon in British post-war entertainment', Wisdom, aged 32, ex-errand boy, ex-page, ex-waiter, was at that time earning £2000 a week simply for appearing in pantomime.

What *was* the overwhelming appeal of this small, battered-looking man in his ill-fitting suit? According to one contemporary commentator, 'He is the reflection of everyone who looks at him. He is the Little Man that Chaplin was, even more pitiful, more twentieth-century, more ineffectual at dealing with life's indignities and complications. He is brow-beaten and helpless. He cannot cope. He falls down because the world overwhelms him. Can this happen to me? his public asks. It not only can: it does. The absence of any "act", the artlessness and roughness of his material, all help to give the illusion that there, but for the grace of Wisdom, go I.'

This was quite a build-up, but clearly it *was* an 'act', or lack of it, that had impressed the Rank Organisation's executive producer, Earl St John, when he tuned in to watch television on Christmas Day, 1951, and saw Wisdom in a festive show. Here was a tempting proposition, he thought. The great thing British films seemed noticeably to lack at that time was an outstanding comedian.

Wisdom, with his knockabout style, smile and generous helping of pathos could be just the answer. It would, however, take courage to experiment with him, for Rank was only too conscious of the mess it had made in trying to put, for example, the great Sid Field on the screen in such failures as *London Town* (1946) and *The Cardboard Cavalier* (1949). Comedians used to 'working' on an audience in the music-hall had proved a problem when it came to the more impersonal mechanics of film-making.

St John eventually won over his colleagues and, after much negotiation, Wisdom signed a seven-year contract with an initial guarantee of three films during a two-year period for the grand sum – and it was quite grand in those days – of £15,000.

Despite his having started at the top, Wisdom's path to film stardom was not particularly smooth. Now in his late sixties, he recalls: 'After I did a test, they paid me for the first film but never actually made it. The test was directed by Ronnie Neame and I did a bit with Petula Clark. I remember the dialogue was that I had to tell her that her eyes were as "light as gossamer". That was the film test for a comedian. No wonder they paid me. Of course, when they got to the second film, they thought, "Well, we can't keep paying out for him", so they decided to do it. So, *Trouble in Store*, though my starring début, was actually the second of the seven for which I'd signed.'

Deputed to guide Wisdom's fortunes in the movies was the equally small and energetic writer-director John Paddy Carstairs, son of the famous British comedian and mimic Nelson Keys, who himself had had a distinguished career in both silents and some early talkies.

Carstairs, who changed his name because everyone expected a son of the great Nelson Keys to be funny, was steeped in the film industry, having been a scriptwriter in Britain and Hollywood from the 'thirties. He was also the director of such popular postwar films as *Sleeping Car to Trieste* and *The Chiltern Hundreds*. Nevertheless Carstairs,

Gump-suited Norman in *One Good Turn*.

Norman flouts authority (David Lodge), in *On the Beat*. Not amused are Terence Alexander and Raymond Huntley.

the ex-public schoolboy who was also a distinguished painter (he exhibited at the Royal Academy) and Wisdom, born in Paddington poverty, did not necessarily add up to a marriage made in heaven, despite their common interests in comedy. According to Wisdom, the first clash came about four days into filming *Trouble in Store* at Pinewood.

'We were doing the shop-dressing scene in what was, supposedly, Selfridges. During a rehearsal I was hanging cups from the teapot spout, putting a jug on the handle, doing everything wrong, and Paddy stopped me, saying, "You don't want to do that, no, no, you're a window-dresser, you should do it right." I said that surely my character was meant to mess everything up, to which he replied, "You do as you're told." I told him I still wanted to try it my way, whereupon he threw his hat on the floor – he used to wear a different hat almost every day – and left the set.

'Ten minutes later he was back and, of course, by now I was in a terrible state of nerves. "Will you do it my way?" he asked. Only if I could also do it the way I wanted and then we'd decide which way was best, I replied. Which is what we did. Rushes the following day were very interesting because the theatre was packed with people who knew about our argument. They laughed quite a lot at Paddy's way because of my facial expressions, but when I did it the wrong way, they laughed like mad.

'Paddy was sitting next to me at this point and he reached over and ruffled my hair, saying, "Norman, in future we talk." From then on we were the greatest of pals. There was this great feeling between us. We gelled nicely and he had the same sense of humour as I did.'

Carstairs, who directed, and co-wrote some of, Wisdom's first six films for Rank, was fond of declaring the comedian would 'do anything, if you dare him'.

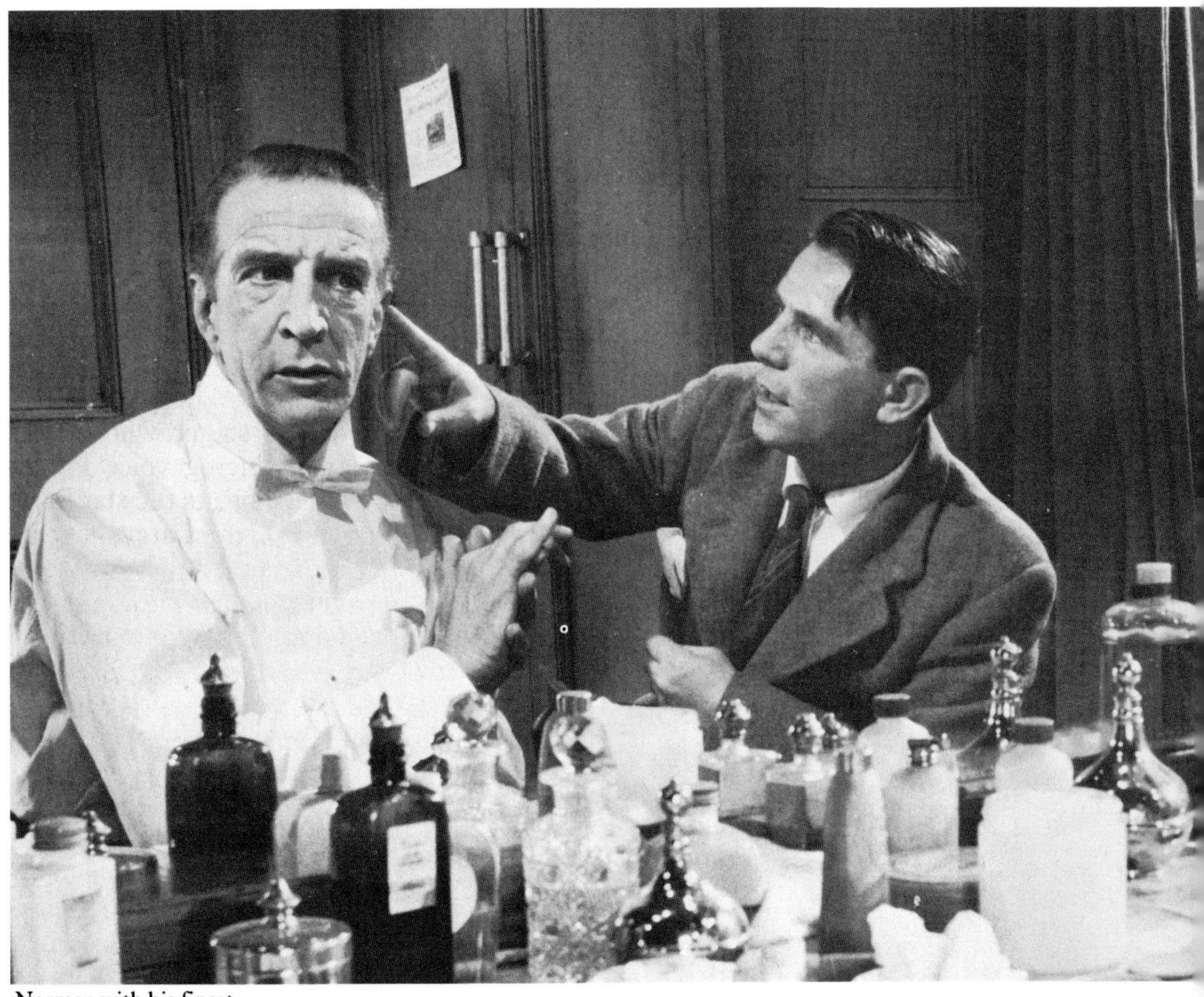

Norman with his finest foil, Jerry Desmonde, just before the dye begins to run in *Follow a Star*.

One of Wisdom's trademarks in the films which had followed him from his popular stage and television appearances was the famous 'gump' suit and peaked cap. This had stemmed from summer season in Scarborough, where Wisdom used to do one show a week for a month. There was a conjuror on the bill, David Nixon (later to become a great television favourite), who found the final show hard-going in terms of gathering new material, so he asked Wisdom if he would pretend to be a member of the audience.

Wisdom explains: 'The idea was he'd invite me on stage, I'd mess up a few tricks, get some laughs and so on. I went into the town and bought a suit for 30 bob and a cap for about a shilling. We did the act and it proved so successful that we were booked into the London Casino at the end of that season. As for the way I used to wear the cap, that came from a television show when the director asked if I'd take it off because it was casting a shadow over my face. But it's part of my uniform, I protested; people were getting to know me that way. "Well,

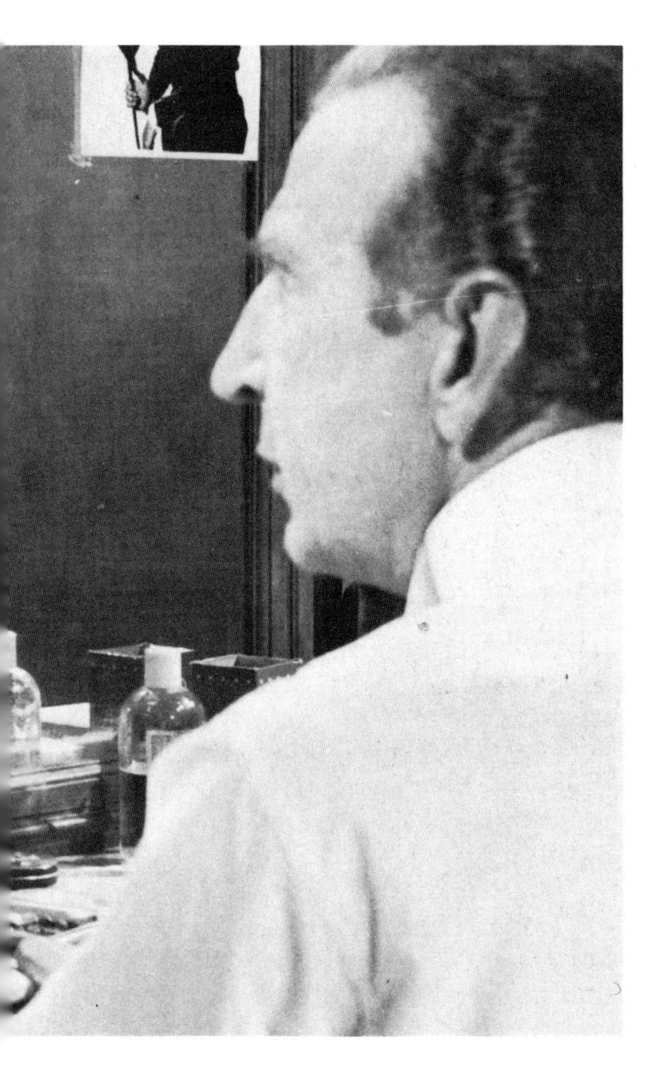

do something. Turn the peak up." Which is what I did. The shadow disappeared and the peak remained up after that.'

Trouble in Store (1953), *One Good Turn* (1954), *Man of the Moment* (1955), *Up in the World* (1956), *Just My Luck* (1957), *The Square Peg* (1958), *Follow a Star* (1959) . . . the 'fifties films followed a tried formula.

Hapless window-dresser, odd-job man, junior clerk, window-cleaner, gormless punter, puny parachutist (though in that film, *The Square Peg*, Wisdom also got his first chance to double up, playing the Nazi General Schreiber as well) or shy singer, they were all Norman – lucky with orphans and cripples, generally unlucky in love and always very much put-upon by the likes of supercilious Jerry Desmonde or pompous Edward Chapman (as the immortal Mr Grimsdale).

Poor Jerry Desmonde, who had also been stooge to Sid Field, would find himself dangling from a tree in *The Early Bird* or the victim of some real messing-about in *Follow a Star*. In the film, Desmonde played Vernon Carew, an ageing singer who 'steals' Wisdom's wonderful singing voice for his stage act. The little man visits the star in his dressing-room and, because Carew is going grey, offers to put some dye on his hair.

'Of course, he was already in his evening dress,' Wisdom recalls, 'without jacket on. The dye went all round his neck and down the front of his shirt and his acting was absolutely marvellous because he went raving mad. There were tears in his eyes from frustration and sheer annoyance. Then the director [Robert Asher, who was to supervise Wisdom's last six films for Rank] said, "Cut." The crew packed up but Jerry kept going. He couldn't help it, he was in a terrible state – and it was absolutely sincere.'

After just his second film, stories began appearing in the press about Wisdom with headlines such as 'I'm a nice chap really.' He was quoted as saying, 'Yes, I know what they have been saying. They say success has made me high-hatted. That I'm a selfish star who doesn't want to give anyone else the limelight in his films. That I'm difficult . . .

'It just isn't true, you know. But I can tell you it's been hurting me deeply. I've been really unhappy. I'm a peace-loving little chap who does just what he's ordered to do. I don't want all the glory or, for that matter, all the blame. All I'm contributing are a few gag suggestions. If they don't like the suggestions they can throw them out. I'm only the star, not the boss.' By the time he was on assignment number six, Wisdom had managed to extract a prominent co-writer credit.

There was more press excitement in the mid-'fifties when a London-based American producer, Irving Allen, announced his company was sinking no less than £500,000 (the Rank comedies cost about £130,000 each) in a major movie to launch Wisdom on an international career. It seems that the comedian's first three films had been flops in the States but that, said Allen, 'was not Wisdom's fault. That's Mr Rank's worry. You must spend money to make good pictures.'

Added one of the producer's assistants: 'Wisdom will conquer America all right. Our pictures are successful because they are more extravagant, have a glamorous setting and show Britain and America.' *An Englishman in Las Vegas*, as the project was 'glamorously' titled, was apparently to have co-starred Edward G. Robinson and Anita Ekberg. It was never made. Wisdom was not to 'conquer' America for at least another decade – until 1967, that is, when he was acclaimed for the Broadway stage show *Walking Happy*, which then did, indeed, lead to his first, and only, Hollywood movie, *The Night They Raided Minsky's*, in which he played a music-hall comic.

Meanwhile, back in Britain, Rank continued churning out the Wisdom fare, one a year, made in black-and-white, released on Boxing Day, all moneyspinners. The company even threw a lunch for him at Grosvenor House, where they presented their diminutive gold-mine with a beautiful silver tray atop golden legs for being the Organisation's top box-office attraction.

Wisdom, the perfectionist, kept fretting. Olive Dodds, director of artists for the company, remembers how he would come and sit in her office and tell her 'how he wanted to play the Hunchback of Nôtre-Dame. He was ambitious and longed to be a straight actor. Never mind the bottom-pinching, he was a fabulous worker.'

On two occasions he went off to make films – one, *The Girl on the Boat*, a period piece derived from P.G. Wodehouse – for another company, but he always returned to the fold. He could not understand why Rank did not shoot his comedies in colour and he very much resented the fact. The company's reasoning was simple – if it could make money with him on monochrome, why bother to switch to more expensive colour?

After ten films for Rank number eleven, *The Early Bird*, and the twelfth and last, 1966's *Press for Time*, finally got the colour treatment. However, Wisdom was again seen to be whingeing in the papers about what he said was the company's refusal to let him have more say in the productions: 'They don't seem to realise that I have grown up and can get laughs without falling down.'

Nevertheless his story idea about a modern-day Dick Whittington who ends up not as Lord Mayor of London but as a ticket tout at Wembley remained on the shelf.

When Norman Wisdom, as butcher's assistant Norman Pitkin in *A Stitch in Time*, is banned from entering hospital to visit little orphaned Lindy, he has to resort to various disguises. One is as an ambulance man. Another (patently confusing Jerry Desmonde, seen here as Sir Hector) is that of a flighty nurse. Wisdom has said that in his opinion slapstick is 'more difficult to perform than straight acting . . . The routines would have to be worked out well in advance so one knew exactly how to make them seem almost spontaneous.'

It was said to have been as a result of Wisdom's perpetual moaning that Rank was determined to find and demonstrate a comedic rival who would not only make them more money but also, perhaps, contrive 'to stop Norman's nonsense'. Rank settled on one of television's top teams, Morecambe and Wise, starring them in three (colour) films between 1964 and 1967 – *The Intelligence Men*, *That Riviera Touch* and *The Magnificent Two*. Although the trio made money, the films had cost too much to make and the profit margin on them was too low for the exercise to continue.

Wisdom now looks back on his thirteen years with Rank with much affection, though admitting that 'a little cog would occasionally get in the wheel, but that happens to everybody.'

His favourite recollection goes back to that first film, *Trouble in Store*, and, more particularly, the song which would always become associated with the Little Man in the gump suit.

'I was doing a show at the Prince of Wales theatre and I decided to write a song for it. I went to the musical director, had it arranged, then put it in the show. The

manager came round and said how dare I change the material. I told him it was *my* act, to which he replied, "This is a show, and anyway, it's an awful song."

'A few months later, I was doing the film and we were on the scene where I'm with Lana Morris and we're trying to feed the swans.

'Paddy Carstairs thought it would be marvellous if we had a song to go in at that point. I told him I'd write one, to which he said he was satisfied with the work I was doing and that I shouldn't mess about trying to write songs too. So I went to the bloke in the music recording department and asked him to take the song, from the theatre show, to the director telling Paddy he'd written it.

'The bloke did this, after which Paddy came over to me and said he thought he had the right song for me. We went over to the studio and the bloke sat down at the piano and sang, "Don't Laugh At Me 'Cos I'm a Fool". "What do you think of that?" Paddy asked me. "Not too keen," I said. Paddy replied that we were going to use it anyway. We didn't tell him until after we'd recorded it that I had actually written the song.'

Below: Morecambe and Wise attempting to be 'The Intelligence Men'; (middle), definitive proof of Ernie's short, fat, hairy legs in a scene from *That Riviera Touch*; (right), Eric makes a suave lover for Margit Saad in *The Magnificent Two*.

The Cleo That Never Was

Cleopatra, one of Hollywood's most famous flops, and perhaps the costliest, started filming at Pinewood on 28 September 1960 and was suspended 52 days later, on 18 November. Just under eleven minutes of usable De Luxe, Todd-AO film were 'in the can'.

This was to be another Roman epic-that-never-was, an eerie echo of an earlier fiasco, Korda's *I, Claudius*, at Denham in 1937, a project which was scrapped owing to a mixture of illness and incompetence.

Pinewood's *Cleopatra* story began towards the end of 1959, when Twentieth Century-Fox sealed a deal with Rank to bring its prestigious production to England. Why the UK? Elizabeth Taylor, signed for the title role, insisted on a European base for tax reasons. Fox was lured because of potential income from the Eady fund.

Whatever the various financial implications, the film would be the biggest ever handled in Britain. The sets alone were to cost more than the entire budgets of the three costliest films made at Pinewood since the studio opened.

Despite a shortage of plasterers – Pinewood had even resorted to advertising on peak-time network television for more workers – the paper palaces of Rome and Alexandria began to take shape during the damp, chill summer of 1960. A remarkable set, representing Alexandria harbour, went up and some million gallons of water went in, augmented by English rains.

Rouben Mamoulian, the 62-year-old Russian-born director – and no stranger to studio fights, having been fired from both *Laura* and *Porgy and Bess* – had spent a year of preparation on *Cleopatra*. He was said to have been physically sick with apprehension when he first saw the bogus city of Alexandria set in the English countryside. His mood was not improved when he learned that Hollywood was insisting that the Egyptian desert scenes be filmed there too.

Ernie Holding, who ran Fox's office in London, was convinced from the beginning that the enterprise was massively unwieldy: 'And it was too big. I remember those designs so well. I had them pasted all round my office. Every time I looked at them I thought, "Christ, we'll never get this done." '

When Elizabeth Taylor checked into the studio, trouble followed. She insisted on having her own Hollywood hairdresser, Sydney Guilaroff. The unions said no. After a dispute that reached out to other studios, the star was told she could have Guilaroff – but only supervising a British hairdresser.

Before a foot of film had been shot, the bill had already passed £1 million, and there were still sixteen shooting weeks to come, at a cost of about $120,000 a *day*.

Shooting started – with Peter Finch cast as Caesar and Stephen Boyd as Mark Antony – and then came the day for the invasion of the 5000 centurions and camp followers for a massive, colourful tableau. Pinewood management had to lay on 28 tube trains from London and there were 30 buses doing a non-stop pick-up from nearby Uxbridge station to the studios.

The harbour of Alexandria on Pinewood's backlot; (inset), Richard Burton and Elizabeth Taylor in the completed version of *Cleopatra*.

Mobile lavatories were hired from Epsom racecourse, catering marquees erected, and food to feed the 5000 was created in mountains.

At 8.30 am they were ready to shoot – except that it was pouring with rain and the weather did not look as if it was clearing up. To cut their losses, the 'call' was abandoned and 5000 extras swept out of the studio, descending on Uxbridge for their refreshment. Pinewood's catering, including 9000 sausage rolls, remained untouched.

Casting itself was a nightmare quite apart from problems with the principals. John Owen was given the job of casting huge crowds – Romans, Egyptians and Nubians – after being given, by the director, some 100 sketches and told: 'I want people like that, facially and physically.' In all, Owen auditioned 10,000 people. 'The only thing that made me wonder whether we would make the film was Mamoulian himself,' Owen recalled. 'He was past it.'

It was Owen who saved the situation over Mark Antony's double and his horse. One of the first scenes shot at Pinewood was to be of Mark Antony, on horseback, leaping from a barge in Alexandria harbour on to the landing stage. The offical stuntman quailed at such a thought. Following a brainwave by the horse-handler, Owen contacted leading showjumper Alan Oliver, who raced from his Oxfordshire bed in the middle of the night to complete the stunt early the following morning.

By this time, Elizabeth Taylor was in the London Clinic with a near-fatal illness necessitating a major operation, and Joan Collins was on standby to take over the role. Fox had decided enough was enough, and pulled the plug on Pinewood's *Cleopatra*. When it cranked up again later in Italy, there was a new director (Joseph Mankiewicz) and two new actors, Rex Harrison (Caesar) and Richard Burton (Mark Antony), to join a now-recovered Elizabeth Taylor.

As they had not used the three large Pinewood stages they had booked, Fox had to pay thousands of pounds in compensation over a further three-month period. Cyril Howard, who was in charge of Rank artists and their contracts at the time, said the company also did rather well out of the 'sub-let' of its star Peter Finch, even though he only filmed for a total of eight days.

According to Ernie Holding, whose office was closed down soon after the *débâcle*: 'The Americans were enthusiastic about the big set on the lot once they had settled for the fact that it wasn't as big as they would have liked. They thought it was an excellent job of work and passed on their compliments to Pinewood. But anyone in the industry who knows anything about it would have realised that shooting towards the end of September on an outside set the size of the one we had just didn't make sense.'

Perhaps the final irony was that even before shooting first began on *Cleopatra* in its ill-fated English sortie, a top-level Hollywood decision had been reached which would, in any case, have precluded that famous final credit line which has decorated so many international movies: 'Made at Pinewood Studios, London, England.'

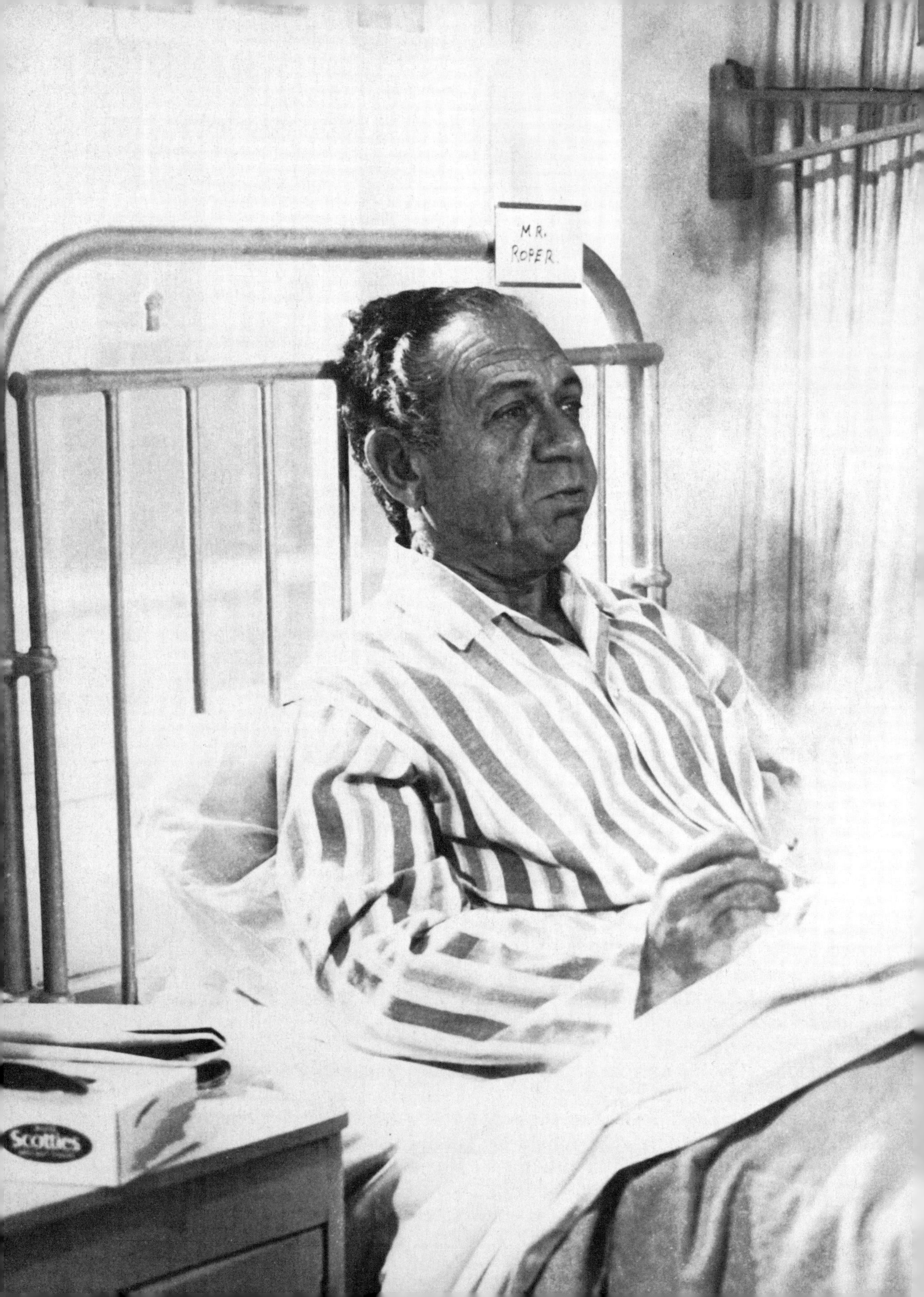
MR.
ROPER.
Scotties

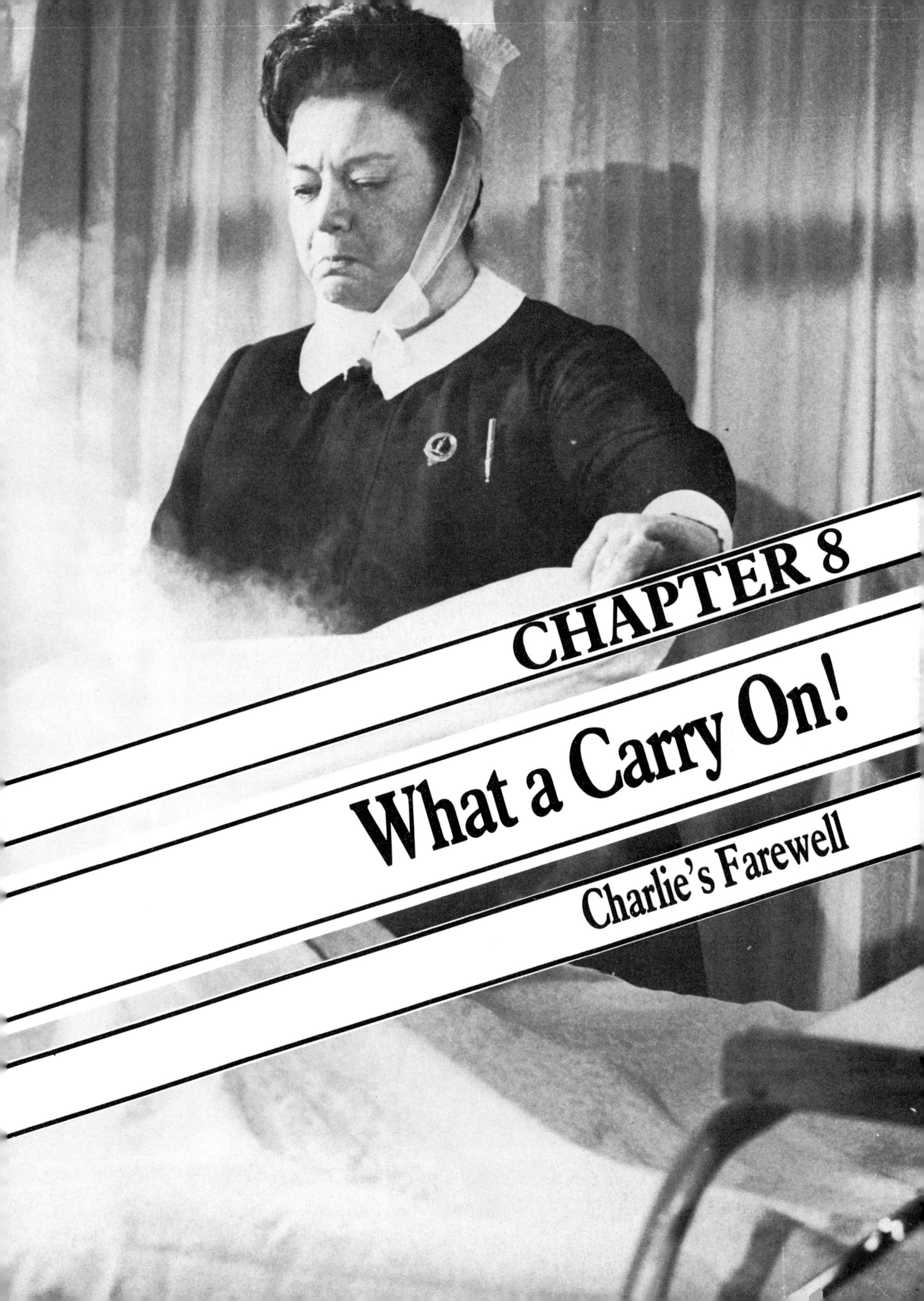
CHAPTER 8
What a Carry On!
Charlie's Farewell

Previous page: Sid James is caught in the act during *Carry On, Doctor* by matron Hattie Jacques; (above), Kenneth Williams and Sid James prepare to fight a duel in *Don't Lose Your Head*.

By the time the Rank Organisation took over the financing of the *Carry On* films in 1966, the series was already a national institution. Twelve had come off the production line, starting in 1958 with *Carry On, Sergeant* (costing a mere £72,000), and they continued at a rate of often two a year, with backing, ironically, from Rank's rivals Anglo Amalgamated (Nat Cohen and Stuart Levy). From the beginning, however, the production base was Pinewood, just as the other constant, over a remarkable 30-year history, was the producer-director team of Peter Rogers and Gerald Thomas.

Rogers had needed a sense of humour from the days when he started out as a producer of religious films for J. Arthur Rank. The films were so bad, he says, that the public were apt to throw tomatoes at the screen. The insult was compounded when Rogers realised that tomatoes were on ration, so it meant people were even prepared to squander food to indicate their disgust.

The *Carry On* formula of puns, slapstick and risqué humour reaped dividends from the start – number two, *Carry On, Nurse* was the top money-maker of 1959 – as did the early establishment of a regular acting team, including Sid James, Barbara Windsor, Joan Sims, Kenneth Connor, Kenneth Williams, Charles Hawtrey and Hattie Jacques. The films, shot on a shoestring, were usually completed in five to six weeks and would generally be scheduled for the spring or autumn since most of the cast were appearing in pantomime or seaside shows at other times of the year.

When Stuart Levy died and his partner, Nat Cohen, wished to move on to grander things, Peter Rogers decided to fall in with Rank. Their first collaboration was *Don't Lose Your Head* (1966), a *Carry On* in all but name. For this, and the subsequent *Follow That Camel*, the company dropped the *Carry On* prefix, presumably because it would have linked the films too closely with the company's rivals. Commercial considerations fairly swiftly prevailed and '*Carry On*' was appended third time out for *Carry On, Doctor*.

When the team settled in to Pinewood for *Don't Lose Your Head* (a spoof on the French Revolution), the pattern was familiar but still funny, thanks to the series' best scriptwriter, Talbot Rothwell. There was Sid James as lisping Sir Rodney Ffing ('with two ffs'), and Kenneth Williams as Citizen Camembert ('I'm the big cheese round here'), not to mention Charles Hawtrey and Peter Butterworth as, respectively, the Duc de Pommfrit and Citizen Bidet.

The poverty of the budgets meant that improvisation was the name of the game. For *Carry On Up the Khyber* (1968), the cast and crew went to Beddgelert, doubling for India, at the foot of Mount Snowdon in Wales. Sixty local farmers were hired as hostile tribesmen, such a cluster of extras prompting Gerald Thomas to declare he felt like Cecil B. DeMille. As warrior chief Bungdit Din, Bernard Bresslaw had to wear make-up so complicated it took him a full two hours to apply the brown gunge. Later, while in pantomime in Newcastle, Bresslaw slipped into a local Indian restaurant for a curry; the proprietor enthused about the *Carry On* films, and *Carry On Up the Khyber* in particular. 'Tell me,' he asked the giant actor, 'did you enjoy my country?'

Kenneth Williams' favourite recollection of Carrying On stems from this particular film. Joan Sims, playing the governor's wife, buxom Lady Joan Ruff-Diamond, had to declare her love for Williams, as the wickedly handsome but villainous Khasi of Kalabar. In mid-declaration, Williams broke wind. How, asked Miss Sims, could this love scene continue with all that farting going on? 'Oh, shut up,' said Williams. 'Valentino used to sound off all the time in *his* love scenes.' Director Thomas quickly chipped in: 'But they were *silent* films then. Yours are now on the soundtrack.'

Carry On Camping (1969) was filmed during a particularly wet autumn and the girls, who needed to wear wellington boots in the muddy fields, had to be filmed from the knees upwards. Brown leaves had to be sprayed green and the grass painted to create the right summery effect.

The script demanded that Barbara Windsor, as the delectable Babs, should lose her bra during a strenuous outdoor aerobics session. First, she demanded a closed set. Then, discovering the shooting was in a field, called for 'a closed field'. The bra was supposed to ping off into Kenneth Williams' face. It was decided to use a stray fishing line to hook the garment but Miss Windsor insisted that a dirty old man (Williams' character) would have *pulled* it off. Williams tried it but only succeeded in pulling the actress down headfirst into the mud. They sponged her down and started all over again with, this time, her hands covering her bare chest. Now, Hattie Jacques, as gym mistress Miss Haggerd, pulled her by the arm, thus exposing her.

Poor Barbara Windsor also found herself victim of a producer's jape during *Carry On Camping*. Directed to walk first through mud and then through a slimy stream, she started her unpleasant trek. Believing it to

Right: Hattie Jacques, followed by Barbara Windsor, leads the girls to the showers in *Carry On Camping*; (far right), affairs of state discussed by Kenneth Williams, Sid James, Charles Hawtrey and Terry Scott in *Carry On, Henry*.

be just a rehearsal – with no microphones active – she began uttering her opinion of Peter Rogers in the choicest language. For a joke, the soundmen recorded it. When the day's rushes were shown, Rogers mischievously decided to play back the soundtrack to the actress, whereupon she became hysterical, expecting instant dismissal.

During the shooting of *Carry On Again, Doctor* (1969), Jim Dale, as the unsubtly named Dr Nookey, attempted a stunt whereby he plummeted down 30 stairs on a hospital trolley. Unfortunately, on each stair a metal bar jarred his arm. 'Everybody thought I was brilliant,' he recalls, 'but my arm swelled up like a balloon and I had to go to hospital to have it treated.'

Carry On Up the Jungle, released the following year, featured Bernard Bresslaw as an African chief, Upsidasi, who had to translate head-hunter Sid James's English into the local lingo. Conscientious as ever, Bresslaw decided to learn a genuine language, Ndebel, because he did not want to be recorded uttering mere gibberish. When he arrived on the set, he expected the cast and extras to be suitably surprised and impressed. But the black extras looked at him quite blankly. They were all from the West Indies. However, his efforts were not entirely in vain. Years later, in a Bournemouth shoe shop, a sales assistant asked

Tourists Kenneth Connor and June Whitfield discover the perils of sleeping in a half-finished hotel, which include being interrupted by Peter Butterworth, in *Carry On Abroad*.

Bresslaw where he had learned Ndebel. That, he recalls, made it all worth while.

For *Carry On Loving* (1970), about the misadventures of a marriage agency, Kenneth Williams, alias Percival Snooper, had to be hit in the face with a cream cake. To make the shot easier, Gerald Thomas ordered someone off camera to hurl it from just six feet away. Williams joked that he wanted someone cross-eyed to throw it, whereupon all hell broke loose. The director tried three times and missed, then Julian Holloway, Bernard Bresslaw and eventually the whole cast joined in, until he was eventually splattered. Amid such frolics, no one was actually sure *who* had hit the actor.

Barbara Windsor's favourite of the series was *Carry On, Henry* (1970), which just happened to coincide with BBC Television's popular six-part historical pageant dealing with the fruity monarch, even if South African-born Sid James was to prove a shade more rough-hewn than Keith Michell. As King's favourite, Bettina, Miss Windsor was let in for some more bawdy activity and again she asked for the set to be cleared. This clearly puzzled one of the Pinewood technicians, who had strolled in from a nearby stage where Ken Russell was putting cast and extras through unspeakable hoops for his controversial *The Devils*.

'What,' he declared, 'a closed set for a bum and tit? You should see what's going on next door for everyone to watch!'

In *Carry On, Matron* (1971), Kenneth Cope had to dress up as a woman, in frilly undies – black knickers, stockings and suspenders. He says he so enjoyed the attention, he ended up flirting with the men and even chased a black extra who was trying to pick him up.

For a scene in *Carry On Abroad* (1972) – set in the fictitious, if faintly recognisable, resort of Elsbels – Sid James had to collect some tickets then pick up a suitcase that was supposed to be empty. For a joke, one of the camera crew decided to fill it with weights. When James flipped the case up, expecting it to be featherlight, he almost toppled over with the weight. Trouper that he was, he first feigned annoyance then joined in the general hilarity.

Barbara Windsor had never ridden a motorbike until she was required to do so, along Brighton Promenade, in *Carry On, Girls* (1973). Gerald Thomas told her she could have as many rehearsals as she liked until she felt completely at ease, but Barbara thought that endless rehearsing would only end up scaring the life out of her, so she decided to get on with it and do it first time with the camera rolling. And it worked.

The following year, 1974, probably spelled the beginning of the end for the series, although there would still be a further four, the last in 1978. The year 1974 saw the début of Greg Smith's *Confessions of . . .* quartet, equally slapstick, obviously youth-oriented and, perhaps the real killer, much more explicitly sexy. If *Carry Ons* were the equivalent of McGill postcards, *Confessions of . . .* (successively *Window Cleaner*, *Pop Performer*, *Driving Instructor* and *From a Holiday Camp*) smacked of 'What the Butler Saw'. A trio of equally saucy, and youthful, titles in producer Stanley Long's *Adventures of . . .* cycle (*Plumber's Mate*, *Private Eye* and *Taxi Driver*) proved simply the final nail in the coffin.

When, once again, Barbara Windsor was asked to expose herself in *Carry On, Dick* – as in Dick Turpin – nobody seemed the least bit interested during filming. 'Doesn't anybody want to look at me?' she asked, poignantly. 'We've seen it all before,' came the chilling retort.

Carry On, Dick (1974) was to be Sid James's last film. The following year, he was not used in *Carry On Behind*. At the time he was appearing weekly in television's hit sitcom *Bless This House*, and there was fear of over-exposure. A year later, he was dead following a heart attack during a stage performance. *Carry On Behind* (1975) not only introduced a crop of new actors, including Windsor Davies (from *It Ain't Half Hot, Mum*) and Ian Lavender (of *Dad's Army*), but also added some international glamour in the form of Elke Sommer. The mix did not prove particularly popular. Even less so was 1976's *Carry On, England*, the 16th and last *Carry On* that would be financed by a now less-than-enchanted Rank. Even Peter Rogers' boast 'We're vulgar, but we're never crude' was now beginning to sound a little hollow.

The final outing to date at Pinewood had been *Carry On, Emmanuelle*, the *raison d'être* of which seemed to be 'if you can't beat the bandwagon, at least climb on it'. The film was financed independently, and Rogers and Thomas used a young Australian scriptwriter, Lance Peters, a pretty newcomer, Suzanne Danielle, as the man-devouring heroine, and just three of the original *Carry On* stars, Kenneth Williams, Joan Sims and Kenneth Connor. The public stayed away in droves, presumably signifying that it preferred its sex straight, not spoofed.

The actors who made the series knew they would never become millionaires, regular though the work may have been. As Barbara Windsor once said: 'Nobody's going to get rich playing in *Carry Ons*. Anybody doing them strictly for money is in trouble. The reason we do them is that it's such a great team.'

Peter Rogers, who may admit to having become wealthy from his *Carry On* connection, summed up the 30 years with typical succinctness: 'To have made the series is not an achievement – it's a bloody liberty.'

Right: Barbara Windsor and Sid James share the joys of highway robbery in *Carry On, Dick*, 26th in the series. When Babs had to strip for one scene, no one seemed particularly interested.

Caught in a dig are Elke Sommer and Kenneth Williams in *Carry On Behind*; (far right), sergeant major Windsor Davies bawls out orders on behalf of his curiously-clad commanding officer, Kenneth Connor, in *Carry On, England*.

Charlie's Farewell

After the critical box-office disaster of Charlie Chaplin's savagely anti-American film *A King in New York* (1957), made in England in the wake of his self-imposed exile from the country that had been his home since 1913, most people believed the great man had finally retired from the industry. Chaplin was on his way to the London première of *Limelight* (1952) when he was notified that the US Attorney General had instructed the immigration authorities not to issue Chaplin a re-entry visa unless he submitted himself to the then rampant House Un-American Activities Committee to clear himself of alleged Communist leanings. Chaplin, a Cockney born in 1889, determined from that moment never to return to the States and settled instead in Switzerland. *A King in New York* – a satirical swipe at the American way of life – was his filmic riposte, made from a bitter desire for revenge rather than for reasons of commercial potential. The film features Chaplin as the deposed King Shahdov, who takes refuge in New York.

Almost another decade had gone by when Chaplin, now aged 77, and father of eight, suddenly emerged from 'retirement' and returned to his native England to make yet another movie, at Pinewood. Called *A Countess from Hong Kong*, it was backed, ironically, by a generous slice of American money, from Universal. For the first time Chaplin worked in colour, widescreen and with international stars – Marlon Brando and Sophia Loren. Though writer, director and composer as usual, Chaplin was not the film's producer: this chore he entrusted to his friend Jerome Epstein.

The film opens with a subtitle: 'As a result of two World Wars, Hong Kong was crowded with refugees . . .' and then proceeds to tell the comic story of an exiled Russian countess (Loren) who meets an American diplomat (Brando) while working

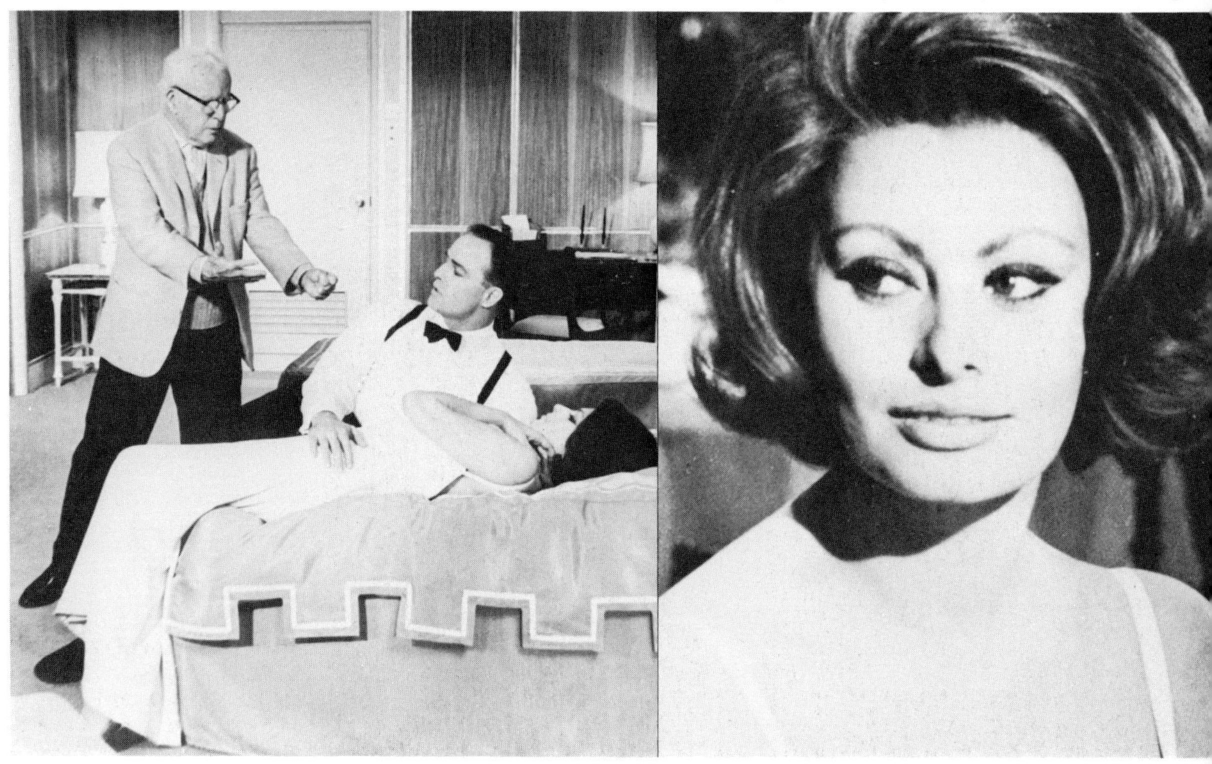

as a dance escort. When he has to sail home for a new post, she smuggles herself on board ship and he next encounters her as a stowaway in his cabin. The resulting action is mostly taken up with the diplomat's efforts to conceal the countess from the authorities on board.

Brando, in mid-stream during a mercurial career, seemed a curious choice for this farcical comedy, but as he said: 'When a man of his [Chaplin's] stature in the industry writes a script for you, you can hardly refuse. Why he should think of me for comedy, I haven't the faintest idea. But he said I was the only one who could play it.'

The real problem was that the script was hardly new. It was based on *White Russian*, a film Chaplin had written 30 years earlier for his then wife, Paulette Goddard, and shelved. Its age clearly showed and Chaplin's film-making methods did not help either. He followed his usual practice of acting out every part for his players. Brando, honed in his own very individual Method style, felt insulted – and let it show in a sullen performance. He declared that it was not too long into production before he felt he wanted to tell the Master that it all seemed 'a terrible mistake'. Loren, however, remained constantly diligent. Chaplin's own lot was not made any easier when he slipped and broke an ankle during filming.

Asked during shooting why he insisted on continuing his film-making career, Chaplin said that it was what 'has always sustained me, the place where I have really existed and has been my work. I care about my work; it's the best thing I do.'

Reviews and box office confirmed the worst. *A Countess From Hong Kong* was a failure on both counts.

Chaplin gave himself a cameo in the film. He appears as a sea-sick steward on deck with Brando. He opens the door for the actor but says nothing. Chaplin left films as he had entered them more than fifty years earlier – in silence.

Far left: Chaplin directs Brando and Loren; (left), Loren and Brando in a scene from *A Countess from Hong Kong*.

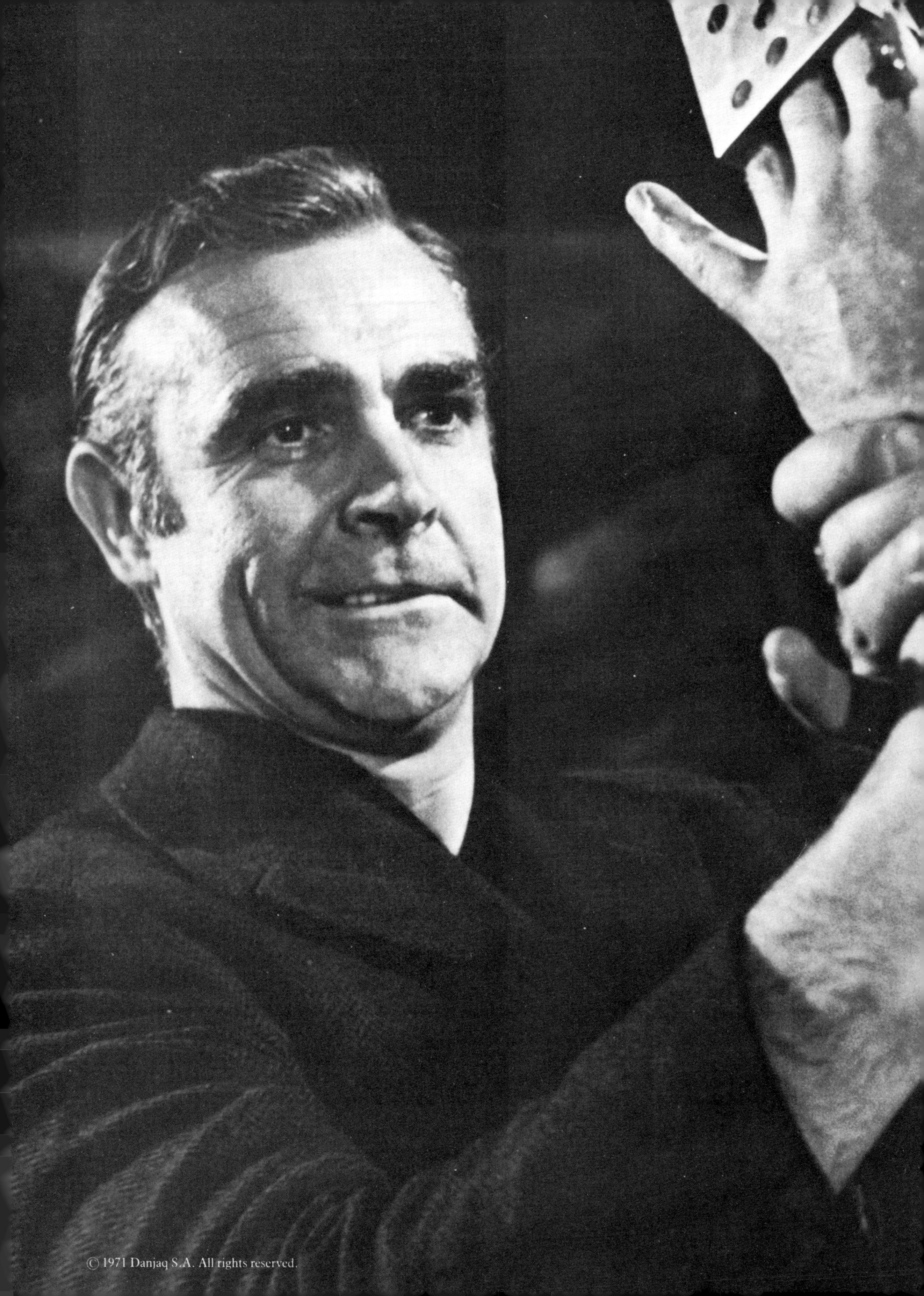

CHAPTER 9

Bond and Beyond: Pinewood 2

Angels with Creamy Faces

The Pinewood story of the 'sixties, 'seventies and, for that matter, of the 'eighties, revolves principally around the *James Bond* saga for, as production generally has waxed and waned over the years, as producers have come and gone, 007 has remained a fixed point in an ever-changing age.

Production of all fifteen official Bond films has been based in Buckinghamshire, from *Dr No* in 1962, which cost less than a million dollars, to 1986's *The Living Daylights*, the cost of which must be counted in megabucks. The series is estimated to have been watched by more than a *billion* people worldwide.

When Harry Saltzman and his partner Albert 'Cubby' Broccoli started the ball rolling they surely cannot have envisaged that the sequence would last more than a quarter of a century and employ a quartet of agents with the famous 'licence to kill' – Sean Connery, George Lazenby, Roger Moore and Timothy Dalton.

Whatever expense was spared on the début *Dr No*, with Connery *versus* Joseph Wiseman, was made up for with attractive Jamaican locations and ingenious production design at the studio of Ken Adam, which included the villain's laboratory and an enormous aquarium.

With the instant success of the first, United Artists supplied a bigger budget second time round, for *From Russia with Love* (1963). This title journeyed to Istanbul but also made full use of the studio – even its lawns, transformed into a training camp

Previous page: Sean Connery has his man fingered in *Diamonds Are Forever*; (left), Connery corners the lovely Daniela Bianchi in *From Russia with Love*. The film had a couple of memorable villains in Lotte Lenya (as Rosa Klebb) and Robert Shaw (as Red Grant).

for the dreaded SPECTRE organisation.

Ken Adam spent four days at Fort Knox in Kentucky researching for his elaborate re-creation of the federal gold depository in five acres at Pinewood for *Goldfinger* (1964), which dollar-for-dollar may be the most successful Bond film yet.

'If,' said Adam, 'the gold bullion seems unrealistically piled, it's because I decided to capture people's imagination by stacking it forty feet into the air. In reality, it should only be stacked two foot six inches up because of the weight.'

The *Bond* budget had increased almost six-fold by 1965, the year of *Thunderball*, which included £200,000 for one item – Largo's luxury yacht *Disco Volante*. Next, on *You Only Live Twice* (1967), just one set, the volcano, cost the same as the *entire* budget of *Dr No*. The volcano (see also page 88) was so high it could be seen three miles away and was wide enough to fly a helicopter in.

When the lid slid off it revealed a 66-foot rocket-launching pad, helicopter platforms, offices and a maze of tunnels. It contained literally miles of tubular steel, 700 tons of structural steel and 200 tons of plaster. An approach road and platform consumed half-a-million tubular couplings and 800 railway sleepers (at 16*s* 9*d* each).

Sean Connery stepped down for *On Her Majesty's Secret Service* (1969) to be replaced by the one-hit-wonder George Lazenby, who moved aside when Connery returned for *Diamonds Are Forever* (1971), featuring a lavish Pinewood penthouse for villainous Ernst Stavro Blofeld.

The Bond/Miss Moneypenny relationship has always been an enigma – so here, in *For Your Eyes Only*, Roger Moore and Lois Maxwell look suitably enigmatic. It was the first 007 film in which the original author, Ian Fleming, was uncredited.

The arrival of Roger Moore in *Live and Let Die* (1973), followed by *The Man With the Golden Gun* (1974), saw the main emphasis switch to spectacular locations such as Louisiana and Thailand before *The Spy Who Loved Me* (1977) signalled the start of 007's real megadollar era.

'Cubby' Broccoli had, by now, gone solo and part of the film's £13 million expenditure was £1½ million on the world's largest silent stage, the 007 stage, designed originally to house three nuclear submarines. Measuring 374 feet long, 160 feet wide and 53 feet wide, and built over the old back-lot tank, it was also a remarkable legacy to the site of so much cinema success.

Moonraker (1979), filmed mostly in France for tax reasons, *For Your Eyes Only* (1981), *Octopussy* (1983), *A View to a Kill* (1985) and *The Living Daylights* have continued the reciprocal relationship. It is one Cyril Howard treasures dearly, and no wonder for all the work and income it generates.

Howard, who has served 45 years with Rank, including the past 38 at Pinewood itself, became managing director in 1976 on the death of a great character, E.A.R. 'Kip' Herren. Herren, a large man fond of wearing immense cardigans, would hurtle round the studio and, colleagues still recall, on approaching someone in a corridor would bellow, 'Who let you in?' The daunting greeting was actually a form of welcome.

'Every time a *Bond* film starts – even years they shoot, odd years they distribute – it seems to liven up the place,' commented Howard. 'When Cubby returns there's a different atmosphere. Everyone's buoyant.' This is perhaps understandable when you realise that Howard has an overall pay-roll of about 600, of which nearly 400 are manual grades. The place, for instance, still maintains almost 100 carpenters. And yet, in its 50 years, Pinewood has had just five hours of strikes – two of which were over well within a day.

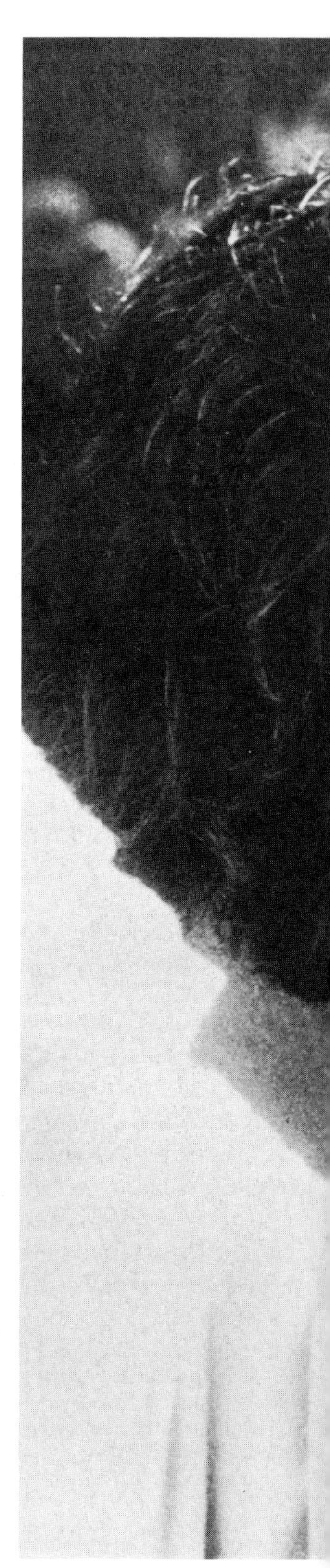

Barry Foster and Alec McCowen follow the directions of the Master, Alfred Hitchcock, during filming of Universal's *Frenzy* at Pinewood. Above: Ken Marshall braves the Pinewood swamp in Columbia's *Krull*; (right), Oliver Reed and Vanessa Redgrave in a moment from Warner's *The Devils*.

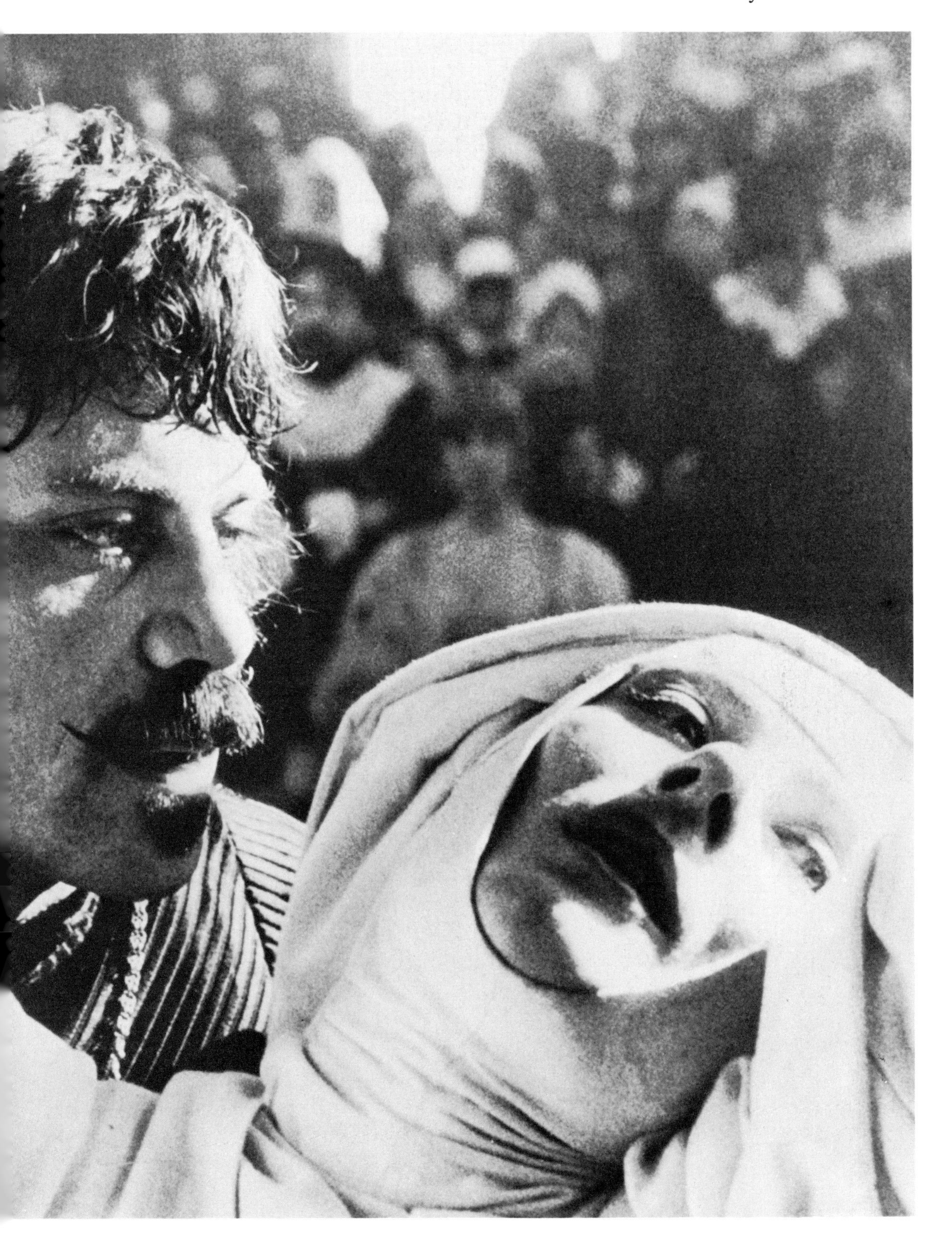

There was once a time, however, when the studio had more than a thousand workers on its books and operated 24 hours a day on two shifts.

That all changed in 1969, the year the Americans pulled out of British-based production *en masse* following the euphoric Swinging 'Sixties – a time when, remarked one film-maker, if you were British, long-haired and under 30, the Americans would give you a movie to direct.

Howard reaped the whirlwind: 'Production contracted almost to nothing and we lost a whole battery of feature films on which we were dependent. It was a nasty time and there were a lot of redundancies.'

Another infamous date etched on his memory is 27 June 1984 – the day the 007 stage burned down. It was during the filming of Ridley Scott's extravagant fantasy *Legend*. Cast and crew had broken for lunch and, as they completed their break, a gas bottle on the set 'wept' and caught a spark. The result was a million-pound blaze. Yet, within months, a new 007 stage had arisen literally from the ashes of the old edifice.

Another date which provokes mixed memories is 1976. During the year Howard was aware, as filming on *The Spy Who Loved Me* drew to a close, that there was

painfully little in the pipeline. He had resisted all ideas of going 'four-wall' – that is, making Pinewood simply a shell into which producers brought their own personnel, like Shepperton and Elstree studios – and was determined to keep it a full-facility complex. However, he had an overhead to cover.

'We were going down the swanee and I was paddling the canoe. Then the phone rang and it was *Superman*. We'd already turned down the film once because we had the Bond film and there was no space. The producers had gone off to Italy but that proved unsatisfactory. They returned to Shepperton, but the complex there wasn't going to be big enough for their needs. This time I welcomed them with open arms.'

Superman, which transformed the 007 stage into the wondrous Fortress of Solitude, came to Pinewood and filled the studio. Alternating with the *Bond*s, there then followed from the father-and-son producer team Alexander and Ilya Salkind *Superman 2*, *Superman 3*, *Supergirl* and, less super but just as fantastic, *Santa Claus – The Movie*.

Framed on Cyril Howard's wall is a spectacular *Daily Mail* centre spread of 15 August 1983 which proclaims 'How *Supergirl* changed the face of Britain' above the ex-

Left: Alice Playten and Peter O'Farrell are hidden under remarkable make-up for Ridley Scott's fantasy *Legend*; (above), David Huddleston made a cuddly Santa in the Salkinds' *Santa Claus – The Movie*.

planatory subhead 'The £250,000 transformation scene that brought America's Mid-West to a slice of Buckinghamshire.' Aerial and ground shots display, quite startlingly, the production designer's art and Pinewood's scope as 'Main Street, Mid Vale, Illinois' stretches across ten acres complete with 'Popeye's Famous Fried Chicken and Biscuit Parlour' and 'The Little Chapel of the Roses.'

But then the studio is perfectly used to this kind of re-creation. Even as *Supergirl* was preparing to 'fly', a 30-foot-high Vesuvius was being readied to erupt elsewhere on the lot for the American television miniseries *The Last Days of Pompeii*.

The main administration block has had its fair share of transformations too – from an embassy being stormed by the SAS in Euan Lloyd's production *Who Dares Wins* to a gutted ruin in Lionel Jeffries' fantasy *The Amazing Mr Blunden*. Close by was built a lavish swimming-pool for Paramount's *Great Gatsby*, with Robert Redford and Mia Farrow. Baron Bomburst's castle in *Chitty Chitty Bang Bang* and Laurence Olivier's house in *Sleuth* are just two more Pinewood creations that have dazzled cinemagoers.

But where does art end and life begin? Not too long ago, there was a car chase through Pinewood studio streets punctuated by gunshots. People working indoors thought it sounded incredibly realistic.

In fact, it was part of a real-life wages snatch, and the shots were real too. A studio security man threw himself at the gunman's car and was seriously wounded in the stomach. Though he recovered, happily, the loot never was.

Far top right: Laurence Olivier and Michael Caine in *Sleuth*; (far bottom right), a slice of American Mid-West in South Bucks for *Supergirl*.
Right: Robert Redford and Mia Farrow in *The Great Gatsby*.

Daily Mail

Angels with Creamy Faces

'Made-in-Britain' film musicals have been a rare enough commodity. Yet during 1975 no less than three were in production at Pinewood. Bryan Forbes' *The Slipper and the Rose*, composed by the Sherman Brothers (of *Mary Poppins* fame), was a charming version of the Cinderella story with Richard Chamberlain and Gemma Craven. *The Bawdy Adventures of Tom Jones*, derived from an obscure American stage show, was a rather less than charming insult to Henry Fielding.

The third, Alan Parker's *Bugsy Malone*, by far the cheapest of the three to make, was quite simply unique. Thirty-year-old Parker, a prolific maker of television commercials and writer-director of some sensitive TV films, conceived the idea for a Hollywood gangster pastiche played entirely by children.

After American composer Paul Williams had agreed to score Parker's début feature, co-producers David Puttnam (who already had a considerable track record with such films as *That'll Be the Day* and *Stardust*) and Alan Marshall, who had worked with the director in commercials, set about raising the money.

Bugsy Malone started filming as soon as the schools broke up for the summer holidays. The film was eventually completed on a laughably tiny budget of £531,000. This was made up of contributions from Rank, Paramount and the National Film Finance Corporation, not to mention second mortgages on the film-makers' homes.

Left: Scott Baio in the title role and Paul Murphy as Leroy lead the creamy-faced kids in the splurge-gun finale from *Bugsy Malone*; 'We don't need no education' suggest the faceless pupils in MGM's *Pink Floyd – The Wall*, which was derived from the Floyd's best-selling concept album.

Between mid-July and the end of September, 300–400 children between the ages of eight and fourteen came and went as Parker directed a series of hilarious setpieces – from Fat Sam's Grand Slam Speakeasy featuring the great climactic 'splurge-gun' battle, with cream substituting for bullets, to a pedal-car chase through nearby Black Park (council-owned land to the West of Pinewood that has doubled for almost anywhere in dozens of films).

The kids, including Jodie Foster and Scott Baio, who have both gone on to become considerable stars, were allowed to work only three-and-a-half hours a day, so there had to be a two-shift system. Main scenes would be shot in the morning; some background material or a dance number in the afternoon.

The financial success of *Bugsy Malone* was very gratifying for all concerned but unfortunately – such are the thought processes of film-makers worldwide – someone in Rank then assumed that childlike fantasies with music were the secret of box-office success and a substantial investment was committed to making a film about the Wombles. Directed by Lionel Jeffries (who some years earlier had made the hit *Railway Children*), *Wombling Free* received the barest release, was sold to television with almost indecent haste and generally proved an expensive failure.

Parker and Marshall must have quite liked their Pinewood experience, for a couple of years later they moved their company there. But their second film at the studio, in 1982, could not have provided a greater contrast with *Bugsy*, apart from a musical connection.

Pink Floyd – The Wall, starring Bob Geldof, was an imaginative interpretation of the best-selling rock album. Violent, sexy and anarchic, it cost $12 million to make.

CHAPTER 10

The Beat Goes On

Previous page: Gabriel Byrne and Denholm Elliott in an acclaimed Rank film of the 'eighties, *The Defence of the Realm*; (above), Michael Caine created anti-hero Harry Palmer in *The Ipcress File*, a co-production between Rank and Universal.

Visiting the Rank Organisation's headquarters in South Street, London W1 is, suggests Sir Richard Attenborough, 'a fairly daunting experience, even if one is not on a quest for hard cash. The two opaque glass-panelled nine-foot-high doors are protected by thick black glossy painted bars. There is a brass door-bell – polished every hour, one would think – which almost dares one to press it.'

On such a quest, nearly a quarter of a century ago, to raise cash for his *Gandhi* project, Attenborough pressed the bell 'with trembling hand. After a few moments the door was opened by a conservatively uniformed commissionaire and I announced that I had an appointment with the Chairman.

'I paced up and down the black and white chessboard marble floor of the hall while a phone call was made to Mr Davis's secretary. After another few moments I was taken up the massive black marble staircase. It reminded me of "Xanadu" in *Citizen Kane*, and, when I was finally shown into the Chairman's office, I was even a little surprised to see John Davis there rather than Orson Welles.'

Whether Welles/Kane would have been more sympathetic to the cause, Attenborough does not hazard a guess. Certainly he received pretty short shrift from Davis, who had finally attained the top job at the Organisation in 1962 on the retirement of the good Lord Rank.

Why on earth make a film about someone like Gandhi? Most people know nothing about him, and anyway, would they really be very interested?

That was just for starters.

Attenborough must be 'totally insane', 'nobody in India would let him make it' and 'nobody will want to see it.'

Nevertheless, 'because we have done well together' and with something short of munificence, Davis pressed a cheque for £5000 on Attenborough so that he could at least continue researching and developing the subject.

'If you set it up,' Davis told the film-maker, 'I would like you to repay us; if not, then you needn't bother.' The cheque was repaid a number of years ago.

By 1960, Davis had turned the great debts of 1949 into more than modest profits. This entailed slimming down the cinema chain and, most crucially, backing the American copying company Xerox as well as diversifying into a broader range of leisure services including bingo and hotels. On the film side, it was only the production facilities that could regularly report healthy profits.

Rank Film Laboratories, consistently profitable since their purchase from Denham in 1945, were re-equipped with new processing technology which enabled them to overtake Technicolor as the most successful labs in western Europe.

The great sufferer was film production, which had dwindled to a trickle by the end of the 'sixties and was all but non-existent by the mid-'seventies. While continuing to finance the *Carry On* series, Rank's total investment in production in the five years up to 1976 had only been at the rate of about £1¼ million a year, which nevertheless enabled it to back some five Hammer films, *The Shout* and *Tarka the Otter* (both of which revived the company's liaison with the NFFC).

So it was with something approaching astonishment when in May 1977 (the year Davis retired as chairman to become president until his final exit from the company in 1983) the industry learned that Rank was about to do a *volte-face* and go back into film-making with a vengeance.

Rank Productions, run by Edmond Chilton, a genial, chubby former equipment salesman, and Tony Williams – slight, bespectacled and a graduate of the company's own management-training scheme – were to make initially nine new films, including four produced by the hustling Michael Klinger, who had made two of Roman Polanski's best 'sixties films, *Repulsion* and *Cul-de-Sac*.

A year after Rank's momentous announcement, the Klinger package was said to be 'well and truly off' because financial arrangements had not, apparently, 'worked out'.

From Betty Box and Ralph Thomas were to come *The Persian Ransom* and *The Red Hot Ferrari*, both with glittering casts. Neither were made. With United Artists, Rank was going to finance a remake of the classic Bogart thriller *The Big Sleep*. This ended up as a Lord Grade-produced film.

However, a remake of the often-filmed John Buchan yarn, *The 39 Steps*, did go ahead and, people joked at the time, Rank would go on remaking it until they got it right. *The Lady Vanishes* was remade too, though not with Roger Moore and John Cleese as originally announced. Their places were taken by Elliott Gould and Ian Carmichael.

The Eagle's Wing, *Riddle of the Sands*, *Bad Timing*, and *Silver Dream Racer* followed, not all without incident. Anthony Harvey, the director of *The Eagle's Wing*, a lyrical if painfully slow-moving western, professed himself 'extraordinarily depressed' at the way he felt Rank had treated the film following reviews 'which, if you'd written them yourself, couldn't have been better.'

Harvey claimed that Rank 'didn't believe in the film. I would never do another film with them while the present people are in

Right: it never happened in Buchan's original story, but this climax to the second remake of *The 39 Steps*, with Robert Powell on the face of Big Ben, made for much excitement. Unlike the other two film versions, this one used the novel's correct period setting.

Right: Cybill Shepherd and Elliott Gould in a witless remake of *The Lady Vanishes*, which compared very badly with (inset) Hitchcock's peerless version of the thriller starring Michael Redgrave and Margaret Lockwood; (above), Caroline Langrishe and Sam Waterston in the cerebral western *The Eagle's Wing*.

charge.' *Bad Timing*, directed by Nicolas Roeg, had all the makings of a big prestige picture but was effectively doomed after the crushing judgement of the omnipotent George Pinches, the man who actually booked films for Rank cinemas: 'A sick film made by sick people for sick audiences.'

Things were not looking good and when, at the glitzy Cannes Film Festival in May 1980, a new '$50 million' production programme was launched with a couple of sheets of foolscap rather than a champagne-and-canapés shindig, everyone should have smelled a rat.

A month later, the honeymoon was over as Chilton explained that future production plans had been scrapped since it was felt there were better things that could be done with shareholders' money. There was no point Rank 'dabbling its feet' in production – which it had. You have to 'go the whole hog' – which it hadn't, he said. It would seem that the past three years had been merely an aberration.

Oscar-winning producer David Puttnam, whose *HMS Ulysses* project had been one victim of the 'chop', believed that Rank's move raised more general questions about

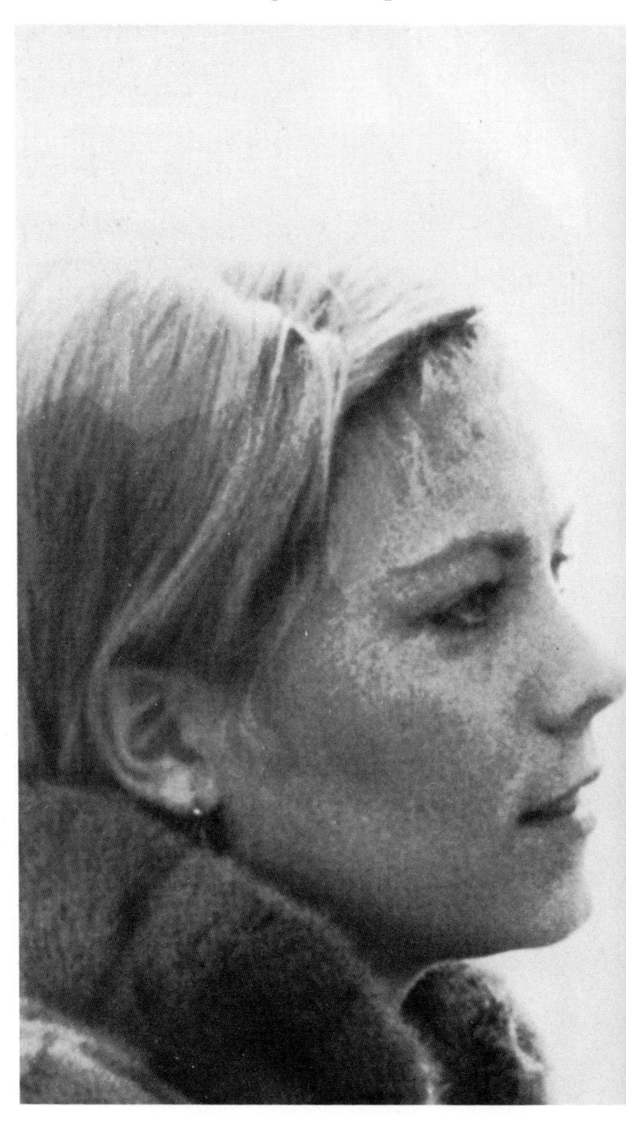

Right: Theresa Russell and Art Garfunkel in *Bad Timing*; (above), David Essex in *Silver Dream Racer*.

British management and, in particular, about levels of competence and courage. Yet for Rank it was probably better this way than to keep just 'a half-assed profile.'

Maybe the most telling comment of all came from writer and newspaper columnist Keith Waterhouse, who summed up reaction to Rank's reversal: 'Ripples of shock ran through Wardour Street on a Richter scale of absolute zero.'

Tony Williams was convinced that the Rank line-up of films 'didn't get the backing and encouragement from the company it should have. It wasn't as successful as it could, and should, have been. It allowed a situation to continue with its theatres in this country where they were, should I say, less than co-operative over the showing of their own films. There was no way that by showing Rank-made films more extensively than they were it could have been in any way against the spirit of the Monopolies Commission, whose earlier judgements had been designed to prevent all the screens being dominated by the company's own pictures.

'On the sheer number of films made alone – perhaps four a year – and the multi-screen

conversions, there was no way the films, even if they had been blockbusters, could have dominated the screens and prevented the product of British independent producers reaching the screen.'

According to Williams, the effect of the company's ambivalent attitude to its own films was to 'affect international confidence, for if the company's *own* films were not able to receive maximum playing time in the company's *own* theatres, then there had to be something very wrong.'

Could a more charismatic production head have succeeded where Williams failed?

'In my view,' he concluded, damningly, 'he would have been confounded by the Rank system.'

What Williams's explanation and excuses did not, arguably, take into account were certain facts of film life.

From way back, the British film industry had been trying to break into the lucrative and massive American domestic market with its own distribution companies.

Two faces of the natural world: (far left), Eric Porter and *The Belstone Fox*; (above), *Tarka the Otter*.

Gaumont-British tried it in the 1930s and Rank attempted the same in the 1950s, without success.

Rank Film Distributors chose a different path in the 1960s when it financed and distributed a number of films as co-productions with major US companies – *The Heroes of Telemark* with Columbia and *The Ipcress File* with Universal, for example. This way, the films obtained proper US distribution but the price to be paid was that the American partner expected to have the final decision on script, director and cast: a sometimes bitter fact of life recognised by experienced film-industry personnel, but anathema to would-be film moguls whose only knowledge of films could be said to have been gleaned from cinema auditoria.

The feeling was that delusions of grandeur and the belief that the more money spent, the better the entertainment caused Ed Chilton and his cohorts to ignore the advice of the distributors and exhibitors and to squander shareholders' money on

WHOLE FRESH
CHICKEN

Tommy Cannon, Suzanne Danielle and Bobby Ball in *The Boys in Blue*, an 'eighties offering with a blast from the past.

unsuitable projects which had no hope of achieving anything other than 'art house' distribution in America.

Amid all this gloom at about the turn of the 'eighties, which coincided with continual cinema closures and admission figures sliding inexorably, one telling statement was however generally missed as Ed Chilton heaped the blame on his own fleshy shoulders. He said that the company would be 'increasing its investment via Rank Film Distributors. This policy means that we will have between 10 and 15 per cent of some 10–12 films a year, rather than struggling to finance fully a handful.'

That year Jim Daly moved from running the laboratories to heading a new all-embracing Film and Television Services division. Caution had to be the order of the day. As Daly explains: 'Initially we had a situation where overall the division was barely profitable – the profits for the first year were certainly less than £1 million – and a large part of the problem was Rank Film Distributors (RFD).'

RFD at that time was carrying a sizeable loss, which was the result of the film productions of the preceding three years. Daly continues: 'A large part of the improvement in the division as a whole since that time has been brought about by the turnaround at RFD. We started with an extremely cautious policy, not investing in any further film production and ticking over until we had got ourselves sorted out.

'However, it became obvious very quickly from the point of view of the division as a whole that RFD was a good case for sensible investment . . . Where we are investing in films we can obviously have some influence in where the film might be made and certainly where it might be processed.

'Also, we have the advantage of having distribution rights to the product. So the benefits of investing in film production can accrue not only for RFD directly, but for

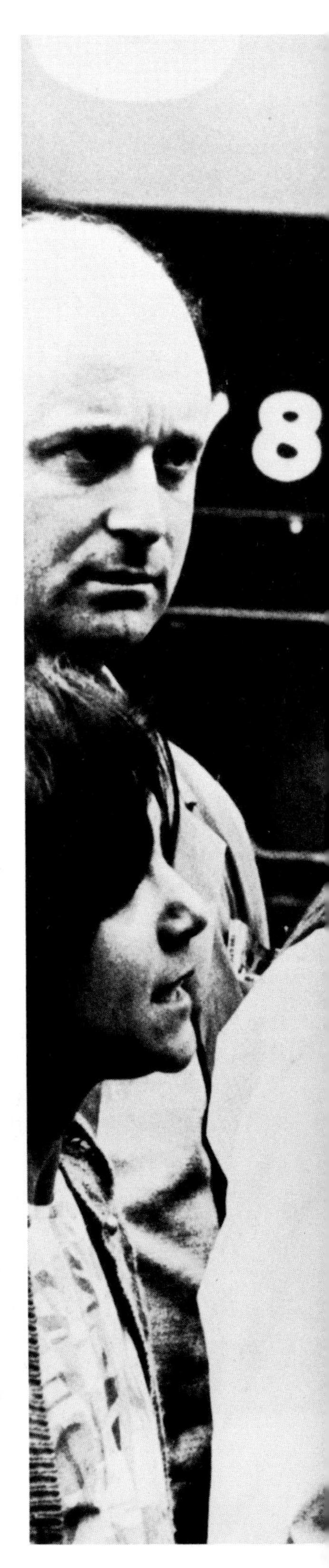

Above: Irina Brook and John Gordon Sinclair in *The Girl in the Picture*; (right), Gary Waldhorn, Warren Mitchell and Bernard Hill gather round Denis Lawson in Jack Rosenthal's comedy *The Chain*.

the studio, the labs, the video duplication business, video servicing and video distribution.'

In the year following Daly's appointment, he put in place a new management team at RFD headed by Fred Turner, whose first task was to secure an output agreement with America's Orion Pictures. Once that was in place other US independents were eager to offer product, which has ensured the flow of profitable films from the States such as *The Terminator*, with Arnold Schwarzenegger, Gene Wilder's *The Woman in Red* and Woody Allen's *The Purple Rose of Cairo* and *Hannah and Her Sisters*.

The real profitability of RFD has come about because the new management has been allowed to put into practice its plan to develop overseas markets by exploiting its substantial library of films on television and video and, in the UK, to take a leading part in the new media of cable television in hotels.

RFD has also increased its own, admittedly low-profile, investment in some new British films: not too many yet, but enough to suggest that, in a precarious production climate, Rank is at least trying.

First dabblings were not promising. *Nutcracker* with its *double-entendre* title boasted Joan Collins as the head of an international ballet company mixed up in defections and

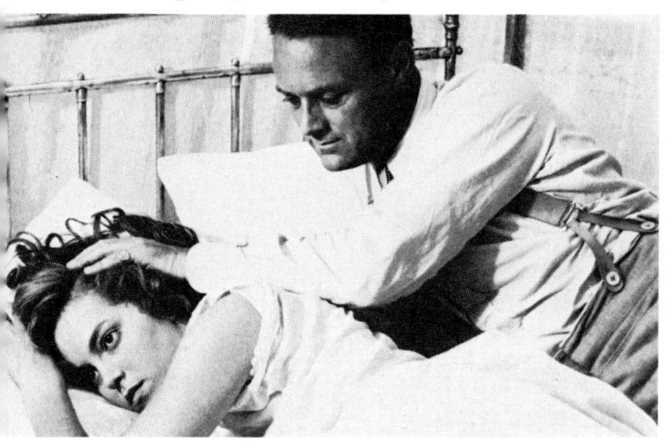

Left: Greta Scacchi and Nickolas Grace in Merchant-Ivory's success *Heat and Dust*. Above: Scacchi and Christopher Cazenove in the film.

no little sex. Joan's *Dynasty* following did not pursue her into cinemas, but it was interesting to note just how far 'Britain's Bad Girl' had come.

The Boys in Blue contained an enormous chunk of *déjà-vu*. Not only did it remind one of the days when Gainsborough used to pop popular comedians of the day into films (in this case Cannon and Ball), but also derived its very plot from just that very 'thirties era.

It was nothing less than an updated – but not so you'd particularly notice – version of Will Hay's *Ask a Policeman*, perhaps not so surprising when you realise that the writer-director was 74-year-old Val Guest, who, as a 26-year-old, had co-written the Will Hay comedy.

The quality had to improve, and it did so dramatically with *Heat and Dust* and *Educating Rita* in 1983. *Heat and Dust*, adapted from her own novel by Ruth Prawer Jhabvala, came from the the durable producer-director team of Ismail Merchant and James Ivory, and contrasted an English girl's search for her roots in India today with the stifling society of the British Raj. Julie Christie, Shashi Kapoor, Christopher Cazenove and, in particular, newcomer Greta Scacchi created an indelible impression.

Educating Rita, with Julie Walters and Michael Caine, brought producer-director Lewis Gilbert directly back into the Rank fold for the first time in nearly 25 years – he had made two popular hits, *Reach for the Sky* and *Carve Her Name With Pride*, for Rank many years ago. At the British Academy Awards, Julie Walters and Michael Caine were named, respectively, best actress and actor (Walters was also nominated for a Hollywood Oscar) while the film itself won the best film trophy. It was also a massive hit for RFD. There was compensation for *Heat and Dust*, apart from healthy box-office returns, in the form of an award for best adapted screenplay.

Since then there have been *Secret Places*, *The Bostonians* (another classy Merchant-Ivory collaboration, with Christopher Reeve and Vanessa Redgrave), Jack Rosenthal's comedy *The Chain*, *Not Quite Jerusalem* (another stage adaptation from Lewis Gilbert, but not a patch on the success of *Rita*), *The Girl in the Picture* (starring John Gordon-Sinclair from *Gregory's Girl*) and a powerful conspiracy thriller, *The Defence of the Realm*, executive-produced by David Puttnam.

By far the biggest financial gamble for Rank – certainly since the short production idyll of the late 'seventies – has been *The Fourth Protocol*, in which RFD invested more than £3 million in exchange for all sorts of rights.

The film is a triumph of perseverance for best-selling author Frederick Forsyth, who was determined, following other movies of his work (*The Day of the Jackal* and *The Odessa File*), to have complete control this time. Not only did he write the screenplay but he also raised the money and, with the film's principal star, Michael Caine, served as executive producer. Also starring in this all-action story of power politics and nuclear threat are Pierce Brosnan, Ned Beatty, Joanna Cassidy and Ian Richardson.

As the continuing story of Rank moves closer to the 1990s, it is worth recalling finally the company founder who, though he would never have admitted to any great knowledge of film-making, regularly proved that with the people he backed he had a popular touch.

'In America,' he once said, 'they like to make pictures about things that might happen once in twenty centuries. We like to make them about reality.'

Left: Julie Walters in award-winning form in *Educating Rita* as the hairdresser with ambitions to better herself through learning.

Left: Sean Connery and Gert Frobe look impressed with Oddjob's skill as a bowler-hat marksman in *Goldfinger*. The impassive manservant was played by Harold Sakata. Above: Bond (Roger Moore) and Scaramanga (Christopher Lee) begin a duel to the death in *The Man with the Golden Gun*.

All action as Bond (Roger Moore) launches a painful attack in ***Moonraker***.

In *Dr No*, the first of the *Bond* films, Sean Connery as 007 indulges in a little romantic chit-chat with his most enduring ally, Miss Moneypenny, played by Lois Maxwell.

On his visit to the villainous Largo's luxurious estate in *Thunderball* (A) Bond (Sean Connery) is given a chance to demonstrate his shooting skills on the skeet range. Largo is played by Adolfo Celi. Bond (George Lazenby) confronts Ernst Stavro Blofeld (Telly Savalas) during a party at the SPECTRE chief's mountain retreat in *On Her Majesty's Secret Service* (B). The lovely Solitaire (Jane Seymour) confesses to Bond (Roger Moore) in *Live and Let Die* (C) that she is secretly pleased to have lost her telepathic gift.

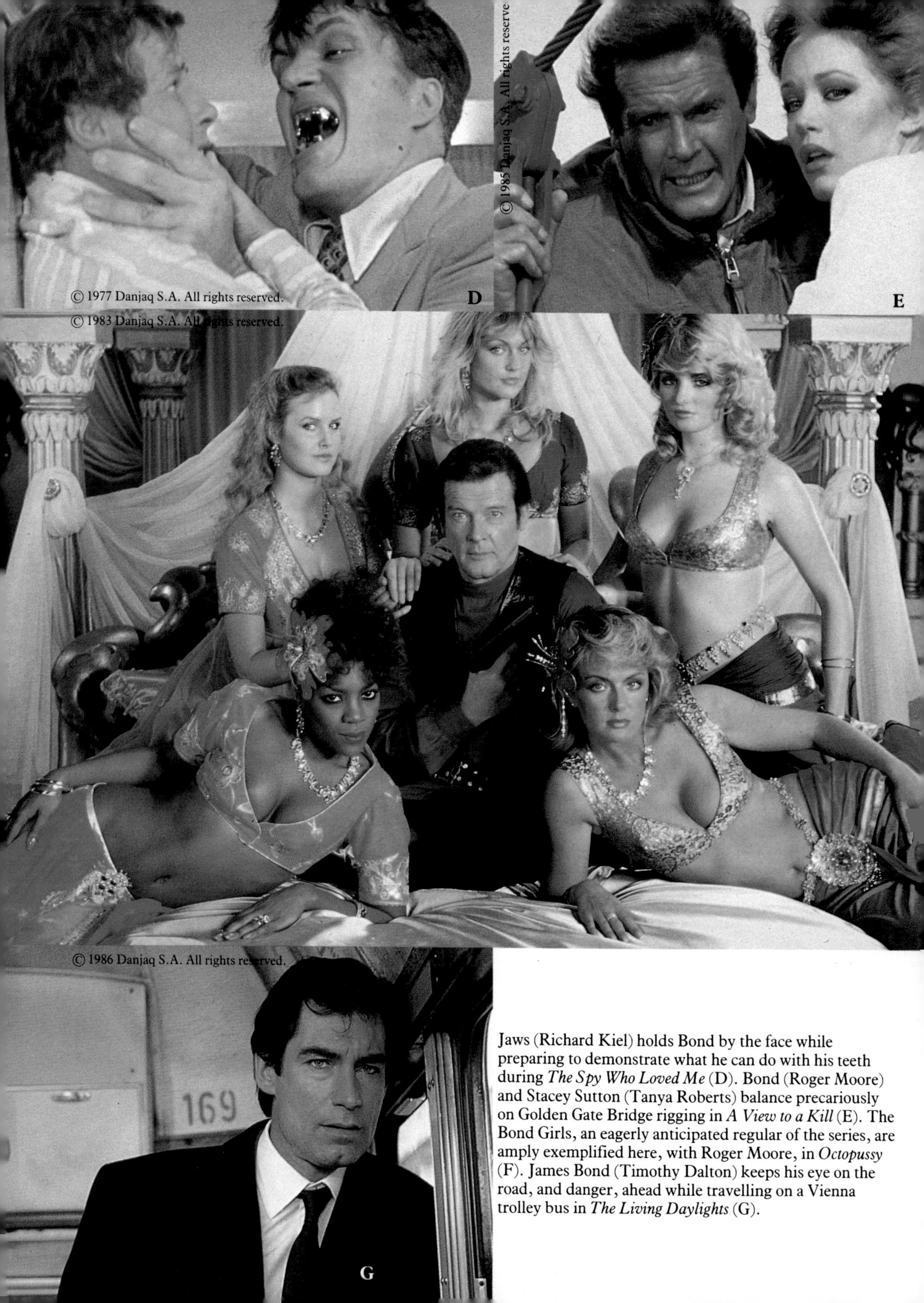

Jaws (Richard Kiel) holds Bond by the face while preparing to demonstrate what he can do with his teeth during *The Spy Who Loved Me* (D). Bond (Roger Moore) and Stacey Sutton (Tanya Roberts) balance precariously on Golden Gate Bridge rigging in *A View to a Kill* (E). The Bond Girls, an eagerly anticipated regular of the series, are amply exemplified here, with Roger Moore, in *Octopussy* (F). James Bond (Timothy Dalton) keeps his eye on the road, and danger, ahead while travelling on a Vienna trolley bus in *The Living Daylights* (G).

Rank's colourful years 2

Kirk Douglas, as Dr Rolf Pedersen, leads a Resistance attack on a German heavy water plant in Norway during *The Heroes of Telemark*.

Rita Tushingham as the brave, but dumb, fur trader's wife in *The Trap*, set in nineteenth-century British Columbia.

Fenn Street school's sexbomb Sharon (Carol Hawkins) teases teacher John Alderton in the sitcom spin-off *Please, Sir!*

Rudolf Nureyev and Margot Fonteyn in the Royal Ballet's production of Kenneth MacMillan's *Romeo and Juliet*, with music by Prokofiev.

Eric Porter looks suitably concerned as another bloody corpse turns up in Hammer's *Hands of the Ripper*.

In the Fortress of Solitude, the vengeful Ursa (Sarah Douglas) puts the boot into Superman (Christopher Reeve) during a scene from Richard Lester's *Superman II*, a Salkind production for Warner Brothers, made at Pinewood in 1979.

Eyebrows shaved, pop-star Pink (Bob Geldof) becomes a Fascist-style dictator in MGM's *Pink Floyd – The Wall*, made at Pinewood in 1981.

Aerial view of Pinewood 1987, showing the 007 stage (top right), model tank and backing (bottom left), and administration offices (bottom right).

Sigourney Weaver, reprising her role as Ripley in James Cameron's sequel to *Alien*, gets some heavy metal help as she takes on the mother beast; 20th Century-Fox's *Aliens* was made at Pinewood in 1985-6.

Cowboys-turned-First-World-War-fliers Scott McGinnis and Jeff Osterhage in Rick Herland's production of *Sky Bandits*, directed by Zoran Perisic at Pinewood in 1985-6.

Pierce Brosnan and Michael Caine in a scene from *The Fourth Protocol*.

The bottle seems to be mightier than the pen for English professor Michael Caine in *Educating Rita*.

Filmography

British feature-length films with which the late Lord Rank and/or one of his companies and his successors have been financially involved from 1935 to 1986

1935

Turn of the Tide *PC*: British National. *P*: John Corfield. *D*: Norman Walker. *S*: L. DuGarde Peach, J.O.C. Orton. *C*: Wilfrid Lawson, Geraldine Fitzgerald, Niall McGinnis, Sam Livesey.
No Monkey Business *PC*: Radius. *P*: Julius Haemann. *D*: Marcel Varnel. *S*: Roger Burford, Val Guest. *C*: Gene Gerrard, June Clyde, Renee Houston, Claude Dampier.
Moscow Nights *PC*: London/Capitol. *P*: Alexander Korda, Alexis Granowski, Max Schach. *D*: Anthony Asquith. *S*: Erich Seipmann. *C*: Laurence Olivier, Penelope Dudley Ward, Harry Baur.
The Iron Duke *PC*: Gaumont. *P*: Michael Balcon. *D*: Victor Saville. *S*: Bess Meredyth. *C*: George Arliss, Gladys Cooper, Emlyn Williams, Ellaline Terriss.
Heat Wave *PC*: Gainsborough. *P*: Jerome Jackson. *D*: Maurice Elvey. *S*: Austin Melford, Leslie Arliss, Jerome Jackson. *C*: Albert Burdon, Cyril Maude, Les Allen, Anna Lee.
Bulldog Jack *PC*: Gaumont. *P*: Michael Balcon. *D*: Walter Forde. *S*: H.C. McNeile, Gerard Fairlie, J.O.C. Orton, Sidney Gilliat. *C*: Jack Hulbert, Fay Wray, Claude Hulbert, Ralph Richardson.
The 39 Steps *PC*: Gaumont. *P*: Ivor Montagu. *D*: Alfred Hitchcock. *S*: Charles Bennett, Ian Hay, Alma Reville. *C*: Robert Donat, Madeleine Carroll, Godfrey Tearle, Lucie Mannheim.
The Clairvoyant *PC*: Gainsborough. *P*: Michael Balcon. *D*: Maurice Elvey. *S*: Charles Bennett, Bryan Edgar Wallace, Robert Edmunds. *C*: Claude Rains, Fay Wray, Jane Baxter, Mary Clare.
Stormy Weather *PC*: Gainsborough. *P*: Michael Balcon. *D*: Tom Walls. *S*: Ben Travers. *C*: Tom Walls, Ralph Lynn, Yvonne Arnaud, Robertson Hare.
Boys Will Be Boys *PC*: Gainsborough. *P*: Michael Balcon. *D*: William Beaudine. *S*: Will Hay, Robert Edmunds. *C*: Will Hay, Gordon Harker, Claude Dampier, Jimmy Hanley, Davy Burnaby.
Car of Dreams *PC*: Gaumont. *P*: Michael Balcon. *D*: Graham Cutts, Austin Melford. *S*: Austin Melford. *C*: John Mills, Grete Mosheim, Robertson Hare, Norah Howard.
The Guv'nor *PC*: Gaumont. *P*: Michael Balcon. *D*: Milton Rosmer. *S*: Maude Howell, Guy Bolton. *C*: George Arliss, Gene Gerrard, Viola Keats, Patric Knowles.
Foreign Affaires *PC*: Gainsborough. *P*: Michael Balcon. *D*: Tom Walls. *S*: Ben Travers. *C*: Tom Walls, Ralph Lynn, Robertson Hare, Norma Varden.

Abbreviations

PC Production Company; *P* Producer; *D* Director; *S* Script; *C* Cast; *ACT* Association of Cinema Technicians; *AFM* Allied Film Makers; *BFM* British Film Makers; *G&S* Greenspan and Seligman Enterprises; *GHW* Gregory, Hake and Walker; *HH* Harold Huth Productions; *IP* Independent Producers; *ITC* Incorporated Television.

1936

Limelight *PC*: Wilcox. *PD*: Herbert Wilcox. *S*: Laura Whetter. *C*: Anna Neagle, Arthur Tracy, Jane Winton, Ellis Jeffreys.
The Improper Duchess *PC*: City. *P*: Maurice Browne. *D*: Harry Hughes. *S*: Harry Hughes, Vernon Harris. *C*: Yvonne Arnaud, Hugh Wakefield, James Carew, Felix Aylmer.
King of the Castle *PC*: City. *P*: Basil Humphrys. *D*: Redd Davis. *S*: George Dewhurst. *C*: June Clyde, Claude Dampier, Billy Milton, Cynthia Stock.
When Knights Were Bold *PC*: Capitol. *P*: Max Schach. *D*: Jack Raymond. *S*: Austin Parker, Douglas Furber. *C*: Jack Buchanan, Fay Wray, Garry Marsh, Kate Cutler.
Public Nuisance Number 1 *PC*: Cecil. *P*: Herman Fellner, Max Schach. *D*: Marcel Varnel. *S*: Roger Burford, Robert Edmunds, Val Guest. *C*: Frances Day, Arthur Riscoe, Claude Dampier, Muriel Aked.
Rhodes of Africa *PC*: Gaumont. *P*: Geoffrey Barkas. *D*: Berthold Viertel. *S*: Michael Barringer, Miles Malleson. *C*: Walter Huston, Oscar Homolka, Basil Sydney, Peggy Ashcroft.
Fame *PC*: Wilcox. *P*: Herbert Wilcox. *D*: Leslie Hiscott. *S*: Michael Barringer, R.P. Weston, Bert Lee, Jack Marks. *C*: Sydney Howard, Muriel Aked, Miki Hood, Brian Lawrence.
Debt of Honour *PC*: British National. *P*: John Corfield. *D*: Norman Walker. *S*: Tom Geraghty, Cyril Campion. *C*: Leslie Banks, Will Fyffe, Geraldine Fitzgerald, Niall McGinnis.
Pot Luck *PC*: Gainsborough. *P*: Michael Balcon. *D*: Tom Walls. *S*: Ben Travers. *C*: Tom Walls, Ralph Lynn, Robertson Hare, Diana Churchill.
Tudor Rose *PC*: Gainsborough. *P*: Michael Balcon. *D*: Robert Stevenson. *S*: Robert Stevenson, Miles Malleson. *C*: Cedric Hardwicke, Nova Pilbeam, John Mills, Felix Aylmer.
The Secret Agent *PC*: Gaumont. *P*: Ivor Montagu. *D*: Alfred Hitchcock. *S*: Charles Bennett, Jesse Lasky Jnr, Alma Reville, Ian Hay. *C*: Madeleine Carroll, Peter Lorre, Robert Young, John Gielgud.
Love in Exile *PC*: Capitol. *P*: Max Schach. *D*: Alfred L. Werker. *S*: Herman Mankiewicz, Roger Burford, Ernest Betts. *C*: Clive Brook, Helen Vinson, Mary Carlisle, Will Fyffe.
The Marriage of Corbal *PC*: Capitol. *P*: Max Schach. *D*: Karl Grune. *S*: S. Fullman. *C*: Nils Asther, Hugh Sinclair, Hazel Terry, Noah Beery.
Where There's a Will *PC*: Gainsborough. *P*: Michael Balcon. *D*: William Beaudine. *S*: Will Hay, Ralph Spence, Robert Edmunds, William Beaudine. *C*: Will Hay, Gina Malo, Hartley Power, Graham Moffatt.
Seven Sinners *PC*: Gaumont. *P*: Michael Balcon. *D*: Albert de Courville. *S*: Frank Launder, Sidney Gilliat, L. DuGarde Peach, Austin Melford. *C*: Edmund Lowe, Constance Cummings, Thomy Bourdelle, Henry Oscar.

Peter Lorre, John Gielgud, Madeleine Carroll and Robert Young in Hitchcock's *Secret Agent*. Previous page: Anna Neagle in *London Melody*.

Everything is Thunder *PC*: Gaumont. *P*: S.C. Balcon. *D*: Milton Rosmer. *S*: Marian Dix, J.O.C. Orton. *C*: Constance Bennett, Oscar Homolka, Douglass Montgomery, Roy Emerton.
East Meets West *PC*: Gaumont. *P*: Haworth Bromley. *D*: Herbert Mason. *S*: Maude Howell. *C*: George Arliss, Lucie Mannheim, Godfrey Tearle, Romney Brent.
Dishonour Bright *PC*: Cecil. *P*: Herman Fellner, Max Schach. *D*: Tom Walls. *S*: Ben Travers. *C*: Tom Walls, Eugene Pallette, Betty Stockfield, Diana Churchill.
Millions *PC*: Wilcox. *P*: Herbert Wilcox. *D*: Leslie Hiscott. *S*: Michael Barringer. *C*: Gordon Harker, Frank Pettingell, Richard Hearne, Jane Carr.
Southern Roses *PC*: Grafton. *P*: Isidore Goldschmidt, Max Schach. *D*: Fred Zelnik. *S*: Ronald Gow. *C*: George Robey, Neil Hamilton, Gina Malo, Chili Bouchier.
Tropical Trouble *PC*: City. *P*: Basil Humphrys. *D*: Harry Hughes. *S*: Vernon Harris. *C*: Douglass Montgomery, Betty Anne Davis, Alfred Drayton, Natalie Hall.
The Secret of Stamboul *PC*: Wainwright. *P*: Richard Wainwright. *D*: Andrew Marton. *S*: Richard Wainwright, Howard Irving Young, Noel Langley. *C*: Valerie Hobson, Frank Vosper, James Mason, Kay Walsh.
Land Without Music *PC*: Capitol. *P*: Max Schach. *D*: Walter Forde. *S*: Rudolph Bernauer, Marian Dix. L. DuGarde Peach. *C*: Richard Tauber, Jimmy Durante, Diana Napier, June Clyde.
This'll Make You Whistle *PC*: Wilcox. *PD*: Herbert Wilcox. *S*: Guy Bolton, Paul Thompson. *C*: Jack Buchanan, Elsie Randolph, Jean Gillie, William Kendall.
You Must Get Married *PC*: City. *P*: Basil Humphrys. *D*: Leslie Pearce. *S*: F. McGrew Willis, Richard Fisher. *C*: Frances Day, Neil Hamilton, Robertson Hare, Wally Patch.
Sabotage *PC*: Gaumont. *P*: Ivor Montagu. *D*: Alfred Hitchcock. *S*: Charles Bennett, Ian Hay, Alma Reville, Helen Simpson, E.V.H. Emmett. *C*: Sylvia Sidney, Oscar Homolka, John Loder, Desmond Tester.
Windbag the Sailor *PC*: Gainsborough. *P*: Michael Balcon. *D*: William Beaudine. *S*: Leslie Arliss, Robert Edmunds, Marriott Edgar, Val Guest. *C*: Will Hay, Moore Marriott, Graham Moffatt, Dennis Wyndham.

1937

Splinters in the Air *PC*: Wilcox. *P*: Herbert Wilcox. *D*: Alfred Goulding. *S*: R.P. Weston, Bert Lee, Jack Marks. *C*: Sydney Howard, Richard Hearne, Stuart Robertson, Ralph Reader.
London Melody *PC*: Wilcox. *PD*: Herbert Wilcox. *S*: Florence Tranter, Monckton Hoffe. *C*: Anna Neagle, Tullio Carminati, Robert Douglas, Horace Hodges.
Head Over Heels *PC*: Gaumont. *P*: Michael Balcon. *D*: Sonnie Hale. *S*: Dwight Taylor, Fred Thompson, Marjorie Gaffney. *C*: Jessie Matthews, Louis Borell, Robert Flemying, Helen Whitney Bourne.
The Great Barrier *PC*: Gaumont. *P*: Gunther Stapenhorst. *D*: Milton Rosmer, Geoffrey Barkas. *S*: Ralph Spence, Michael Barringer, Milton Rosmer. *C*: Richard Arlen, Antoinette Cellier, Barry Mackay, Lilli Palmer.
For Valour *PC*: Capitol. *P*: Max Schach. *D*: Tom Walls. *S*: Ben Travers. *C*: Tom Walls, Ralph Lynn, Veronica Rose, Joan Marion.
The Frog *PC*: Wilcox. *P*: Herbert Wilcox. *D*: Jack Raymond. *S*: Ian Hay, Gerald Elliott. *C*: Gordon Harker, Carol Goodner, Noah Beery, Jack Hawkins.
The Gang Show *PC*: Wilcox. *P*: Herbert Wilcox. *D*: Alfred Goulding. *S*: Marjorie Gaffney. *C*: Ralph Reader, Gina Malo, Stuart Robertson, Richard Ainley.
Our Fighting Navy *PC*: Wilcox. *P*: Herbert Wilcox. *D*: Norman Walker. *S*: Gerald Elliott, Harrison Owens. *C*: H.B. Warner, Richard Cromwell, Robert Douglas, Noah Beery.
Okay for Sound *PC*: Gainsborough. *P*: Edward Black. *D*: Marcel Varnel. *S*: Marriott Edgar, Val Guest, Flanagan & Allen, Nervo & Knox, Naughton & Gold. *C*: Fred Duprez, Enid Stamp-Taylor, Graham Moffatt, Meinhart Maur.
Take My Tip *PC*: Gaumont. *D*: Herbert Mason. *S*: Sidney Gilliat, Michael Hogan, Jack Hulbert. *C*: Jack Hulbert, Cicely Courtneidge, Harold Huth, Frank Cellier.
Sunset in Vienna *PC*: Wilcox. *P*: Herbert Wilcox. *D*: Norman Walker. *S*: Marjorie Gaffney, Harrison Owens. *C*: Tullio Carminati, John Garrick, Lilli Palmer, Edgar Driver.
King Solomon's Mines *PC*: Gaumont. *P*: Geoffrey Barkas. *D*: Robert Stevenson. *S*: Michael Hogan, Roland Pertwee, A.R. Rawlinson, Charles Bennett, Ralph Spence. *C*: Paul Robeson, Cedric Hardwicke, Roland Young, John Loder.
Said O'Reilly to McNab *PC*: Gainsborough. *P*: Edward Black. *D*: William Beaudine. *S*: Leslie Arliss, Marriott Edgar. *C*: Will Mahoney, Will Fyffe, Ellis Drake, Jock McKay.
Gangway *PC*: Gaumont. *P*: Sonnie Hale. *D*: Lesser Samuels, Sonnie Hale. *C*: Jessie Matthews, Barry Mackay, Nat Pendleton, Noel Madison.
Dr Syn *PC*:Gaumont. *D*: Roy William Neill. *S*: Michael Hogan, Roger

Burford. *C*: George Arliss, John Loder, Margaret Lockwood, Roy Emerton.
Command Performance *PC*: Grosvenor. *P*: Harcourt Templeman. *D*: Sinclair Hill. *S*: George Pearson, Michael Hankinson, Sinclair Hill. *C*: Arthur Tracy, Lilli Palmer, Mark Daly, Rae Collett.
School for Husbands *PC*: Wainwright. *P*: Richard Wainwright. *D*: Andrew Marton. *S*: Frederick Jackson, Austin Melford, Gordon Sherry. *C*: Diana Churchill, June Clyde, Rex Harrison, Romney Brent.
Non-Stop New York *PC*: Gaumont. *D*: Robert Stevenson. *S*: Kurt Siodmak, Roland Pertwee, J.O.C. Orton, Derek Twist. *C*: John Loder, Anna Lee, Francis L. Sullivan, Frank Cellier.
Smash and Grab *PC*: Jack Buchanan. *D*: Tim Whelan. *S*: Ralph Spence. *C*: Jack Buchanan, Elsie Randolph, Arthur Margetson, Antony Holles.
Oh, Mr Porter *PC*: Gainsborough. *P*: Edward Black *D*: Marcel Varnel. *S*: Marriott Edgar, Val Guest, J.O.C. Orton, Will Hay. *C*: Will Hay, Moore Marriott, Graham Moffatt, Sebastian Smith.
The Sky's the Limit *PC*: Jack Buchanan. *D*: Lee Garmes, Jack Buchanan. *S*: Jack Buchanan, Douglas Furber. *C*: Jack Buchanan, Mara Loseff, William Kendall, David Hutcheson.
Young and Innocent *PC*: Gaumont. *D*: Alfred Hitchcock. *S*: Charles Bennett, Alma Reville, Anthony Armstrong, Edwin Greenwood, Gerald Savory. *C*: Nova Pilbeam, Derrick de Marney, Percy Marmont, Edward Rigby.
OHMS *PC*: Gaumont. *P*: Geoffrey Barkas. *D*: Raoul Walsh. *S*: Bryan Edgar Wallace, Austin Melford, A.R. Rawlinson. *C*: Wallace Ford, John Mills, Anna Lee, Grace Bradley.

Jean Gillie and Bobby Howes in *Sweet Devil*.

1938

The Lady Vanishes *PC:* Gaumont/Gainsborough. *P*: Edward Black. *D*: Alfred Hitchcock. *S*: Frank Launder, Sidney Gilliat. *C*: Margaret Lockwood, Michael Redgrave, Dame May Whitty, Paul Henreid.
Sweet Devil *PC*: Jack Buchanan. *D*: René Guissart. *S*: Ralph Spence, Geoffrey Kerr. *C*: Bobby Howes, Jean Gillie, William Kendall. Syd Walker.
Owd Bob *PC*: Gainsborough. *P*: Edward Black. *D*: Robert Stevenson. *S*: Michael Hogan, J.B. Williams. *C*: Will Fyffe, John Loder, Margaret Lockwood, Moore Marriott.
Bank Holiday *PC*: Gainsborough. *P*: Edward Black. *D*: Carol Reed. *S*: Rodney Ackland, Roger Burford. *C*: John Lodge, Margaret Lockwood, Hugh Williams, Rene Ray.
Second Best Bed *PC*: Capitol. *P*: Max Schach. *D*: Tom Walls. *S*: Ben Travers. *C*: Tom Walls, Jane Baxter, Veronica Rose, Carl Jaffe.
Sailing Along *PC*: Gaumont. *D*: Sonnie Hale. *S*: Lesser Samuels, Sonnie Hale. *C*: Jessie Matthews, Roland Young, Barry Mackay, Jack Whiting.
Kate Plus Ten *PC*: Wainwright. *P*: Richard Wainwright. *D*: Reginald Denham. *S*: Jack Hulbert, Jeffrey Dell. *C*: Jack Hulbert, Genevieve Tobin, Noel Madison, Francis L. Sullivan.
Strange Boarders *PC*: Gainsborough. *P*: Edward Black. *D*: Herbert Mason. *S*: A.R. Rawlinson, Sidney Gilliat. *C*: Tom Walls, Renée St Cyr, Leon M. Lion, Googie Withers.
Convict 99 *PC*: Gainsborough. *P*: Edward Black. *D*: Marcel Varnel. *S*: Marriott Edgar, Val Guest, Jack Davies, Ralph Smart. *C*: Will Hay, Moore Marriott, Graham Moffatt, Googie Withers.
Kicking the Moon Around *PC*: Vogue. *P*: Herbert Wynne. *D*: Walter Forde. *S*: Angus MacPhail, Roland Pertwee, Michael Hogan, H.Fowler Mear. *C*: Ambrose, Evelyn Dall, Harry Richman, Florence Desmond.
Break the News *PC*: Jack Buchanan. *D*: René Clair. *S*: Geoffrey Kerr. *C*: Jack Buchanan, Maurice Chevalier, June Knight, Marta Labarr.
Alf's Button Afloat *PC*: Gainsborough. *P*: Edward Black. *D*: Marcel Varnel. *S*: Marriott Edgar, Val Guest, Ralph Smart. *C*: The Crazy Gang.
Follow Your Star *PC*: Belgrave. *P*: Harcourt Templeman. *D*: Sinclair Hill. *S*: George Pearson, Stafford Dickens. *C*: Arthur Tracy, Belle Chrystal, Mark Daly, Horace Hodges.
A Spot of Bother *PC*: Pinebrook. *P*: Anthony Havelock-Allan. *D*: David MacDonald. *S*: John Cousins, Stephen Clarkson, A.R. Rawlinson. *C*: Robertson Hare, Alfred Drayton, Sandra Storme, Kathleen Joyce.
Hey! Hey! USA! *PC*: Gainsborough. *P*: Edward Black. *D*: Marcel Varnel. *S*: Marriott Edgar, Val Guest, J.O.C. Orton. *C*: Will Hay, Edgar Kennedy, Tommy Bupp, David Burns.
Crackerjack *PC*: Gainsborough. *P*: Edward Black. *D*: Albert de Courville. *S*: A.R. Rawlinson, Michael Pertwee, Basil Mason. *C*: Tom Walls, Lilli Palmer, Noel Madison, Leon M. Lion.
Lightning Conductor *PC*: Pinebrook. *P*: Anthony Havelock-Allan. *D*: Maurice Elvey. *S*: J. Jefferson Farjeon, Ivor McClaren, Laurence Green. *C*: Gordon Harker, John Lodge, Sally Gray, Ernest Thesiger.
Pygmalion *PC*: Pascal. *P*: Gabriel Pascal. *D*: Anthony Asquith, Leslie Howard. *S*: Anatole de Grunwald, W.P. Lipscomb, Cecil Lewis, Ian Dalrymple. *C*: Leslie Howard, Wendy Hiller, Wilfrid Lawson, Marie Lohr.
Old Bones of the River *PC*: Gainsborough. *P*: Edward Black. *D*: Marcel Varnel. *S*: Marriott Edgar, Val Guest, J.O.C. Orton. *C*: Will Hay, Moore Marriott, Graham Moffatt, Robert Adams.

1939

The Mikado *PC*: G & S. *P*: Geoffrey Toye, Josef Somlo. *D*: Victor Schertzinger. *S*: Geoffrey Toye. *C*: Kenny Baker, Jean Colin, Martyn Green, Sydney Granville.
A Girl Must Live *PC*: Gainsborough. *P*: Edward Black. *D*: Carol Reed. *S*: Frank Launder, Austin Melford. *C*: Margaret

Lockwood, Renee Houston, Lilli Palmer, George Robey.
A Window in London *PC*: G & S. *P*: Josef Somlo, Richard Norton. *D*: Herbert Mason. *S*: Ian Dalrymple, Brigid Cooper. *C*: Michael Redgrave, Sally Gray, Paul Lukas, Hartley Power.
The Arsenal Stadium Mystery *PC*: G & S. *P*: Josef Somlo, Richard Norton. *D*: Thorold Dickinson. *S*: Thorold Dickinson, Donald Bull. *C*: Leslie Banks, Greta Gynt, Ian Maclean, Esmond Knight.
On the Night of the Fire *PC*: G & S. *P*: Josef Somlo. *D*: Brian Desmond Hurst. *S*: Brian Desmond Hurst, Terence Young, Patrick Kirwan. *C*: Ralph Richardson, Diana Wynyard, Romney Brent, Mary Clare.
The Frozen Limits *PC*: Gainsborough. *P*: Edward Black. *D*: Marcel Varnel. *S*: Marriott Edgar, Val Guest, J.O.C. Orton. *C*: The Crazy Gang.

1940

Band Waggon *PC*: Gainsborough. *P*: Edward Black. *D*: Marcel Varnel. *S*: Marriott Edgar, Val Guest. *C*: Arthur Askey, Jack Hylton and his Band, Richard Murdoch, Pat Kirkwood.
For Freedom *PC*: Gainsborough. *P*: Edward Black, Castleton Knight. *D*: Maurice Elvey. *S*: Miles Malleson, Leslie Arliss. *C*: Will Fyffe, Anthony Hume, E.V.H. Emmett, Guy Middleton.
Charley's (Big Hearted) Aunt *PC*: Gainsborough. *P*: Edward Black. *D*: Walter Forde. *S*: Marriott Edgar, Val Guest. *C*: Arthur Askey, Richard Murdoch, Moore Marriott, Graham Moffatt.
Old Bill and Son *PC*: Legeran. *P*: Josef Somlo, Harold Boxall, Alexander Korda. *D*: Ian Dalrymple. *S*: Bruce Bairsfather, Ian Dalrymple. *C*: Morland Graham, John Mills, Mary Clare, Renee Houston.
Gasbags *PC*: Gainsborough. *P*: Edward Black. *D*: Marcel Varnel. *S*: Val Guest, Marriott Edgar. *C*: The Crazy Gang.
Neutral Port *PC*: Gainsborough. *P*: Edward Black. *D*: Marcel Varnel. *S*: J.B. Williams, T.J. Morrison. *C*: Will Fyffe, Leslie Banks, Yvonne Arnaud, Phyllis Calvert.

1941

The Ghost Train *PC*: Gainsborough. *P*: Edward Black. *D*: Walter Forde. *S*: Marriott Edgar, Val Guest. J.O.C. Orton. *C*: Arthur Askey, Richard Murdoch, Kathleen Harrison, Morland Graham.
Major Barbara *PC*: Pascal. *P*: Gabriel Pascal. *D*: Gabriel Pascal, Harold French, David Lean. *S*: Anatole de Grunwald, George Bernard Shaw. *C*: Wendy Hiller, Rex Harrison, Robert Morley, Emlyn Williams.
Cottage to Let *PC*: Gainsborough. *P*: Edward Black. *D*: Anthony Asquith. *S*: Anatole de Grunwald, J.O.C. Orton. *C*: Leslie Banks, Alastair Sim, John Mills, Jeanne de Casalis.
He Found a Star *PC*: John Corfield. *D*: John Paddy Carstairs. *S*: Austin Melford, Brigid Boland. *C*: Vic Oliver, Sarah Churchill, Evelyn Dall, Robert Sansom.
Jeannie *PC*: Tansa. *P*: Marcel Hellman. *D*: Harold French. *S*: Anatole de Grunwald, Roland Pertwee. *C*: Michael Redgrave, Barbara Mullen, Wilfrid Lawson, Kay Hammond.
I Thank You *PC*: Gainsborough. *P*: Edward Black. *D*: Marcel Varnel. *S*: Val Guest, Marriott Edgar. *C*: Arthur Askey, Richard Murdoch, Lily Morris, Moore Marriott.
The 49th Parallel *PC*: Ortus. *P*: John Sutro, Michael Powell. *D*: Michael Powell. *S*: Emeric Pressburger, Rodney

Richard 'Stinker' Murdoch and Arthur Askey look bemused in *Band Waggon*.

Ackland. *C*: Leslie Howard, Raymond Massey, Laurence Olivier, Anton Walbrook.
Hi Gang! *PC*: Gainsborough. *P*: Edward Black. *D*: Marcel Varnel. *S*: Val Guest, Marriott Edgar, J.O.C. Orton, Howard Irving Young. *C*: Bebe Daniels, Ben Lyon, Vic Oliver, Moore Marriott.
Freedom Radio *PC*: Two Cities. *P*: Mario Zampi. *D*: Anthony Asquith. *S*: Basil Woon, Gordon Wellesley, Louis Golding, Anatole de Grunwald, Jeffrey Dell, Brigid Boland. *C*: Clive Brook, Diana Wynyard, Raymond Huntley.

1942

Hard Steel *PC*: GHW. *P*: James B. Sloan. *D*: Norman Walker. *S*: Lydia Hayward. *C*: Wilfrid Lawson, Betty Stockfeld, John Stuart, George Carney.
Back Room Boy *PC*: Gainsborough. *P*: Edward Black. *D*: Herbert Mason. *S*: Val Guest, Marriott Edgar. *C*: Arthur Askey, Richard Murdoch, Moore Marriott, Graham Moffatt.
The Day Will Dawn *PC*: Niksos Films. *P*: Paul Soskin. *D*: Harold French. *S*: Terence Rattigan, Anatole de Grunwald, Patrick Kirwan. *C*: Ralph Richardson, Deborah Kerr, Hugh Williams, Griffith Jones.
Uncensored *PC*: Gainsborough. *P*: Edward Black. *D*: Anthony Asquith. *S*: Wolfgang Wilhelm, Terence Rattigan, Rodney Ackland. *C*: Eric Portman, Phyllis Calvert, Griffith Jones, Raymond Lovell.
The First of the Few *PC*: Misbourne/British Aviation. *P*: Leslie Howard, John Stafford, George King, Adrian Brunel. *D*: Leslie Howard. *S*: Anatole de Grunwald, Miles Malleson. *C*: Leslie Howard, David Niven, Rosamund John, Roland Culver.
Secret Mission *PC*: IP/Excelsior. *P*: Marcel Hellman. *D*: Harold French. *S*: Anatole de Grunwald, Basil Bartlett. *C*: Hugh Williams, James Mason, Michael Wilding, Carla Lehmann.
The Great Mr Handel *PC*: IP/GHW. *P*: James B. Sloan. *D*: Norman Walker. *S*: Gerald Elliott, Victor MacClure. *C*: Wilfrid Lawson, Elizabeth Allan, Malcolm Keen, Michael Shepley.

Elizabeth Allan and Wilfrid Lawson in *The Great Mr Handel*.

In Which We Serve *PC*: Two Cities. *P*: Noel Coward. *D*: Noel Coward, David Lean. *S*: Noel Coward. *C*: Noel Coward, John Mills, Bernard Miles, Celia Johnson.
King Arthur was a Gentleman *PC*: Gainsborough. *P*: Edward Black. *D*: Marcel Varnel. *S*: Val Guest, Marriott Edgar. *C*: Arthur Askey, Evelyn Dall, Anne Shelton, Max Bacon.
Unpublished Story *PC*: Two Cities. *P*: Anthony Havelock-Allan. *D*: Harold French. *S*: Anatole de Grunwald, Patrick Kirwan. *C*: Richard Greene, Valerie Hobson, Basil Redford, Roland Culver.

1943

The Silver Fleet *PC*: IP/Archers. *P*: Michael Powell, Emeric Pressburger, Ralph Richardson. *DS*: Vernon Sewell, Gordon Wellesley. *C*: Ralph Richardson, Googie Withers, Esmond Knight, Beresford Egan.
It's That Man Again *PC*: Gainsborough. *P*: Edward Black. *D*: Walter Forde. *S*: Howard Irving Young, Ted Kavanagh. *C*: Tommy Handley, Greta Gynt, Jack Train, Sidney Keith.
We Dive at Dawn *PC*: Gainsborough. *P*: Edward Black. *D*: Anthony Asquith. *S*: J.B. Williams, Val Valentine, Frank Launder. *C*: Eric Portman, John Mills, Reginald Purdell, Niall McGinnis.
The Gentle Sex *PC*: Two Cities/Concanen. *P*: Derrick de Marney, Leslie Howard. *D*: Leslie Howard, Maurice Elvey. *S*: Moie Charles, Aimee Stuart, Roland Pertwee, Phyllis Rose. *C*: Joan Gates, Jean Gillie, Joan Greenwood, Joyce Howard.
The Life and Death of Colonel Blimp *PC*: IP/Archers. *PDS*: Michael Powell, Emeric Pressburger. *C*: Anton Walbrook, Deborah Kerr, Roger Livesey, Roland Culver.
The Man in Grey *PC*: Gainsborough. *P*: Edward Black. *D*: Leslie Arliss. *S*: Margaret Kennedy, Leslie Arliss, Doreen Montgomery. *C*: Margaret Lockwood, Phyllis Calvert, James Mason, Stewart Granger.
They Met in the Dark *PC*: IP/Excelsior. *P*: Marcel Hellman. *D*: Karel Lamac. *S*: Anatole de Grunwald, Miles Malleson, Basil Bartlett, Victor MacClure, James Seymour. *C*: James Mason, Joyce Howard, Tom Walls, Phyllis Stanley.
Dear Octopus *PC*: Gainsborough. *P*: Edward Black. *D*: Harold French. *S*: R.J. Minney, Patrick Kirwan. *C*: Margaret Lockwood, Michael Wilding, Celia Johnson, Roland Culver.
The Flemish Farm *PC*: Two Cities. *P*: Sydney Box. *D*: Jeffrey Dell. *S*: Jeffrey Dell, Jill Craigie Dell. *C*: Clive Brook, Clifford Evans, Jane Baxter, Philip Friend.
Millions Like Us *PC*: Gainsborough. *P*: Edward Black. *DS*: Frank Launder, Sidney Gilliat. *C*: Eric Portman, Patricia Roc, Anne Crawford, Gordon Jackson.
The Lamp Still Burns *PC*: Two Cities. *P*: Leslie Howard. *D*: Maurice Elvey. *S*: Elizabeth Baron, Roland Pertwee, Major Neilson. *C*: Rosamund John, Stewart Granger, Godfrey Tearle, Sophie Stewart.
The Demi-Paradise *PC*: Two Cities. *P*: Anatole de Grunwald. *D*: Anthony Asquith. *S*: Anatole de

Stanley Holloway and Robert Newton in *This Happy Breed*.

Grunwald. *C*: Laurence Olivier, Penelope Dudley-Ward, Leslie Henson, Marjorie Fielding.

1944

Bees in Paradise *PC*: Gainsborough. *P*: Edward Black. *D*: Val Guest. *S*: Val Guest, Marriott Edgar. *C*: Arthur Askey, Anne Shelton, Peter Graves, Max Bacon.
On Approval *PC*: IP. *P*: Sydney Box, Clive Brook. *D*: Clive Brook. *S*: Clive Brook, Terence Young. *C*: Clive Brook, Beatrice Lillie, Googie Withers, Roland Culver.
Tawny Pipit *PC*: Two Cities. *DS*: Bernard Miles, Charles Saunders. *C*: Bernard Miles, Rosamund John, Niall McGinnis, Jean Gillie.
This Happy Breed *PC*: Two Cities. *P*: Noel Coward, Anthony Havelock-Allan. *D*: David Lean. *S*: David Lean, Ronald Neame, Anthony Havelock-Allan. *C*: Robert Newton, Celia Johnson, John Mills, Kay Walsh.
Fanny by Gaslight *PC*: Gainsborough. *P*: Edward Black. *D*: Anthony Asquith. *S*: Doreen Montgomery, Aimee Stuart. *C*: Phyllis Calvert, James Mason, Wilfrid Lawson, Stewart Granger.
A Canterbury Tale *PC*: IP/Archers. *PDS*: Michael Powell, Emeric Pressburger. *C*: Eric Portman, Sheila Sim, Dennis Price, Sgt John Sweet.
The Way Ahead *PC*: Two Cities. *P*: John Sutro, Norman Walker. *D*: Carol Reed. *S*: Eric Ambler, Peter Ustinov. *C*: David Niven, Raymond Huntley, William Hartnell, Stanley Holloway.
Give Us the Moon *PC*: Gainsborough. *P*: Edward Black. *DS*: Val Guest. *C*: Vic Oliver, Peter Graves, Margaret Lockwood, Roland Culver.
2,000 Women *PC*: Gainsborough. *P*: Edward Black. *D*: Frank Launder. *S*: Frank Launder, Sidney Gilliat. *C*: Phyllis Calvert, Flora Robson, Patricia Roc, Renee Houston.
Mr Emmanuel *PC*: Two Cities. *P*: William Sistrom. *D*: Harold French. *S*: Gordon Wellesley, Norman Ginsberg. *C*: Felix Aylmer, Greta Gynt, Wolf Rilla, Peter Mullins.
Love Story *PC*: Gainsborough. *P*: Harold Huth. *D*: Leslie Arliss. *S*: Leslie Arliss, Doreen Montgomery, Rodney Ackland. *C*: Margaret Lockwood, Stewart Granger, Patricia Roc, Tom Walls.
Don't Take it to Heart *PC*: Two Cities. *P*: Sydney Box. *DS*: Jeffrey Dell. *C*: Richard Greene, Patricia Medina, Alfred Drayton, Edward Rigby.
Madonna of the Seven Moons *PC*: Gainsborough. *P*: R.J. Minney. *D*: Arthur Crabtree. *S*: Roland Pertwee, Brock Williams. *C*: Phyllis Calvert, Stewart Granger, Patricia Roc, Peter Glenville.
English Without Tears *PC*: Two Cities. *P*: Anatole de Grunwald, Sydney Box. *D*: Harold French. *S*: Terence Rattigan, Anatole de Grunwald. *C*: Michael Wilding, Penelope Ward, Lilli Palmer, Claude Dauphin.

1945

Waterloo Road *PC*: Gainsborough. *P*: Edward Black. *DS*: Sidney Gilliat. *C*: John Mills, Stewart Granger, Alastair Sim, Joy Shelton.
Henry V *PC*: Two Cities. *PD*: Laurence Olivier. *S*: Laurence Olivier, Alan Dent. *C*: Laurence Olivier, Robert Newton, Leslie Banks, Renee Asherson.
A Place of One's Own *PC*: Gainsborough. *P*: R.J. Minney. *D*: Bernard Knowles. *S*: Brock Williams. *C*: Margaret Lockwood, James Mason, Barbara Mullen, Dennis Price.
Blithe Spirit *PC*: Two Cities/Cineguild. *P*: Anthony Havelock-Allan. *D*: David Lean. *S*: David Lean, Ronald Neame, Anthony Havelock-Allan. *C*: Rex Harrison, Constance Cummings, Kay Hammond, Margaret Rutherford.
They Were Sisters *PC*: Gainsborough. *P*: Harold Huth. *D*: Arthur Crabtree. *S*: Roland Pertwee. *C*: Phyllis Calvert, James Mason, Hugh Sinclair, Anne Crawford.
The Way to the Stars *PC*: Two Cities. *P*: Anatole de Grunwald. *D*: Anthony Asquith. *S*: Terence Rattigan, Anatole de

Grunwald. *C*: Michael Redgrave, John Mills, Rosamund John, Douglass Montgomery.
I'll Be Your Sweetheart *PC*: Gainsborough. *P*: Louis Levy. *D*: Val Guest. *S*: Val Guest, Val Valentine. *C*: Margaret Lockwood, Vic Oliver, Michael Rennie, Peter Graves.
Johnny Frenchman *PC*: Ealing. *P*: Michael Balcon. *D*: Charles Frend. *S*: T.E.B. Clarke. *C*: Françoise Rosay, Tom Walls, Patricia Roc, Ralph Michael.

Rex Harrison and Lilli Palmer in *The Rake's Progress*.

They Knew Mr Knight *PC*: IP/GHW. *P*: James B. Sloan. *D*: Norman Walker. *S*: Norman Walker, Victor MacClure. *C*: Mervyn Johns, Nora Swinburne, Alfred Drayton, Joyce Howard.
Dead of Night *PC*: Ealing. *P*: Sidney Cole, John Croydon. *D*: Basil Dearden, Cavalcanti, Robert Hamer, Charles Crichton. *S*: Angus MacPhail, John Baines, T.E.B. Clarke. *C*: Mervyn Johns, Miles Malleson, Googie Withers, Basil Radford, Sally Anne Howes, Michael Redgrave, Frederick Valk.
The Seventh Veil *PC*: Theatrecraft/Ortus. *P*: John Sutro, Sydney Box. *D*: Compton Bennett. *S*: Muriel and Sydney Box. *C*: James Mason, Ann Todd, Herbert Lom, Hugh McDermott.
I Know Where I'm Going *PC*: IP/Archers. *PDS*: Michael Powell, Emeric Pressburger. *C*: Roger Livesey, Wendy Hiller, Pamela Brown, Nancy Price.
Brief Encounter *PC*: IP/Cineguild. *P*: Anthony Havelock-Allan, Ronald Neame. *D*: David Lean. *S*: David Lean, Ronald Neame. *C*: Trevor Howard, Celia Johnson, Stanley Holloway, Joyce Carey.
The Wicked Lady *PC*: Gainsborough. *P*: R.J. Minney. *D*: Leslie Arliss. *S*: Leslie Arliss, Aimee Stuart, Gordon Glennon. *C*: Margaret Lockwood, James Mason, Patricia Roc, Griffith Jones.
Pink String and Sealing Wax *PC*: Ealing. *P*: Michael Balcon. *D*: Robert Hamer. *S*: Diana Morgan, Roland Pertwee. *C*: Googie Withers, Mervyn Johns, Gordon Jackson, Sally Ann Howes.
The Rake's Progress *PC*: IP/Individual. *P*: Frank Launder, Sidney Gilliat. *D*: Sidney Gilliat. *S*: Frank Launder, Sidney Gilliat. *C*: Rex Harrison, Lilli Palmer, Godfrey Tearle, Griffith Jones.
Here Comes the Sun *PC*: John Baxter. *D*: John Baxter. *S*: Geoffrey Orme. *C*: Bud Flanagan, Chesney Allen, Elsa Tee, Joss Ambler.

1946

Caesar and Cleopatra *PC*: IP/Pascal. *D*: Gabriel Pascal. *S*: George Bernard Shaw, Marjorie Deans, W.P. Lipscomb. *C*: Vivien Leigh, Claude Rains, Stewart Granger, Flora Robson.
The Captive Heart *PC*: Ealing. *P*: Michael Relph. *D*: Basil Dearden. *S*: Angus MacPhail. Guy Morgan. *C*: Michael Redgrave, Mervyn Johns, Basil Radford, Jack Warner.
Caravan *PC*: Gainsborough. *P*: Harold Huth. *D*: Arthur Crabtree. *S*: Roland Pertwee. *C*: Stewart Granger, Jean Kent, Anne Crawford, Dennis Price, Robert Helpmann.
Bedelia *PC*: John Corfield. *P*: Isadore Goldsmith. *D*: Lance Comfort. *S*: Vera Caspary, Herbert Victor, Moie Charles, Roy Ridley, Isadore Goldsmith. *C*: Margaret Lockwood, Ian Hunter, Barry K. Barnes, Anne Crawford.
The Years Between *PC*: Sydney Box. *D*: Compton Bennett. *S*: Muriel and Sydney Box. *C*: Michael Redgrave, Valerie Hobson, Flora Robson, Felix Aylmer.
Beware of Pity *PC*: Two Cities. *P*: W.P. Lipscomb. *D*: Maurice Elvey. *S*: W.P. Lipscomb, Elizabeth Baron, Margaret Steen. *C*: Lilli Palmer, Albert Lieven, Cedric Hardwicke, Gladys Cooper.
I See a Dark Stranger *PC*: IP/Individual. *P*: Frank Launder, Sidney Gilliat. *D*: Frank Launder. *S*: Frank Launder, Sidney Gilliat, Wolfgang Wilhelm. *C*: Deborah Kerr, Trevor Howard, Raymond Huntley, Michael Howard.
Men of Two Worlds *PC*: Two Cities. *P*: John Sutro. *D*: Thorold Dickinson. *S*: Thorold Dickinson, Herbert Victor. *C*: Phyllis Calvert, Eric Portman, Robert Adams, Orlando Martins.
London Town *PC*: Wesley Ruggles. *D*: Wesley Ruggles. *S*: Elliot Paul, Sigfried Herzig, Val Guest. *C*: Sid Field, Greta Gynt, Tessie O'Shea, Claude Hulbert.
The Magic Bow *PC*: Gainsborough. *P*: R.J. Minney. *D*: Bernard Knowles. *S*: Roland Pertwee, Norman Ginsbury. *C*: Stewart Granger, Phyllis Calvert, Jean Kent, Dennis Price.
The Overlanders *PC*: Ealing. *P*: Ralph Smart. *DS*: Harry Watt. *C*: Chips Rafferty, John Nugent Hayward, Daphne Campbell, John Fernside.
Carnival *PC*: Two Cities. *P*: John Sutro, William Sassoon. *D*: Stanley Haynes. *S*: Stanley Haynes, Peter Ustinov, Eric Maschwitz, Guy Green. *C*: Sally Gray, Michael Wilding, Stanley Holloway, Bernard Miles.
A Matter of Life and Death *PC*: IP/The Archers. *PDS*: Michael Powell, Emeric Pressburger. *C*: David Niven, Kim Hunter, Roger Livesey, Raymond Massey.
School for Secrets *PC*: Two Cities. *P*: Peter Ustinov, George H. Brown. *DS*: Peter Ustinov. *C*: Ralph Richardson, Raymond Huntley, Richard Attenborough, Marjorie Rhodes.
Green for Danger *PC*: IP/Individual. *P*: Frank Launder, Sidney Gilliat. *D*: Sidney Gilliat. *S*: Sidney Gilliat, Claude Gerney. *C*: Sally Gray, Trevor Howard, Rosamund John, Alastair Sim.
Great Expectations *PC*: IP/Cineguild. *P*: Anthony Havelock-Allan, Ronald Neame. *D*: David Lean. *S*: Ronald Neame, Kay Walsh, David Lean, Cecil McGivern, Anthony Havelock-Allan. *C*: John Mills, Valerie Hobson, Finlay Currie, Bernard Miles.
Daybreak *PC*: Triton. *P*:

Sydney Box. *D*: Compton Bennett. *S*: Muriel and Sydney Box. *C*: Ann Todd, Eric Portman, Maxwell Reed.

1947

Hungry Hill *PC*: Two Cities. *P*: William Sistrom. *D*: Brian Desmond Hurst. *S*: Daphne du Maurier, Terence Young, Francis Crowdy. *C*: Margaret Lockwood, Dennis Price, Cecil Parker, Michael Denison.
Odd Man Out *PC*: Two Cities. *PD*: Carol Reed. *S*: F.L. Green, R.C. Sheriff. *C*: James Mason, Robert Newton, Kathleen Ryan, Robert Beatty.
The Root of all Evil *PC*: Gainsborough. *P*: Harold Huth. *DS*: Brock Williams. *C*: Phyllis Calvert, Michael Rennie, John McCallum, Moore Marriott.
Hue and Cry *PC*: Ealing. *P*: Henry Cornelius. *D*: Charles Crichton. *S*: T.E.B. Clarke. *C*: Alastair Sim, Jack Warner, Valerie White, Harry Fowler.
Nicholas Nickleby *PC*: Ealing. *P*: John Croydon. *D*: Cavalcanti. *S*: John Dighton. *C*: Cedric Hardwicke, Alfred Drayton, Derek Bond, Sally Ann Howes.
The Man Within *PC*: Production Film Service. *PS*: Muriel and Sydney Box. *D*: Bernard Knowles. *C*: Richard Attenborough, Michael Redgrave, Jean Kent, Joan Greenwood.
Black Narcissus *PC*: IP/ The Archers. *PDS*: Michael Powell, Emeric Pressburger. *C*: Deborah Kerr, Sabu, David Farrar, Flora Robson.
Take My Life *PC*: IP/ Cineguild. *P*: Anthony Havelock-Allan. *D*: Ronald Neame. *S*: Winston Graham, Valerie Taylor, Margaret Kennedy. *C*: Hugh Williams, Greta Gynt, Marius Goring, Francis L. Sullivan.

Kathleen Ryan and Stewart Granger in *Captain Boycott*.

The Brothers *PC*: Triton. *P*: Sydney Box. *D*: David MacDonald. *S*: Muriel and Sydney Box, David MacDonald, Paul Vincent Carroll. *C*: Patricia Roc, Will Fyffe, Maxwell Reed, Finlay Currie.
Bush Christmas *PC*: Ralph Smart. *DS*: Ralph Smart. *C*: Chips Rafferty, John Fernside, Stan Tolshurst, Helen Grieve.
Dear Murderer *PC*: Gainsborough. *P*: Betty Box. *D*: Arthur Crabtree. *S*: Muriel and Sydney Box, Peter Rogers. *C*: Eric Portman, Greta Gynt, Dennis Price, Jack Warner.
The Loves of Joanna Godden *PC*: Ealing. *P*: Sidney Cole. *D*: Charles Frend. *S*: H.E. Bates, Angus MacPhail. *C*: Googie Withers, Jean Kent, John McCallum, Derek Bond.
Frieda *PC*: Ealing. *P*: Michael Relph. *D*: Basil Dearden. *S*: Ronald Millar, Angus MacPhail. *C*: David Farrar, Glynis Johns, Mai Zetterling, Flora Robson.
The Upturned Glass *PC*: Triton. *P*: Sydney Box, James Mason. *D*: Lawrence Huntington. *S*: J.P. Monaghan, Pamela Kellino. *C*: James Mason, Rosamund John, Pamela Kellino, Ann Stephens.
Holiday Camp *PC*: Gainsborough. *P*: Sydney Box. *D*: Ken Annakin. *S*: Muriel and Sydney Box, Peter Rogers, Mabel and Denis Constanduros, Ted Willis. *C*: Flora Robson, Dennis Price, Jack Warner, Hazel Court.
Jassy *PC*: Gainsborough. *P*: Sydney Box. *D*: Bernard Knowles. *S*: Dorothy and Campbell Christie, Geoffrey Kerr. *C*: Margaret Lockwood, Patricia Roc, Dennis Price, Dermot Walsh.
Master of Bankdam *PC*: Holbein. *P*: Nat Bronsten, Walter Forde, Edward Dryhurst. *D*: Walter Forde. *S*: Edward Dryhurst, Moie Charles. *C*: Anne Crawford, Dennis Price, Tom Walls, Stephen Murray.
Captain Boycott *PC*: IP/ Individual. *P*: Frank Launder, Sidney Gilliat. *D*: Frank Launder. *S*: Frank Launder, Wolfgang Wilhelm, Paul Vincent Carroll, Patrick Campbell. *C*: Stewart Granger, Kathleen Ryan, Cecil Parker, Robert Donat.
The October Man *PC*: Two Cities. *PS*: Eric Ambler. *D*: Roy Baker. *C*: John Mills, Joan Greenwood, Edward Chapman, Joyce Carey.
Fame is the Spur *PC*: Two Cities. *P*: John Boulting. *D*: Roy Boulting. *S*: Nigel Balchin. *C*: Michael Redgrave, Rosamund John, Bernard Miles, Carla Lehmann.
Uncle Silas *PC*: Two Cities. *P*: Josef Somlo, Laurence Irving. *D*: Charles Frank. *S*: Ben Travers. *C*: Jean Simmons, Katina Paxinou, Derrick de Marney, Derek Bond.
The White Unicorn *PC*: John Corfield. *P*: Harold Huth. *D*: Bernard Knowles. *S*: Robert Westerby, A.R. Rawlinson, Moie Charles. *C*: Margaret Lockwood, Dennis Price, Ian Hunter, Joan Greenwood.
The End of the River *PC*: IP/Archers. *P*: Michael Powell, Emeric Pressburger. *D*: Derek Twist. *S*: Wolfgang Wilhelm. *C*: Sabu, Bibi Ferreira, Esmond Knight, Robert Douglas.
The Woman in the Hall *PC*: IP/Wessex. *P*: Ian Dalrymple. *D*: Jack Lee. *S*: G.B. Stern, Ian Dalrymple, Jack Lee. *C*: Ursula Jeans, Jean Simmons, Cecil Parker, Jill Raymond.
It Always Rains on Sunday *PC*: Ealing. *P*: Henry Cornelius. *D*: Robert Hamer. *S*: Robert Hamer, Henry Cornelius, Angus MacPhail. *C*: Googie Withers, John McCallum, Edward Chapman, Jimmy Hanley.
When the Bough Breaks *PC*: Gainsborough. *P*: Betty Box. *D*: Lawrence Huntington. *S*: Muriel and Sydney Box, Peter Rogers. *C*: Patricia Roc, Rosamund John, Bill Owen, Patrick Holt.

1948

The Mark of Cain *PC*: Two Cities. *P*: W.P. Lipscomb. *D*: Brian Desmond Hurst.

S: W.P. Lipscomb, Francis Crowdy, Christianna Brand, *C*: Eric Portman, Sally Gray, Patrick Holt, Dermot Walsh.
Vice Versa *PC*: Two Cities. *P*: Peter Ustinov, George H. Brown. *DS*: Peter Ustinov. *C*: Roger Livesey, Kay Walsh, Anthony Newley, David Hutcheson.
Easy Money *PC*: Gainsborough. *P*: Frank Bundy. *D*: Bernard Knowles. *S*: Muriel and Sydney Box. *C*: Greta Gynt, Dennis Price, Jack Warner, Mervyn Johns.
Against the Wind *PC*: Ealing. *P*: Sidney Cole. *D*: Charles Crichton. *S*: T.E.B. Clarke, Michael Pertwee, Paul Vincent Carroll. *C*: Robert Beatty, Jack Warner, Simone Signoret, Gordon Jackson.
Blanche Fury *PC*: IP/ Cineguild. *P*: Anthony Havelock-Allan. *D*: Marc Allegret. *S*: Audrey Erskine Lindop, Hugh Mills, Cecil McGivern. *C*: Stewart Granger, Valerie Hobson, Walter Fitzgerald, Michael Gough.
Miranda *PC*: Gainsborough *P*: Betty Box. *D*: Ken Annakin. *S*: Peter Blackmore, Denis Waldock. *C*: Googie Withers, Glynis Johns, Griffith Jones, John McCallum.
Broken Journey *PC*: Gainsborough. *P*: Sydney Box. *D*: Ken Annakin. *S*: Robert Westerby. *C*: Phyllis Calvert, Margot Grahame, James Donald, Francis L. Sullivan.
One Night With You *PC*: Two Cities. *P*: Josef Somlo. *D*: Terence Young. *S*: Caryl Brahms, S.J. Simon. *C*: Nino Martini, Patricia Roc, Bonar Colleano, Hugh Wakefield.
Good Time Girl *PC*: Triton. *P*: Sydney Box, Samuel Goldwyn. *D*: David MacDonald. *S*: Muriel and Sydney Box, Ted Willis. *C*: Jean Kent, Dennis Price, Griffith Jones, Flora Robson.
Corridor of Mirrors *PC*: Apollo. *P*: Rudolph Cartier. *D*: Terence Young. *S*: Rudolph Cartier, Edana Romney. *C*: Eric Portman, Edana Romney, Barbara Mullen, Hugh Sinclair.
The Calendar *PC*: Gainsborough. *P*: Anthony Darnborough. *D*: Arthur Crabtree. *S*: Geoffrey Kerr. *C*: Greta Gynt, John McCallum, Raymond Lovell, Sonia Holm.

Trevor Howard and Ann Todd in *The Passionate Friends*.

Hamlet *PC*: Two Cities. *PD*: Laurence Olivier. *C*: Laurence Olivier, Eileen Herlie, Basil Sydney, Jean Simmons.
My Sister and I *PC*: Burnham. *P*: John Corfield, Harold Huth. *D*: Harold Huth. *S*: A.R. Rawlinson, Joan Rees, Michael Medwin, Robert Westerby. *C*: Sally Ann Howes, Barbara Mullen, Dermot Walsh, Hazel Court.
Oliver Twist *PC*: IP/ Cineguild. *P*: Anthony Havelock-Allan. *D*: David Lean. *S*: David Lean, Stanley Haynes. *C*: Alec Guinness, Robert Newton, John Howard Davies, Kay Walsh.
My Brother's Keeper *PC*: Gainsborough. *P*: Anthony Darnborough. *D*: Alfred Roome, Roy Rich. *S*: Frank Harvey. *C*: Jack Warner, Jane Hylton, David Tomlinson, Bill Owen.
The Red Shoes. *PC*: IP/ The Archers. *PD*: Michael Powell, Emeric Pressburger. *S*: Emeric Pressburger, Keith Winter. *C*: Anton Walbrook, Marius Goring, Moira Shearer, Robert Helpmann.
London Belongs to Me *PC*: IP/Individual. *P*: Frank Launder, Sidney Gilliat. *D*: Sidney Gilliat. *S*: Sidney Gilliat, J.B. Williams. *C*: Richard Attenborough, Alastair Sim, Fay Compton, Stephen Murray.
Mr Perrin and Mr Traill *PC*: Two Cities. *P*: Alexander Galperson. *D*: Lawrence Huntington. *S*: L.A.G. Strong. T.J. Morrison. *C*: Marius Goring, David Farrar, Greta Gynt, Raymond Huntley.
Saraband for Dead Lovers *PC*: Ealing. *P*: Michael Relph. *D*: Michael Relph, Basil Dearden. *S*: John Dighton, Alexander Mackendrick. *C*: Stewart Granger, Joan Greenwood, Françoise Rosay, Flora Robson.
The Weaker Sex *PC*: Two Cities. *P*: Paul Soskin. *D*: Roy Baker. *S*: Esther McCracken, Paul Soskin. *C*: Ursula Jeans, Cecil Parker, Joan Hopkins, Derek Bond.
The Blind Goddess *PC*: Gainsborough. *P*: Betty Box. *D*: Harold French. *S*: Muriel and Sydney Box. *C*: Eric Portman, Anne Crawford, Hugh Williams, Michael Denison.
Esther Waters *PC*: IP/ Wessex. *P*: Ian Dalrymple. *D*: Ian Dalrymple, Peter Proud. *S*: Michael Gordon, William Rose, Gerard Tyrell. *C*: Kathleen Ryan, Dirk Bogarde, Cyril Cusack, Ivor Barnard.
Sleeping Car to Trieste *PC*: Two Cities. *P*: George H. Brown. *D*: John Paddy Carstairs. *S*: Allan MacKinnon, William Douglas Home. *C*: Jean Kent, Albert Lieven, Derrick de Marney, Paul Dupuis.
Woman Hater *PC*: Two Cities. *P*: William Sistrom. *D*: Terence Young. *S*: Robert Westerby, Nicholas Phipps. *C*: Stewart Granger, Edwige Feuillere, Ronald Squire, Jeanne de Casalis.
Quartet *PC*: Gainsborough. *P*: Anthony Darnborough. *D*: Ken Annakin, Arthur Crabtree, Harold French, Ralph Smart. *S*: R.C. Sheriff. *C*: Cecil Parker, George Cole, Dirk Bogarde, Basil Radford, Mervyn Johns, Mai Zetterling.
Here Come the Huggetts *PC*: Gainsborough. *P*: Betty Box. *D*: Ken Annakin. *S*: Muriel and Sydney Box, Peter Rogers, Mabel and Denis Constanduros. *C*: Jack Warner, Kathleen Harrison, Jane Hylton, Susan Shaw.
It's Hard to be Good *PC*: Two Cities. *P*: John Gossage. *DS*: Jeffrey Dell. *C*: Anne Crawford, Jimmy Hanley, Raymond Huntley, Lana Morris.
Another Shore *PC*: Ealing. *P*: Ivor Montagu. *D*: Charles Crichton. *S*: Walter Meade. *C*: Robert Beatty, Stanley Holloway, Moira Lister, Michael Medwin.
Scott of the Antarctic *PC*: Ealing. *P*: Sidney Cole. *D*: Charles Frend. *S*: Ivor Montagu, Walter Meade, Mary Hayley Bell. *C*: John Mills, Derek Bond, Harold Warrender, James Robertson Justice.
The Fool and the Princess *PC*: Merton Park. *P*: Frank Hoare. *DS*: William Hammond. *C*: Bruce Lester, Lesley Brook, Adina Mandlova, Irene Handl.
Look Before You Love *PC*: Burnham. *P*: John

Corfield, Harold Huth. *S*: Reginald Long. *C*: Margaret Lockwood, Griffith Jones, Norman Wooland, Phyllis Stanley.
Once a Jolly Swagman *PC*: Pinewood/Wessex. *P*: Ian Dalrymple. *D*: Jack Lee. *S*: Jack Lee, William Rose, Cliff Gordon. *C*: Dirk Bogarde, Bonar Colleano, Renee Asherson, Bill Owen.
Portrait from Life. *PC*: Gainsborough. *P*: Anthony Darnborough. *D*: Terence Fisher. *S*: Muriel and Sydney Box, Frank Harvey. *C*: Mai Zetterling, Robert Beatty, Guy Rolfe, Herbert Lom.

1949

Warning to Wantons *PC*: Aquila. *PD*: Donald B. Wilson. *S*: Donald B. Wilson, James Laver. *C*: Harold Warrender, Anne Vernon, David Tomlinson, Sonia Holm.
Third Time Lucky *PC*: Kenilworth/Alliance. *P*: Mario Zampi. *D*: Gordon Parry. *S*: Gerald Butler. *C*: Glynis Johns, Dermot Walsh, Charles Goldner, Harcourt Williams.
Eureka Stockade *PC*: Ealing. *P*: Leslie Norman. *D*: Harry Watt. *S*: Harry Watt, Walter Greenwood, Ralph Smart. *C*: Chips Rafferty, Jane Barrett, Gordon Jackson, Jack Lambert.
Once Upon a Dream *PC*: Triton. *P*: Anthony Darnborough. *D*: Ralph Thomas. *S*: Patrick Kirwan, Victor Katona. *C*: Googie Withers, Griffith Jones, Guy Middleton, Raymond Lovell.
The Passionate Friends *PC*: Pinewood/Cineguild. *P*: Eric Ambler. *D*: David Lean. *S*: Eric Ambler, David Lean, Stanley Haynes. *C*: Ann Todd, Claude Rains, Trevor Howard, Betty Ann Davies.
Vote for Huggett *PC*: Gainsborough. *P*: Betty Box. *D*: Ken Annakin. *S*: Mabel and Denis Constanduros, Allan Mackinnon. *C*: Jack Warner, Kathleen Harrison, Susan Shaw, Petula Clark.
The History of Mr Polly *PC*: Two Cities. *P*: John Mills. *DS*: Anthony Pelissier. *C*: John Mills, Sally Ann Howes, Finlay Currie, Betty Ann Davies.
All Over Town *PC*: Pinewood/Wessex. *P*: Ian Dalrymple. *D*: Derek Twist. *S*: Derek Twist, Michael Gordon, Inez Holden, Stafford Byrne. *C*: Norman Wooland, Sarah Churchill, Cyril Cusack, Fabia Drake.
The Blue Lagoon *PC*:Pinewood/Individual. *P*: Frank Launder, Sidney Gilliat. *D*: Frank Launder. *S*: Frank Launder, John Baines, Michael Hogan. *C*: Jean Simmons, Donald Houston, Noel Purcell, Cyril Cusack.
Fools Rush In *PC*: Pinewood. *P*: Aubrey Baring. *D*: John Paddy Carstairs. *S*: Geoffrey Kerr. *C*: Sally Ann Howes, Guy Rolfe, Nora Swinburne, Nigel Buchanan.
Bad Lord Byron. *PC*: Triton. *P*: Aubrey Baring. *D*: David Macdonald. *S*: Terence Young, Anthony Thorne, Peter Quennell, Lawrence Kitchen, Paul Holt. *C*: Dennis Price, Mai Zetterling, Joan Greenwood, Linden Travers.

Jean Simmons and Laurence Olivier in *Hamlet*.

Floodtide *PC*: Aquila. *P*: Donald B. Wilson. *D*: Frederick Wilson. *S*: George Blake, Donald B. Wilson. *C*: Gordon Jackson, Rona Anderson, John Laurie, Jack Lambert.
It's Not Cricket *PC*: Gainsborough. *P*: Betty Box. *D*: Alfred Roome. Roy Rich. *S*: Bernard McNab. Lyn Lockwood, Gerard Bryant. *C*: Basil Radford, Naunton Wayne, Susan Shaw, Maurice Denham.
A Boy, a Girl and a Bike *PC*: Gainsborough. *P*: Ralph Keene. *D*: Ralph Smart. *S*: Ted Willis. *C*: John McCallum, Honor Blackman, Patrick Holt, Diana Dors.
Passport to Pimlico *PC*: Ealing. *P*: E.V.H. Emmett. *D*: Henry Cornelius. *S*: Henry Cornelius, T.E.B. Clarke. *C*: Stanley Holloway, Hermione Baddeley, Margaret Rutherford, Paul Dupuis.
The Huggetts Abroad *PC*: Gainsborough. *P*: Betty Box. *D*: Ken Annakin. *S*: Mabel and Denis Constanduros, Ted Willis, Gerard Bryant. *C*: Jack Warner, Kathleen Harrison, Susan Shaw, Petula Clark.
Adam and Evelyne *PC*: Two Cities. *PD*: Harold French. *D*: Noel Langley, Lesley Storm, George Barraud, Nicholas Phipps. *C*: Stewart Granger, Jean Simmons, Helen Cherry, Joan Swinstead.
The Perfect Woman *PC*: Two Cities. *P*: George Black, Alfred Black. *D*: Bernard Knowles. *S*: Bernard Knowles, George Black, J.B. Boothroyd. *C*: Patricia Roc, Stanley Holloway, Nigel Patrick, Miles Malleson.
Stop Press Girl *PC*: Aquila. *P*: Donald B. Wilson. *D*: Michael Barry. *DS*: T.J. Morrison, Basil Thomas. *C*: Sally Ann Howes, Gordon Jackson, Basil Radford, Naunton Wayne.
Marry Me *PC*: Gainsborough. *P*: Betty Box. *D*: Terence Fisher. *S*: Lewis Gilbert, Denis Waldock. *C*: Derek Bond, Susan Shaw, Patrick Holt, Carol Marsh.
Christopher Columbus *PC*: Gainsborough. *P*: Frank Bundy. *D*: David Macdonald. *S*: Cyril Roberts, Muriel and Sydney Box. *C*: Fredric March, Florence Eldridge, Francis L. Sullivan, Linden Travers.
Whisky Galore *PC*: Ealing. *P*: Monja Danischewsky. *D*: Alexander Mackendrick. *S*: Compton Mackenzie, Angus MacPhail. *C*: Basil Radford, Joan Greenwood, James Robertson Justice, Gordon Jackson.
Kind Hearts and Coronets *PC*: Ealing. *P*: Michael Relph. *D*: Robert Hamer. *S*: Robert Hamer, John Dighton. *C*: Dennis Price, Alec Guinness, Valerie Hobson, Joan Greenwood.
Poet's Pub *PC*: Aquila. *P*: Donald B. Wilson *D*:

Frederick Wilson. *S*: Diana Morgan. *C*: Derek Bond, Rona Anderson, James Robertson Justice, Barbara Murray.
Helter Skelter *PC*: Gainsborough. *P*: Anthony Darnborough. *D*: Ralph Thomas. *S*: Patrick Campbell, Jan Read, Gerard Bryant. *C*: Carol Marsh, David Tomlinson, Mervyn Johns, Peter Hammond.
Don't Ever Leave Me *PC*: Triton. *P*: Sydney Box. *D*: Arthur Crabtree. *S*: Robert Westerby. *C*: Jimmy Hanley, Petula Clark, Hugh Sinclair, Linden Travers.
Madness of the Heart *PC*: Two Cities. *P*: Richard Wainwright. *DS*: Charles Bennett. *C*: Margaret Lockwood, Maxwell Reed, Kathleen Byron, Paul Dupuis.
Tottie True *PC*: Two Cities. *P*: Hugh Stewart. *D*: Brian Desmond Hurst. *S*: C. Denis Freeman. *C*: Jean Kent, James Donald, Hugh Sinclair, Lana Morris.
Train of Events *PC*: Ealing. *P*: Michael Relph. *D*: Sidney Cole, Charles Crichton. *S*: Basil Dearden, Angus MacPhail, T.E.B. Clarke, Ronald Millar. *C*: Valerie Hobson, Jack Warner, John Clements, Irina Baronova.
The Lost People *PC*: Gainsborough. *P*: Gordon Wellesley. *D*: Bernard Knowles, Muriel Box. *S*: Bridget Boland, Muriel Box. *C*: Dennis Price, Mai Zetterling, Richard Attenborough, Siobhan McKenna.
Dear Mr Prohack *PC*: Pinewood/Wessex. *P*: Ian Dalrymple. *D*: Thornton Freeland. *S*: Ian Dalrymple, Donald Bull. *C*: Cecil Parker, Glynis Johns, Hermione Baddeley, Dirk Bogarde.
The Chiltern Hundreds *PC*: Two Cities. *P*: George H. Brown. *D*: John Paddy Carstairs. *S*: William Douglas-Home, Patrick Kirwan. *C*: Cecil Parker, A.E. Matthews, David Tomlinson, Lana Morris.
Diamond City *PC*: Gainsborough. *P*: Frank Bundy. *D*: David Macdonald. *S*: Roger Bray, Roland Pertwee. *C*: David Farrar, Honor Blackman, Diana Dors, Niall McGinnis.
Give Us This Day *PC*: Plantagenet. *P*: Rod Geiger, Nat Bronsten. *D*: Edward Dmytryk. *S*: Ben Barzman, John Penn. *C*: Sam Wanamaker, Lea Padovani, Kathleen Ryan, Bonar Colleano.

Sid Field as *The Cardboard Cavalier*.

The Spider and the Fly *PC*: Pinewood/Mayflower. *P*: Maxwell Setton, Aubrey Baring. *D*: Robert Hamer. *S*: Robert Westerby. *C*: Eric Portman, Guy Rolfe, Nadia Gray, Edward Chapman.
A Run for Your Money *PC*: Ealing. *P*: Leslie Norman. *D*: Charles Frend. *S*: Charles Frend, Leslie Norman, Richard Hughes, Diana Morgan. *C*: Donald Houston, Moira Lister, Alec Guinness, Meredith Edwards.
The Romantic Age *PC*: Pinnacle. *P*: Edward Dryhurst, Eric L'Epine Smith. *D*: Edmond T. Greville. *S*: Edward Dryhurst, Peggy Barwell. *C*: Mai Zetterling, Hugh Williams, Margot Grahame, Petula Clark.
Boys in Brown *PC*: Gainsborough. *P*: Anthony Darnborough. *DS*: Montgomery Tully. *C*: Jack Warner, Richard Attenborough, Dirk Bogarde, Jimmy Hanley.
The Rocking Horse Winner *PC*: Two Cities. *P*: John Mills. *DS*: Anthony Pelissier. *C*: John Mills, Valerie Hobson, John Howard Davies, Ronald Squire.
Traveller's Joy *PC*: Gainsborough. *P*: Anthony Darnborough. *D*: Ralph Thomas. *S*: Allan Mackinnon, Bernard Quayle. *C*: John McCallum, Googie Withers, Yolande Donlan, Maurice Denham.
The Cardboard Cavalier *PC*: Two Cities. *PD*: Walter Forde. *S*: Noel Langley. *C*: Sid Field, Margaret Lockwood, Mary Clare, Jerry Desmonde.

1950

The Blue Lamp *PC*: Ealing. *P*: Michael Relph. *D*: Basil Dearden. *S*: T.E.B. Clarke, Alexander Mackendrick. *C*: Jack Warner, Jimmy Hanley, Dirk Bogarde, Robert Flemying.
Golden Salamander *PC*: Pinewood. *P*: Alexander Galperson. *D*: Ronald Neame. *S*: Victor Canning, Ronald Neame, Lesley Storm. *C*: Trevor Howard, Anouk Aimée, Herbert Lom, Walter Rilla.
Madeleine *PC*: Pinewood/ Cineguild. *P*: Stanley Haynes. *D*: David Lean. *S*: Stanley Haynes, Nicholas Phipps. *C*: Ann Todd, Norman Wooland, Guy Desny, Leslie Banks.
Morning Departure *PC*: Jay Lewis. *P*: Leslie Parkyn. *D*: Roy Baker. *S*: William Fairchild. *C*: John Mills, Richard Attenborough, Nigel Patrick, Lana Morris.
The Astonished Heart *PC*: Gainsborough. *P*: Anthony Darnborough. *D*: Anthony Darnborough, Terence Fisher. *S*: Noel Coward. *C*: Noel Coward, Celia Johnson, Margaret Leighton, Joyce Carey.
They Were Not Divided *PC*: Two Cities. *P*: Herbert Smith. *DS*: Terence Young. *C*: Edward Underdown, Ralph Clanton, Helen Cherry, Sheila Andrews.
The Reluctant Widow *PC*: Two Cities. *P*: Gordon Wellesley. *D*: Bernard Knowles. *S*: Gordon Wellesley, J.B. Boothroyd. *C*: Jean Kent, Guy Rolfe, Paul Dupuis, Lana Morris.
Prelude to Fame *PC*: Two Cities. *P*: Donald B. Wilson. *D*: Fergus McDonell. *S*: Robert Westerby. *C*: Guy Rolfe, Kathleen Ryan, Kathleen Byron, Jeremy Spenser.
So Long at the Fair *PC*: Gainsborough. *P*: Betty Box. *D*: Anthony Darnborough, Terence Fisher. *S*: Hugh Mills, Anthony Thorne. *C*: Jean Simmons, Dirk Bogarde, David Tomlinson, Honor Blackman.
Dance Hall *PC*: Ealing. *P*: E.V.H. Emmett. *D*: Charles Crichton. *S*: E.V.H. Emmett, Alexander Mackendrick, Diana Morgan. *C*: Donald Houston, Bonar Colleano, Petula Clark, Natasha Parry.
Tony Draws a Horse *PC*: Pinnacle. *P*: Brock Williams, Harold Richmond. *D*: John Paddy Carstairs. *S*: Brock Williams. *C*: Cecil Parker, Anne Crawford, Derek Bond, Barbara Murray.

Waterfront *PC*: Conqueror. *P*: Paul Soskin. *D*: Michael Anderson. *S*: John Brophy, Paul Soskin. *C*: Robert Newton, Kathleen Harrison, Susan Shaw, Richard Burton.
Bitter Springs *PC*: Ealing. *P*: Leslie Norman. *D*: Ralph Smart. *S*: W.P. Lipscomb, Monja Danichewsky. *C*: Tommy Trinder, Chips Rafferty, Gordon Jackson, Jean Blue.
Trio *PC*: Gainsborough. *P*: Anthony Darnborough. *D*: Ken Annakin, Harold French. *S*: R.C. Sheriff, Noel Langley. *C*: James Hayter, Anne Crawford, Jean Simmons, Michael Rennie, Roland Culver, Kathleen Harrison.
Cage of Gold *PC*: Ealing. *P*: Michael Relph. *D*: Basil Dearden. *S*: Jack Whittingham, Paul Stein. *C*: Jean Simmons, David Farrar, James Donald, Herbert Lom.
The Woman in Question *PC*: Javelin. *P*: Teddy Baird. *D*: Anthony Asquith. *S*: John Cresswell. *C*: Jean Kent, Dirk Bogarde, John McCallum, Susan Shaw.
The Magnet *PC*: Ealing. *P*: Sidney Cole. *D*: Charles Frend. *S*: T.E.B. Clarke. *C*: Stephen Murray, Kay Walsh, William Fox, Meredith Edwards.
The Clouded Yellow *PC*: Carillon. *P*: Betty Box. *D*: Ralph Thomas. *S*: Eric Ambler. *C*: Jean Simmons, Trevor Howard, Sonia Dresdel, Maxwell Reed.
Highly Dangerous *PC*: Two Cities. *P*: Anthony Darnborough. *D*: Roy Baker. *S*: Eric Ambler, *C*: Margaret Lockwood, Dane Clark, Marius Goring, Naunton Wayne.

1951

The Adventurers *PC*: Mayflower. *P*: Maxwell Setton, Aubrey Baring. *D*: David Macdonald. *S*: Robert Westerby. *C*: Dennis Price, Jack Hawkins, Siobhan Mackenna, Peter Hammond.
Blackmailed. *PC*: HH. *P*: Harold Huth. *D*: Marc Allegret. *S*: Hugh Mills, Roger Vadim. *C*: Mai Zetterling, Dirk Bogarde, Fay Compton, Robert Flemying.
The Dark Man *PC*: Independent Artists. *P*: Julian Wintle. *DS*: Jeffrey Dell. *C*: Edward Underdown, Maxwell Reed, Natasha Parry, William Hartnell.
Pool of London *PC*: Ealing. *P*: Michael Relph. *D*: Basil Dearden. *S*: Jack Whittingham, John Eldridge. *C*: Bonar Colleano, Susan Shaw, Renee Asherson, Earl Cameron.
The Browning Version *PC*: Javelin. *P*: Teddy Baird. *D*: Anthony Asquith. *S*: Terence Rattigan. *C*: Michael Redgrave, Jean Kent, Nigel Patrick, Ronald Howard.
White Corridors *PC*: Vic. *P*: Joseph Janni, John Croydon. *D*: Pat Jackson. *S*: Pat Jackson, Jan Read. *C*: Googie Withers, Godfrey Tearle, James Donald, Petula Clark.
The Lavender Hill Mob *PC*: Ealing. *P*: Michael Truman. *D*: Charles Crichton. *S*: T.E.B. Clarke. *C*: Alex Guinness, Stanley Holloway, Sidney James, Alfie Bass
Hotel Sahara *PC*: Tower. *P*: George H. Brown. *D*: Ken Annakin. *S*: George H. Brown, Patrick Kirwan. *C*: Yvonne de Carlo, Peter Ustinov, David Tomlinson.
The Man in the White Suit *PC*: Ealing. *P*: Sidney Cole. *D*: Alexander Mackendrick. *S*: Roger Macdougall, Alexander Mackendrick, John Dighton. *C*: Alec Guinness, Joan Greenwood, Cecil Parker, Michael Gough.
Valley of the Eagles *PC*: Independent Sovereign. *P*: Nat Bronsten, George Willoughby. *DS*: Terence Young. *C*: Jack Warner, Nadia Gray, John McCallum, Anthony Dawson.
Appointment with Venus *PC*: British Film Makers. *P*: Betty Box. *D*: Ralph Thomas. *S*: Nicholas Phipps. *C*: David Niven, Glynis Johns, George Coulouris, Barry Jones.
High Treason *PC*: Conqueror. *P*: Paul Soskin. *D*: Roy Boulting. *S*: Frank Harvey, Roy Boulting. *C*: André Morell, Liam Redmond, Mary Morris, Kenneth Griffith.
Where No Vultures Fly *PC*: Leslie Norman. *D*: Harry Watt. *S*: Ralph Smart, W.P. Lipscomb, Leslie Norman. *C*: Anthony Steel, Dinah Sheridan, Harold Warrender, Meredith Edwards.
Encore *PC*: Two Cities/ Paramount. *P*: Anthony Darnborough. *D*: Harold French, Pat Jackson, Anthony Pelissier. *S*: T.E.B. Clarke, Arthur Macrae, Eric Ambler. *C*: Nigel Patrick, Kay Walsh, Glynis Johns, Terence Morgan, Roland Culver.

1952

His Excellency *PC*: Ealing. *P*: Michael Truman. *D*: Robert Hamer. *S*: W.P. Lipscomb, Robert Hamer. *C*: Eric Portman, Cecil Parker, Helen Cherry, Susan Stephen.
Secret People *PC*: Ealing. *P*: Sidney Cole. *D*: Thorold Dickinson. *S*: Thorold Dickinson, Wolfgang Wilhelm. *C*: Valentina Cortese. Serge Reggiani, Audrey Hepburn, Charles Goldner.
Hunted. *PC*: BFM/ Independent Artists. *P*: Julian Wintle. *D*: Charles Crichton. *S*: Jack Whittingham. *C*: Dirk Bogarde, Kay Walsh, Elizabeth Sellars, Jon Whiteley.
The Card *PC*: BFM. *P*: John Bryan. *D*: Ronald Neame. *S*: Eric Ambler. *C*: Alec Guinness, Valerie Hobson, Glynis Johns, Petula Clark.
I Believe in You *PC*: Ealing. *P*: Michael Relph. *D*: Basil Dearden. *S*:

Jean Simmons and Michael Rennie in *Trio*.

Michael Relph, Basil Dearden, Jack Whittingham, Nicholas Phipps. *C*: Cecil Parker, Celia Johnson, Harry Fowler, Joan Collins.
Curtain Up *PC*: Constellation. *P*: Robert Garrett. *D*: Ralph Smart. *S*: Michael Pertwee, Jack Davies. *C*: Robert Morley, Margaret Rutherford, Kay Kendall, Olive Sloane.
The Importance of Being Earnest *PC*: BFM/Javelin. *P*: Teddy Baird. *DS*: Anthony Asquith. *C*: Michael Redgrave, Michael Denison, Edith Evans, Joan Greenwood.
Something Money Can't Buy *PC*: BFM/Vic. *P*: Joseph Janni. *D*: Pat Jackson. *S*: James Lansdale Hodson, Pat Jackson. *C*: Patricia Roc, Anthony Steel, Moira Lister, A.E. Matthews.
Penny Princess *PC*: Conquest. *P*: Val Guest, Frank Godwin. *DS*: Val Guest. *C*: Yolande Donlan, Dirk Bogarde, Mary Clare, A.E. Matthews.
Mandy *PC*: Ealing. *P*: Leslie Norman. *D*: Alexander Mackendrick *S*: Jack Whittingham, Nigel Balchin. *C*: Jack Hawkins, Phyllis Calvert, Terence Morgan, Mandy Miller.
Meet Me Tonight *PC*: BFM. *P*: Anthony Havelock-Allan. *D*: Anthony Pellisier. *S*: Noel Coward. *C*: Valerie Hobson, Nigel Patrick, Kay Walsh, Stanley Holloway.
The Planter's Wife *PC*: Pinnacle. *P*: John Stafford. *D*: Ken Annakin. *S*: Peter Proud, Guy Elmes. *C*: Claudette Colbert, Jack Hawkins, Anthony Steel, Ram Gopal.
Venetian Bird *PC*: BFM. *P*: Betty Box. *D*: Ralph Thomas. *S*: Victor Canning. *C*: Richard Todd, Eva Bartok, John Gregson, George Coulouris.
The Gentle Gunman *PC*: Ealing. *P*: Michael Relph. *D*: Basil Dearden. *S*: Roger Macdougall. *C*: John Mills, Dirk Bogarde, Robert Beatty, Elizabeth Sellars.
It Started in Paradise *PC*: BFM. *P*: Sergei Nolbandov, Leslie Parkyn. *D*: Compton Bennett. *S*: Marghanita Laski, Hugh Hastings. *C*: Jane Hylton, Ian Hunter, Terence Morgan, Muriel Pavlow.
Made in Heaven *PC*: BFM/Fanfare. *P*: George H. Brown. *D*: John Paddy Carstairs. *S*: William Douglas-Home. *C*: David Tomlinson, Petula Clark, Sonja Ziemann, A.E. Matthews.

1953

The Long Memory *PC*: Europa. *P*: Hugh Stewart. *D*: Robert Hamer. *S*: Robert Hamer, Frank Harvey. *C*: John Mills, John McCallum, Elizabeth Sellars, Eva Berg.
The Net *PC*: Two Cities. *P*: Anthony Darnborough. *D*: Anthony Asquith. *S*: William Fairchild. *C*: Phyllis Calvert, James Donald, Robert Beatty, Herbert Lom.
Top of the Form *PC*: BFM. *P*: Paul Soskin. *D*: John Paddy Carstairs. *S*: John Paddy Carstairs, Patrick Kirwan, Ted Willis. *C*: Ronald Shiner, Harry Fowler, Alfie Bass, Jacqueline Pierreaux.
The Titfield Thunderbolt *PC*: Ealing. *P*: Michael Truman. *D*: Charles Crichton. *S*: T.E.B. Clarke. *C*: Stanley Holloway, George Relph, Naunton Wayne, John Gregson.
Street Corner *PC*: London Independent. *P*: Sydney Box, William MacQuitty. *D*: Muriel Box. *S*: Muriel and Sydney Box. *C*: Anne Crawford, Peggy Cummins, Rosamund John, Terence Morgan.
Desperate Moment *PC*: BFM/Fanfare. *P*: George H. Brown. *D*: Compton Bennett. *S*: George H. Brown, Patrick Kirwan. *C*: Dirk Bogarde, Mai Zetterling, Philip Friend, Albert Lieven.
The Final Test *PC*: ACT. *P*: R.J. Minney. *D*: Anthony Asquith. *S*: Terence Rattigan. *C*: Jack Warner, Robert Morley, Brenda Bruce, Ray Jackson.
The Cruel Sea *PC*: Ealing. *P*: Leslie Norman. *D*: Charles Frend. *S*: Eric Ambler. *C*: Jack Hawkins, Donald Sinden, Denholm Elliott, John Stratton.
Turn the Key Softly *PC*: Chiltern. *P*: Maurice Cowan. *D*: Jack Lee. *S*: John Brophy, Maurice Cowan. *C*: Yvonne Mitchell, Joan Collins, Kathleen Harrison.
Genevieve *PC*: Sirius. *PD*: Henry Cornelius. *S*: William Rose. *C*: Dinah Sheridan, John Gregson, Kenneth More, Kay Kendall.
The Malta Story *PC*: BFM/Theta. *P*: Peter de Sarigny. *D*: Brian Desmond Hurst. *S*: William Fairchild, Nigel Balchin. *C*: Alec Guinness, Jack Hawkins, Anthony Steel, Flora Robson.
The Square Ring *PC*: Ealing. *P*: Michael Relph. *D*: Basil Dearden. *S*: Robert Westerby, Peter Myers, Alec Grahame. *C*: Jack Warner, Robert Beatty, Maxwell Reed, Bill Owen.
Wheel of Fate *PC*: Kenilworth. *PD*: Francis Searle. *S*: Guy Elmes. *C*: Patric Doonan, Sandra Dorne, Bryan Forbes, John Horsley.
Always a Bride *PC*: Clarion. *P*: Robert Garrett. *D*: Ralph Smart. *S*: Ralph Smart, Peter Jones. *C*: Peggy Cummins, Terence Morgan, Ronald Squire, James Hayter.
A Day to Remember *PC*: Group. *P*: Betty Box. *D*: Ralph Thomas. *S*: Robin Estridge. *C*: Stanley Holloway, Joan Rice, Odile Versois, Donald Sinden.
Personal Affair *PC*: Two Cities. *P*: Anthony Darnborough. *DS*: Anthony Pelissier. *C*: Gene Tierney, Leo Genn, Glynis Johns, Pamela Brown.
Small Town Story *PC*: Almanak. *P*: Otto Kreisler, Ken Bennett. *D*: Montgomery Tully. *S*: George Fisher. *C*: Donald Houston, Susan Shaw, Alan Wheatley, Kent Walton.
Meet Mr Lucifer *PC*: Ealing. *P*: Monja Danichewsky. *D*: Anthony Pelissier. *S*: Monja Danichewsky, Peter Myers, Alec Grahame. *C*: Stanley Holloway, Peggy Cummins, Jack Watling, Barbara Murray.
Trouble in Store *PC*: Two Cities. *P*: Maurice Cowan. *D*: John Paddy Carstairs. *S*: John Paddy Carstairs, Maurice Cowan, Ted Willis. *C*: Norman Wisdom, Margaret Rutherford, Moira Lister, Derek Bond.
The Kidnappers *PC*: Group. *P*: Sergei Nolbandov, Leslie Parkyn. *D*: Philip Leacock. *S*: Neil Paterson. *C*: Duncan Macrae, Adrienne Corri, Jon Whiteley, Vincent Winter.

1954

The Million Pound Note *PC*: Group. *P*: John Bryan. *D*: Ronald Neame. *S*: Jill Craigie. *C*: Gregory Peck, Jane Griffiths, Ronald Squire, A.E. Matthews.
The Love Lottery *PC*: Ealing. *P*: Monja Danichewsky. *D*: Charles

A cross-Channel line-up for *A Day to Remember*: Peter Jones, Edward Chapman, James Hayter, Stanley Holloway, Harry Fowler, Meredith Edwards, Donald Sinden and Bill Owen.

Crichton. *S*: Harry Kurnitz. *C*: David Niven, Peggy Cummins, Anne Vernon, Herbert Lom.
The Maggie *PC*: Ealing. *P*: Michael Truman. *D*: Alexander Mackendrick. *S*: William Rose. *C*: Paul Douglas, Alex Mackenzie, James Copeland, Abe Barker.
You Know What Sailors Are *PC*: Group. *P*: Julian Wintle, Peter Rogers. *D*: Ken Annakin. *S*: Peter Rogers. *C*: Akim Tamiroff, Donald Sinden, Sarah Lawson, Naunton Wayne.
Fast and Loose *PC*: Group. *P*: Teddy Baird. *D*: Gordon Parry. *S*: A.R. Rawlinson, Ben Travers. *C*: Stanley Holloway, Kay Kendall, Brian Reece, Charles Victor.
Star of My Night *PC*: Kenilworth. *P*: The Danzigers. *D*: Paul Dickson. *S*: Paul Tabori. *C*: Griffith Jones, Kathleen Byron, Hugh Williams, Pauline Olsen.
Doctor in the House *PC*: Group. *P*: Betty Box. *D*: Ralph Thomas. *S*: Richard Gordon, Nicholas Phipps, Ronald Wilkinson. *C*: Dirk Bogarde, Kenneth More, Muriel Pavlow, James Robertson Justice.
West of Zanzibar *PC*: Eagle/Schlesinger. *P*: Leslie Norman. *D*: Harry Watt. *S*: Jack Whittingham, Max Catto. *C*: Anthony Steel, Sheila Sim, Edric Connor, Orlando Martins.
Forbidden Cargo *PC*: London Independent. *PS*: Sydney Box. *D*: Harold French. *C*: Nigel Patrick, Elizabeth Sellars, Terence Morgan, Greta Gynt.
The Rainbow Jacket *PC*: Ealing. *P*: Michael Relph. *D*: Basil Dearden. *S*: T.E.B. Clarke. *C*: Kay Walsh, Bill Owen, Edward Underdown, Fella Edmonds.
The Seekers *PC*: Group/ Fanfare. *P*: George H. Brown. *D*: Ken Annakin. *S*: William Fairchild. *C*: Jack Hawkins, Glynis Johns, Noel Purcell, Inia te Wiata.
Up to His Neck *PC*: Group. *P*: Hugh Stewart. *D*: John Paddy Carstairs. *S*: John Paddy Carstairs, Patrick Kirwan, Ted Willis, Maurice Cowan. *C*: Ronald Shiner, Laya Raki, Harry Fowler, Brian Rix.
The Beachcomber *PC*: London Independent. *P*: William MacQuitty. *D*: Muriel Box. *S*: Sydney Box. *C*: Robert Newton, Glynis Johns, Donald Sinden, Paul Rogers.
The Young Lovers *PC*: Group. *P*: Anthony Havelock-Allan. *D*: Anthony Asquith. *S*: Robin Estridge. *C*: Odile Versois, David Knight, Joseph Tomelty, David Kossoff.
Romeo and Juliet *PC*: Verona. *P*: Joseph Janni, Sandro Ghenzi. *DS*: Renato Castellani. *C*: Laurence Harvey, Susan Shentall, Flora Robson, Norman Wooland.
The Purple Plain *PC*: Two Cities. *P*: John Bryan. *D*: Robert Parrish. *S*: Eric Ambler. *C*: Gregory Peck, Win Min Than, Brenda de Banzie, Bernard Lee.
Lease of Life *PC*: Ealing. *P*: Jack Rix. *D*: Charles Frend. *S*: Eric Ambler. *C*: Robert Donat, Kay Walsh, Denholm Elliott, Adrienne Corri.
Mad About Men *PC*: Group. *P*: Betty Box. *D*: Ralph Thomas. *S*: Peter Blackmore. *C*: Glynis Johns, Donald Sinden, Margaret Rutherford.
The Divided Heart *PC*: Ealing. *P*: Michael Truman. *D*: Charles Crichton. *S*: Jack Whittingham, Richard Hughes. *C*: Cornell Borchers, Yvonne Mitchell, Armin Dahlen, Alexander Knox.
One Good Turn *PC*: Two Cities. *P*: Maurice Cowan. *D*: John Paddy Carstairs. *S*: Maurice Cowan, John Paddy Carstairs, Ted Willis. *C*: Norman Wisdom, Joan Rice, Shirley Abicair, Thora Hird.

1955

To Paris With Love *PC*: Two Cities. *P*: Anthony Darnborough. *D*: Robert Hamer. *S*: Robert Buckner. *C*: Alec Guinness, Odile Versois, Vernon Gray, Elina Labourdette.
Simba *PC*: Group. *P*: Peter de Sarigny. *D*: Brian Desmond Hurst. *S*: John Baines, Robin Estridge. *C*: Dirk Bogarde, Donald Sinden, Virginia McKenna, Earl Cameron.
Out of the Clouds *PC*: Ealing. *P*: Michael Relph. *D*: Basil Dearden. *S*: Michael Relph, John

Eldridge, Rex Rienits. *C*: Anthony Steel, Robert Beatty, David Knight, Margo Lorenz.
As Long as They're Happy *PC*: Group. *P*: Raymond Stross. *D*: J. Lee Thompson. *S*: Alan Melville. *C*: Jack Buchanan, Jeannie Carson, Janette Scott, Brenda de Banzie.
The Night My Number Came Up *PC*: Ealing. *P*: Tom Morahan. *D*: Leslie Norman. *S*: R.C. Sheriff. *C*: Michael Redgrave, Sheila Sim, Alexander Knox, Denholm Elliott.
Above Us the Waves *PC*: London Independent. *P*: Sydney Box, William MacQuitty. *D*: Ralph Thomas. *S*: Robin Estridge. *C*: John Mills, John Gregson, Donald Sinden, James Robertson Justice.
Passage Home *PC*: Group. *P*: Julian Wintle. *D*: Roy Baker. *S*: William Fairchild. *C*: Anthony Steel, Peter Finch, Diane Cilento, Cyril Cusack.
The Ship that Died of Shame *PC*: Ealing. *P*: Michael Relph. *D*: Basil Dearden. *S*: Michael Relph, Basil Dearden, John Whiting. *C*: Richard Attenborough, George Baker, Bill Owen, Virginia McKenna.
Doctor at Sea *PC*: Group. *P*: Betty Box. *D*: Ralph Thomas. *S*: Richard Gordon, Nicholas Phipps, Jack Davies. *C*: Dirk Bogarde, Brenda de Banzie, Brigitte Bardot, James Robertson Justice.
Value for Money *PC*: Group. *P*: Sergei Nolbandov. *D*: Ken Annakin. *S*: R.F. Delderfield, William Fairchild. *C*: John Gregson, Diana Dors, Susan Stephen, Derek Farr.
The Woman for Joe *PC*: Group. *P*: Leslie Parkyn. *D*: George More O'Ferrall. *S*: Neil Paterson. *C*: Diane Cilento, George Baker, David Kossoff, Jimmy Kairoubi.
Man of the Moment *PC*: Group. *P*: Hugh Stewart. *D*: John Paddy Carstairs. *S*: John Paddy Carstairs, Vernon Sylvaine. *C*: Norman Wisdom, Lana Morris, Belinda Lee, Jerry Desmonde.
Touch and Go *PC*: Ealing. *P*: Seth Holt. *D*: Michael Truman. *S*: William Rose. *C*: Jack Hawkins, Margaret Johnston, Roland Culver, John Fraser.
Simon and Laura *PC*: Group. *P*: Teddy Baird. *D*: Muriel Box. *S*: Peter Blackmore. *C*: Peter Finch, Kay Kendall, Muriel Pavlow, Hubert Gregg.
An Alligator Named Daisy *PC*: Group. *P*: Raymond Stross. *D*: J. Lee Thompson. *S*: Jack Davies. *C*: Donald Sinden, Diana Dors, Jean Carson, James Robertson Justice.
The Ladykillers *PC*: Ealing. *P*: Seth Holt. *D*: Alexander Mackendrick. *S*: William Rose. *C*: Alec Guinness, Cecil Parker, Katie Johnson, Peter Sellers.
All for Mary *PC*: Rank. *P*: Paul Soskin. *D*: Wendy Toye. *S*: Paul Soskin, Peter Blackmore, Alan Melville. *C*: Nigel Patrick, David Tomlinson, Kathleen Harrison, Jill Day.

Peter Finch and Virginia McKenna in *A Town Like Alice*.

1956

Lost *PC*: Rank. *P*: Vivian Cox, Sydney Box. *D*: Guy Green. *S*: Janet Green. *C*: David Farrar, David Knight, Julia Arnall, Eleanor Summerfield.
Jumping for Joy *PC*: Rank. *P*: Raymond Stross. *D*: John Paddy Carstairs. *S*: Jack Davies, Henry Blyth. *C*: Frankie Howerd, Stanley Holloway. A.E. Matthews, Tony Wright.
A Town Like Alice *PC*: Vic. *P*: Joseph Janni. *D*: Jack Lee. *S*: W.P. Lipscomb, Richard Mason. *C*: Virginia McKenna, Peter Finch, Marie Lohr, Renee Houston.
Who Done It? *PC*: Ealing. *P*: Michael Relph. *D*: Basil Dearden. *S*: T.E.B. Clarke. *C*: Benny Hill, Belinda Lee, David Kossoff, Garry Marsh.
The Black Tent *PC*: Rank. *P*: William MacQuitty. *D*: Brian Desmond Hurst. *S*: Robin Maugham, Bryan Forbes. *C*: Anthony Steel, Donald Sinden, Anna Maria Sandri, André Morell.
The Feminine Touch *PC*: Ealing. *P*: Jack Rix. *D*: Pat Jackson. *S*: Ian McCormick. *C*: George Baker, Belinda Lee, Delphi Lawrence, Adrienne Corri.
The Long Arm *PC*: Ealing. *P*: Tom Morahan. *D*: Charles Frend. *S*: Robert Barr, Janet Green, Dorothy and Campbell Christie. *C*: Jack Hawkins, John Stratton, Dorothy Alison, Geoffrey Keen.
Reach for the Sky *PC*: Pinnacle. *P*: Daniel Angel. *D*: Lewis Gilbert. *S*: Lewis Gilbert, Vernon Harris. *C*: Kenneth More, Muriel Pavlow, Lyndon Brook, Lee Patterson.
Jacqueline *PC*: Rank. *P*: George H. Brown. *D*: Roy Baker. *S*: Patrick Kirwan, Liam O'Flaherty, Catherine Cookson, Patrick Campbell. *C*: John Gregson, Kathleen Ryan, Jacqueline Ryan, Noel Purcell.
Eyewitness *PC*: Rank. *P*: Sydney Box. *D*: Muriel Box. *S*: Janet Green. *C*: Donald Sinden, Muriel Pavlow, Belinda Lee, David Knight.
House of Secrets *PC*: Rank. *P*: Julian Wintle, Vivian Cox. *D*: Guy Green. *S*: Robert Buckner, Bryan Forbes. *C*: Michael Craig, Julia Arnall, Brenda de Banzie, Barbara Bates.
Checkpoint *PC*: Rank. *P*: Betty Box. *D*: Ralph Thomas. *S*: Robin Estridge. *C*: Anthony Steel, Odile Versois, Stanley Baker, James Robertson Justice.
The Battle of the River Plate *PC*: Arcturus. *PDS*: Michael Powell, Emeric Pressburger. *C*: John Gregson, Anthony Quayle, Peter Finch, Bernard Lee.
The Spanish Gardener *PC*: Rank. *P*: John Bryan. *D*: Philip Leacock. *S*: John Bryan, Lesley Storm. *C*: Dirk Bogarde, Jon Whiteley, Michael Hordern, Cyril Cusack.
Tiger in the Smoke *PC*: Rank. *P*: Leslie Parkyn. *D*: Roy Baker. *S*: Anthony Pelissier. *C*: Donald Sinden, Muriel Pavlow, Tony Wright, Bernard Miles.
Up in the World *PC*: Rank. *P*: Hugh Stewart. *D*: John Paddy Carstairs. *S*: Jack Davies, Peter Blackmore, Henry Blyth. *C*: Norman

Wisdom, Maureen Swanson, Jerry Desmonde, Michael Caridia.
The Big Money *PC*: Rank. *P*: Joseph Janni. *D*: John Paddy Carstairs. *S*: John Baines, Patrick Campbell. *C*: Ian Carmichael, Belinda Lee, Kathleen Harrison, Robert Helpmann.

1957

Ill Met By Moonlight *PC*: Vega. *PDS*: Michael Powell, Emeric Pressburger. *C*: Dirk Bogarde, David Oxley, Marius Goring, Cyril Cusack.
The Secret Place *PC*: Rank. *P*: John Bryan, Anthony Perry. *D*: Clive Donner. *S*: Linette Perry. *C*: Belinda Lee, Ronald Lewis, Michael Brooke, Michael Gwynne.
True as a Turtle *PC*: Rank. *P*: Peter de Sarigny. *D*: Wendy Toye. *S*: John Coates, Jack Davies, Nicholas Phipps. *C*: John Gregson, June Thorburn, Cecil Parker, Keith Michell.
Doctor at Large *PC*: Rank. *P*: Betty Box. *D*: Ralph Thomas. *S*: Richard Gordon, Nicholas Phipps. *C*: Dirk Bogarde, Muriel Pavlow, Donald Sinden, James Robertson Justice.
High Tide at Noon *PC*: Rank. *P*: Julian Wintle. *D*: Philip Leacock. *S*: Neil Paterson. *C*: William Sylvester, Betta St John, Michael Craig, Flora Robson.
The Crooked Sky *PC*: Luckwin. *P*: Bill Luckwell, Derek Winn. *D*: Henry Cass. *S*: Norman Hudis. *C*: Wayne Morris, Karin Booth, Anton Diffring, Bruce Seton.
Miracle in Soho *PC*: Rank. *PS*: Emeric Pressburger. *D*: Julian Amyes. *C*: John Gregson, Belinda Lee, Cyril Cusack, Peter Illing.
Hell Drivers *PC*: Rank/ Aqua. *P*: Benjamin Fisz. *D*: Cy Endfield. *S*: Cy Endfield, John Kruse. *C*: Stanley Baker, Herbert Lom, Patrick McGoohan, Peggy Cummins.

Belinda Lee and John Gregson in *A Miracle in Soho.*

Manuela *PC*: Foxwell. *D*: Guy Hamilton. *S*: William Woods, Guy Hamilton. *C*: Pedro Armendariz, Trevor Howard, Elsa Martinelli, Donald Pleasence.
Across the Bridge. *PC*: IPF. *P*: John Stafford. *D*: Ken Annakin. *S*: Guy Elmes, Denis Freeman. *C*: Rod Steiger, David Knight, Marla Landi, Noel Willman.
Seven Thunders *PC*: Dial. *P*: Daniel Angel. *D*: Hugo Fregonese. *S*: John Baines. *C*: Stephen Boyd, James Robertson Justice, Kathleen Harrison, Tony Wright.
Campbell's Kingdom *PC*: Rank. *P*: Betty Box. *D*: Ralph Thomas. *S*: Robin Estridge, Hammond Innes. *C*: Dirk Bogarde, Stanley Baker, Michael Craig, Barbara Murray.
Robbery Under Arms *PC*: Rank. *P*: Joseph Janni. *D*: Jack Lee. *S*: W.P. Lipscomb, Alexander Baron. *C*: Peter Finch, Ronald Lewis, Maureen Swanson, David McCallum.
The One That Got Away *PC*: Rank. *P*: Julian Wintle. *D*: Roy Baker. *S*: Howard Clewes. *C*: Hardy Kruger, Colin Gordon, Michael Goodliffe, Terence Alexander.
Just My Luck *PC*: Rank. *P*: Hugh Stewart. *D*: John Paddy Carstairs. *S*: Alfred Shaughnessy, Peter Blackmore. *C*: Norman Wisdom, Margaret Rutherford, Jill Dixon, Leslie Phillips.
Dangerous Exile *PC*: Rank. *P*: George H. Brown. *D*: Brian Desmond Hurst. *S*: Robin Estridge. *C*: Louis Jourdan, Belinda Lee, Keith Michell, Richard O'Sullivan.
The Naked Truth *PC*: Anglofilm/Rank. *PD*: Mario Zampi. *S*: Michael Pertwee. *C*: Peter Sellers, Terry Thomas, Peggy Mount, Shirley Eaton.
Windom's Way *PC*: Rank. *P*: John Bryan. *D*: Ronald Neame. *S*: Jill Craigie. *C*: Peter Finch, Mary Ure, Natasha Parry, Robert Flemying.

1958

Violent Playground *PC*: Rank. *P*: Michael Relph. *D*: Basil Dearden. *S*: James Kennaway. *C*: Stanley Baker, Peter Cushing, Anne Heywood, David McCallum.
The Gypsy and the Gentleman *PC*: Rank. *P*: Maurice Cowan. *D*: Joseph Losey. *S*: Janet Green. *C*: Melina Mercouri, Keith Michell, Patrick McGoohan, Flora Robson.
A Tale of Two Cities *PC*: Rank. *P*: Betty Box. *D*: Ralph Thomas. *S*: T.E.B. Clarke. *C*: Dirk Bogarde, Dorothy Tutin, Cecil Parker, Stephen Murray.
Carve Her Name with Pride *PC*: Keyboard. *P*: Daniel Angel. *D*: Lewis Gilbert. *S*: Lewis Gilbert, Vernon Harris. *C*: Virginia McKenna, Paul Scofield, Jack Warner, Denise Grey.
Rooney *PC*: Rank. *P*: George H. Brown. *D*: George Pollock. *S*: Patrick Kirwan. *C*: John Gregson, Muriel Pavlow, Barry Fitzgerald, June Thorburn.
Innocent Sinners *PC*: Rank. *P*: Hugh Stewart. *D*: Philip Leacock. *S*: Rumer Godden, Neil Paterson. *C*: Flora Robson, David Kossoff, Barbara Mullen, Catherine Lacey.
Heart of a Child *PC*: Beaconsfield. *P*: Alfred Shaughnessy. *D*: Clive Donner. *S*: Leigh Vance. *C*: Jean Anderson, Donald Pleasence, Richard Williams, Maureen Pryor.
The Wind Cannot Read *PC*: Rank. *P*: Betty Box. *D*: Ralph Thomas. *S*: Richard Mason. *C*: Dirk Bogarde, Yoko Tani, John Fraser, Ronald Lewis.
A Night to Remember *PC*: Rank. *P*: William MacQuitty. *D*: Roy Baker. *S*: Eric Ambler. *C*: Kenneth More, David McCallum, Jill Dixon, Laurence Naismith.
Nor the Moon by Night *PC*: IPF. *P*: John Stafford. *D*: Ken Annakin. *S*: Guy Elmes. *C*: Belinda Lee, Michael Craig, Patrick McGoohan, Anna Gaylor.
Sea Fury *PC*: Rank/Aqua. *P*: Benjamin Fisz. *D*: Cy Endfield. *S*: Cy Endfield, John Kruse. *C*: Stanley Baker, Victor McLaglen, Luciana Paluzzi, Gregoire Aslan.
Rockets Galore *PC*: Rank. *P*: Basil Dearden. *D*: Michael Relph. *S*: Monja Danichewsky. *C*: Jeannie Carson, Donald Sinden, Roland Culver, Noel Purcell.
Passionate Summer *PC*: Briar. *P*: Kenneth Harper, George Willoughby. *D*: Rudolph Cartier. *S*: Joan Henry. *C*: Virginia McKenna, Bill Travers, Yvonne Mitchell, Alexander Knox.
Sea of Sand *PC*: Tempean. *P*: Robert Baker, Monty Berman. *D*: Guy Green. *S*:

Robert Westerby. *C*: Richard Attenborough, John Gregson, Michael Craig, Vincent Ball.
Floods of Fear *PC*: Rank. *P*: Sydney Box. *D*: Charles Crichton. *S*: Charles Crichton, Vivienne Knight. *C*: Howard Keel, Anne Heywood, Cyril Cusack, Harry H. Corbett.
The Square Peg *PC*: Rank. *P*: Hugh Stewart. *D*: John Paddy Carstairs. *S*: Jack Davies, Henry Blyth, Norman Wisdom, Eddie Leslie. *C*: Norman Wisdom, Honor Blackman, Edward Chapman, Hattie Jacques.
Bachelor of Hearts *PC*: Independent Artists. *P*: Vivian Cox, Julian Wintle, Leslie Parkyn. *D*: Wolf Rilla. *S*: Leslie Bricusse, Frederic Raphael. *C*: Hardy Kruger, Sylvia Sims, Ronald Lewis, Eric Barker.

1959

The Captain's Table *PC*: Rank. *P*: Joseph Janni. *D*: Jack Lee. *S*: John Whiting, Bryan Forbes, Nicholas Phipps. *C*: John Gregson, Peggy Cummins, Donald Sinden, Nadia Gray.
Operation Amsterdam *PC*: Rank. *P*: Maurice Cowan. *D*: Michael McCarthy. *S*: Michael McCarthy, John Eldridge. *C*: Peter Finch, Eva Bartok, Tony Britton, Alexander Knox.
Hidden Homicide *PC*: Bill and Michael Luckwell. *P*: Derek Winn. *D*: Tony Young. *S*: Tony Young, Bill Luckwell. *C*: Griffith Jones, James Kenney, Patricia Laffan, Bruce Seton.
Too Many Crooks *PC*: Rank. *P*: Mario and Giulio Zampi. *D*: Mario Zampi. *S*: Michael Pertwee. *C*: Terry-Thomas, George Cole, Brenda de Banzie, Bernard Bresslaw.
The 39 Steps *PC*: Rank. *P*: Betty Box. *D*: Ralph Thomas. *S*: Frank Harvey, from a scenario by Charles Bennett, Ian Hay, Alma Reville. *C*: Kenneth More, Tania Elg, Brenda de Banzie, Barry Jones.
Whirlpool *PC*: Rank. *P*: George Pitcher. *D*: Lewis Allen. *S*: Lawrence P. Bachmann. *C*: Juliette Greco, O.W. Fischer, Muriel Pavlow, William Sylvester.
Sapphire *PC*: Artna. *P*: Michael Relph. *D*: Basil Dearden. *S*: Janet Green, Lukas Heller. *C*: Nigel Patrick, Yvonne Mitchell, Michael Craig, Paul Massie.
The Heart of a Man *PC*: Everest. *P*: Anna Neagle. *D*: Herbert Wilcox. *S*: Jack Trevor Story, Pamela Bower. *C*: Frankie Vaughan, Anne Heywood, Tony Britton, Anthony Newley.

Hardy Kruger and Sylvia Sims in *Bachelor of Hearts*.

Ferry to Hong Kong *PC*: Rank. *P*: George Maynard. *D*: Lewis Gilbert. *S*: Lewis Gilbert, Vernon Harris, John Mortimer. *C*: Curt Jurgens, Orson Welles, Sylvia Sims, Jeremy Spenser.
Upstairs and Downstairs *PC*: Rank. *P*: Betty Box. *D*: Ralph Thomas. *S*: Frank Harvey. *C*: Michael Craig, Anne Heywood, Mylène Demongeot, James Robertson Justice.
Blind Date *PC*: Independent Artists. *P*: David Deutsch. *D*: Joseph Losey. *S*: Ben Barzman, Millard Lampell. *C*: Hardy Kruger, Stanley Baker, Micheline Presle, Robert Flemying.
The Night We Dropped a Clanger *PC*: Four Star. *P*: David Henley. *D*: Darcy Conyers. *S*: John Chapman. *C*: Brian Rix, Cecil Parker, William Hartnell, Leslie Phillips.
North West Frontier *PC*: Rank. *P*: Marcel Hellman. *D*: J. Lee Thompson. *S*: Robin Estridge. *C*: Kenneth More, Lauren Bacall, Herbert Lom, Wilfrid Hyde-White.
SOS Pacific *PC*: Rank. *P*: John Nasht, Patrick Filmer-Sankey. *D*: Guy Green. *S*: Robert Westerby. *C*: Richard Attenborough, Pier Angeli, John Gregson, Eva Bartok.
Desert Mice *PC*: Artna. *P*: Michael Relph, Sydney Box. *D*: Basil Dearden. *S*: David Climie. *C*: Alfred Marks, Sidney James, Dick Bentley, Patricia Bredin.
Follow a Star *PC*: Rank. *P*: Hugh Stewart. *D*: Robert Asher. *S*: Jack Davies, Henry Blyth, Norman Wisdom. *C*: Norman Wisdom, June Laverick, Jerry Desmonde, Hattie Jacques.
Tiger Bay *PC*: Independent Artists. *P*: John Hawkesworth. *D*: J. Lee Thompson. *S*: John Hawksworth, Shelley Smith. *C*: John Mills, Horst Buchholz, Hayley Mills, Yvonne Mitchell.

1960

Too Young to Love *PC*: Beaconsfield. *P*: Herbert Smith, Sydney Box. *D*: Muriel Box. *S*: Muriel and Sydney Box. *C*: Thomas Mitchell, Pauline Hahn, Joan Miller, Austin Willis.
The Shakedown *PC*: Ethiro. *P*: Norman Williams. *D*: John Lemont. *S*: John Lemont, Leigh Vance. *C*: Terence Morgan, Hazel Court, Donald Pleasence, Robert Beatty.
The Royal Ballet *PC*: Rank/Poetic. *PD*: Paul Czinner. *C*: Margot Fonteyn, Michael Soames, Bryan Ashbridge, Julia Farron, the Royal Ballet Company and the Covent Garden Orchestra.
Conspiracy of Hearts *PC*: Rank. *P*: Betty Box. *D*: Peter Rogers. *S*: Robert Presnell Jnr. *C*: Lilli Palmer, Sylvia Sims, Yvonne Mitchell, Ronald Lewis.
Faces in the Dark *PC*: Penington/Eady. *P*: Jon Penington. *D*: David Eady. *S*: Ephraim Kogan, John Tully. *C*: John Gregson, Mai Zetterling, John Ireland, Michael Denison.
Your Money or Your Wife *PC*: Ethiro. *P*: Norman Williams. *D*: Anthony Simmons. *S*: Ronald Jeans. *C*: Donald Sinden, Peggy Cummins, Richard Wattis, Peter Reynolds.
The League of Gentlemen *PC*: Allied Film Makers. *P*: Michael Ralph. *D*: Basil Dearden. *S*: Bryan Forbes. *C*: Jack Hawkins, Nigel Patrick, Richard Attenborough, Roger Livesey.
Beyond the Curtain *PC*: Martin. *P*: John Martin. *D*: Compton Bennett. *S*: Compton Bennett, John Cresswell. *C*: Richard Greene, Eva Bartok, Marius Goring, Lucie Mannheim.
The Challenge *PC*: Alexandra. *P*: John Temple-Smith. *DS*: John Gilling. *C*: Jayne Mansfield, Anthony Quayle, Carl Mohner, Peter Reynolds.
Never Let Go *PC*: Independent Artists. *P*: Peter de Sarigny. *D*: John Guillermin. *S*: Alun

Alan Barnes, Diane Holgate and Hayley Mills in *Whistle Down the Wind*.

Falconer. *C*: Peter Sellers, Richard Todd, Elisabeth Sellars, Adam Faith.
Make Mine Mink *PC*: Rank. *P*: Hugh Stewart. *D*: Robert Asher. *S*: Michael Pertwee, Peter Blackmore. *C*: Terry-Thomas, Athene Seyler, Hattie Jacques, Billie Whitelaw.
Snowball *PC*: Independent Artists. *P*: Julian Wintle, Leslie Parkyn. *D*: Pat Jackson. *S*: Anne Francis. *C*: Gordon Jackson, Kenneth Griffith, Zena Walker, Daphne Anderson.
Doctor in Love *PC*: Rank. *P*: Betty Box. *D*: Ralph Thomas. *S*: Nicholas Phipps. *C*: Michael Craig, Leslie Phillips, Carole Lesley, James Robertson Justice.
Piccadilly Third Stop *PC*: Ethiro. *P*: Norman Williams. *D*: Wolf Rilla. *S*: Leigh Vance. *C*: Terence Morgan, Yoko Tani, Mai Zetterling, William Hartnell.
Man in the Moon *PC*: Excalibur/AFM. *P*: Michael Relph. *D*: Basil Dearden. *S*: Bryan Forbes, Michael Relph. *C*: Kenneth More, Shirley Anne Field, Michael Hordern, Charles Gray.
The Bulldog Breed *PC*: Rank. *P*: Hugh Stewart. *D*: Robert Asher. *S*: Jack Davies, Henry Blyth, Norman Wisdom. *C*: Norman Wisdom, Ian Hunter, David Lodge, Robert Urquhart.

1961

The Singer Not the Song *PC*: Rank. *P*: Roy Baker, Jack Hanbury. *D*: Roy Baker. *S*: Nigel Balchin. *C*: Dirk Bogarde, John Mills, Mylène Demongeot, Laurence Naismith.
No Love for Johnnie *PC*: Five Star. *P*: Betty Box. *D*: Ralph Thomas. *S*: Nicholas Phipps, Mordecai Richler. *C*: Peter Finch, Stanley Holloway, Donald Pleasence, Billie Whitelaw.
Very Important Person *PC*: Julian Wintle, Leslie Parkyn. *D*: Ken Annakin. *S*: Jack Davies. *C*: James Robertson Justice, Leslie Phillips, Stanley Baxter, Eric Sykes.
Flame in the Streets *PC*: Rank/Somerset. *P*: Roy Baker, Jack Hanbury. *D*: Roy Baker. *S*: Ted Willis. *C*: John Mills, Sylvia Sims, Brenda de Banzie, Earl Cameron.
Whistle Down the Wind *PC*: AFM/Beaver. *P*: Richard Attenborough. *D*: Bryan Forbes. *S*: Keith Waterhouse, Willis Hall. *C*: Hayley Mills, Bernard Lee, Alan Bates, Norman Bird.
Information Received *PC*: United co-production. *P*: John Clein, George Maynard. *D*: Robert Lynn. *S*: Paul Ryder. *C*: Sabina Sesselman, William Sylvester, Hermione Baddeley, Edward Underdown.
No, My Darling Daughter *PC*: Rank/Five Star. *P*: Betty Box. *D*: Ralph Thomas. *S*: Frank Harvey. *C*: Michael Redgrave, Michael Craig, Roger Livesey, Juliet Mills.
Victim *PC*: Parkway/AFM. *P*: Michael Relph. *D*: Basil Dearden. *S*: Janet Green, John McCormick. *C*: Dirk Bogarde, Sylvia Sims, Dennis Price, Nigel Stock.
In the Doghouse *PC*: Rank. *P*: Hugh Stewart. *D*: Darcy Conyers. *S*: Michael Pertwee. *C*: Leslie Phillips, Peggy Cummins, Hattie Jacques, James Booth.

1962

All Night Long *PC*: Rank. *P*: Bob Robert, Michael Relph. *D*: Basil Dearden. *S*: Nel King, Peter Achilles. *C*: Patrick McGoohan, Keith Michell, Betsy Blair, Paul Harris. *Music*: Dave Brubeck, Johnny Dankworth, Charlie Mingus, Tubby Hayes.
A Pair of Briefs *PC*: Rank. *P*: Betty Box. *D*: Ralph Thomas. *S*: Nicholas Phipps. *C*: Michael Craig, Mary Peach, Brenda de Banzie, James Robertson Justice.
The Traitors *PC*: Ello. *P*: James O'Connolly, Joe Levy. *S*: James O'Connolly. *D*: Robert Tronson. *C*: Patrick Allen, James Maxwell, Ewan Roberts, Jacqueline Ellis.
Tiara Tahiti *PC*: Rank. *P*: Ivan Foxwell. *D*: Ted Kotcheff. *S*: Geoffrey Cotterell, Ivan Foxwell, Mordechai Richler. *C*: James Mason, John Mills, Claude Dauphin, Herbert Lom.
Life for Ruth *PC*: AFM. *P*: Michael Relph. *D*: Basil Dearden. *S*: Janet Green, John McCormick. *C*: Michael Craig, Patrick McGoohan, Janet Munro, Paul Rogers.
The Day of the Triffids *PC*: Security. *P*: Philip Yordan, George Pitcher. *D*: Steve Sekeley. *S*: Philip Yordan. *C*: Howard Keel, Nicole Maurey, Janette Scott, Kieron Moore.
Der Rosenkavalier *PC*: Poetic/Rank. *PD*: Paul Czinner. *C*: Elisabeth Schwarzkopf, Sena Jurinac, Anneliese Rothenburger, Otto Edelman; a Salzburg Festival performance, Herbert von Karajan conducting the Vienna Philharmonic Orchestra, Vienna State Opera Chorus/ Opera Ballet and Mozarteum Orchestra.
Band of Thieves *PC*: Filmvale. *P*: Lance Comfort, Bill Chalmers, Harold Shampan. *D*: Peter Bezencenet. *S*: Lyn Fairhurst. *C*: Acker Bilk and his Band, Jimmy Thompson, Jennifer Jayne, Geoffrey Sumner.
Billy Budd *PC*: Anglo-Allied. *P*: Millard Kaufman, Ronald Lubin. *D*: Peter Ustinov. *S*: Peter Ustinov, Robert Rossen. *C*: Robert Ryan, Terence Stamp, Melvyn Douglas, Peter Ustinov.
The Wild and the Willing *PC*: Rank. *P*: Betty Box. *D*: Ralph Thomas. *S*: Nicholas Phipps, Mordechai Richler. *C*: Virginia Maskell, Paul Rogers, Ian McShane, Samantha Eggar.
Stranglehold *PC*: Argo. *P*: Jack Lamont, David Henley. *D*: Lawrence Huntington. *S*: Guy Elmes. *C*: MacDonald Carey, Barbara Shelley, Philip Friend, Nadja Regin.
The Fur Collar *PC*: Albatross. *PDS*: Lawrence Huntington. *C*: John Bentley, Martin Benson, Philip Friend, Nadja Regin.
The Fast Lady *PC*: Independent Artists. *P*:

Julian Wintle, Leslie Parkyn. *D*: Ken Annakin. *S*: Jack Davies, Henry Blyth. *C*: James Robertson Justice, Leslie Phillips, Stanley Baxter, Julie Christie.
On the Beat *PC*: Rank. *P*: Hugh Stewart. *D*: Robert Asher. *S*: Jack Davies, Norman Wisdom, Eddie Leslie. *C*: Norman Wisdom, Jennifer Jayne, Raymond Huntley, David Lodge.
Waltz of the Toreadors *PC*: Independent Artists. *P*: Peter de Sarigny. *D*: John Guillermin. *S*: Wolf Mankowitz. *C*: Peter Sellers, Dany Robin, John Fraser, Cyril Cusack.

1963

This Sporting Life *PC*: Independent Artists. *P*: Albert Fennell, Karel Reisz. *D*: Lindsay Anderson. *S*: David Storey. *C*: Richard Harris, Rachel Roberts, Alan Badel, William Hartnell.
Bitter Harvest *PC*: Independent Artists. *P*: Albert Fennell. *D*: Peter Graham Scott. *S*: Ted Willis. *C*: Janet Munro, John Stride, Alan Badel, Anne Cunningham.
The Bay of St Michel *PC*: Trionyx. *PD*: John Ainsworth. *S*: Christopher Davis. *C*: Keenan Wynn, Mai Zetterling, Ronald Howard, Rona Anderson.
Call Me Bwana *PC*: Eon. *P*: Harry Saltzman, Albert Broccoli. *D*: Gordon Douglas. *S*: Nate Monaster, Joanna Harwood. *C*: Bob Hope, Anita Ekberg, Edie Adams, Lionel Jeffries.
80,000 Suspects *PC*: Rank. *P*: Val Guest, Frank Sherwin Green. *DS*: Val Guest. *C*: Yolande Donlan, Claire Bloom, Richard Johnson, Cyril Cusack.
Doctor in Distress *PC*: Rank. *P*: Betty Box. *D*: Ralph Thomas. *S*: Nicholas Phipps, Richard Scott Thorn. *C*: Dirk Bogarde, Samantha Eggar, James Robertson Justice, Mylène Demongeot.
The Eyes of Annie Jones *PC*: Parroch/McCallum/API. *P*: Neil McCallum, Jack Parsons. *D*: Reginald Le Borg. *S*: Louis Vittes. *C*: Richard Conte, Francesca Annis, Joyce Carey, Myrtle Reed.
Live It Up *PC*: Three Kings. *PD*: Lance Comfort. *S*: Lyn Fairhurst. *C*: David Hemmings, Heinz Burt, Joan Newell, Veronica Hurst.
Farewell Performance *PC*: Sevenay. *P*: Jim O'Connolly. *D*: Robert Tronson. *S*: Aileen Burke, Leone Stuart, Jim O'Connolly. *C*: David Kernan, Delphi Lawrence, Frederick Jaeger, Derek Francis.
The Informers *PC*: Rank. *P*: William MacQuitty. *D*: Ken Annakin. *S*: Alun Falconer, Paul Durst. *C*: Nigel Patrick, Margaret Whiting, Harry Andrews, Colin Blakely.
A Stitch in Time *PC*: Rank. *P*: Hugh Stewart. *D*: Robert Asher. *S*: Jack Davies, Norman Wisdom, Eddie Leslie, Henry Blyth. *C*: Norman Wisdom, Edward Chapman, Jeanette Sterke, Jerry Desmonde.
Father Came Too *PC*: Independent Artists. *P*: Julian Wintle, Leslie Parkyn. *D*: Peter Graham Scott. *S*: Jack Davies, Henry Blyth. *C*: James Robertson Justice, Leslie Phillips, Stanley Baxter, Sally Smith.
Hot Enough for June *PC*: Rank. *P*: Betty Box. *D*: Ralph Thomas. *S*: Lukas Heller. *C*: Dirk Bogarde, Sylva Koscina, Robert Morley, Leo McKern.

1964

Seance on a Wet Afternoon *PC*: AFM/Beaver. *P*: Richard Attenborough, Bryan Forbes. *DS*: Bryan Forbes. *C*: Richard Attenborough, Kim Stanley, Nanette Newman, Patrick Magee.
The Beauty Jungle *PC*: Rank. *PD*: Val Guest. *S*: Val Guest, Robert Muller. *C*: Ian Hendry, Janette Scott, Ronald Fraser, Edmund Purdom.
The High Bright Sun *PC*: Rank. *P*: Betty Box. *D*: Ralph Thomas. *S*: Ian Stuart Black, Bryan Forbes. *C*: Dirk Bogarde, Susan Strasberg, George Chakiris, Denholm Elliott.

Janette Scott is centre of attention in *The Beauty Jungle*.

1965

The Intelligence Men *PC*: Rank. *P*: Hugh Stewart. *D*: Robert Asher. *S*: Sid Green, Dick Hills. *C*: Morecambe and Wise, William Franklyn, April Olrich.
Be My Guest *PC*: Three Kings/Harold Shampan Filmusic. *PD*: Lance Comfort. *S*: Lyn Fairhurst. *C*: David Hemmings, Avril Angers, Joyce Blair, Andrea Monet.
The Ipcress File *PC*: Lowndes/Steven. *P*: Charles Kasher, Harry Saltzman. *D*: Sidney J. Furie. *C*: Michael Caine, Nigel Green, Guy Doleman, Sue Lloyd.
The Heroes of Telemark *PC*: Benton. *P*: Benjamin Fisz. *D*: Anthony Mann. *S*: Ivan Moffat, Ben Barzman. *C*: Kirk Douglas, Richard Harris, Ulla Jacobson, Michael Redgrave.
Sky West and Crooked *PC*: John Mills. *P*: Jack Hanbury. *D*: John Mills. *S*: John Prebble. Mary Hayley Bell. *C*: Hayley Mills, Ian McShane, Laurence Naismith, Geoffrey Bayldon.
The Early Bird *PC*: Rank. *P*: Hugh Stewart. *D*: Robert Asher. *S*: Jack Davies, Norman Wisdom, Henry Blyth, Eddie Leslie. *C*: Norman Wisdom, Edward Chapman, Jerry Desmonde, Paddie O'Neill.
Dateline Diamonds *PC*: Viscount. *P*: Harold Shampan, Harry Benn. *D*: Jeremy Summers. *S*: Tudor Gates. *C*: William Lucas, Kenneth Cope, George Mikell, Conrad Phillips.
Doctor in Clover *PC*: Rank. *P*: Betty Box. *D*: Ralph Thomas. *S*: Jack Davies. *C*: Leslie Phillips, James Robertson Justice, Shirley Anne Field, John Fraser.
I Was Happy Here *PC*: Partisan. *P*: Roy Millichip. *D*: Desmond Davis. *S*: Edna O'Brien, Desmond

Davis. *C*: Sarah Miles, Cyril Cusack, Julian Glover, Sean Caffrey.

1966

That Riviera Touch *PC*: Rank. *P*: Hugh Stewart. *D*: Cliff Owen. *S*: Sid Green, Dick Hills. *C*: Morecambe and Wise, Suzanne Lloyd, Paul Stassino.
The Sandwich Man *PC*: Titan. *P*: Peter Newbrook. *D*: Robert Hartford-Davis. *S*: Robert Hartford-Davis, Michael Bentine. *C*: Michael Bentine, Dora Bryan, Harry H. Corbett, Norman Wisdom.
They're a Weird Mob *PC*: Williamson/Powell International. *PD*: Michael Powell. *D*: Richard Imrie. *C*: Walter Chiari, Clare Dunne, Chips Rafferty, Alida Chelli.
The Trap *PC*: Parallel. *P*: George H. Brown. *D*: Sidney Hayers. *S*: David Osborn. *C*: Rita Tushingham, Oliver Reed, Rex Sevenoaks, Barbara Chilcott.
Romeo and Juliet *PC*: Poetic. *PD*: Paul Czinner. *C*: Margot Fonteyn, Rudolph Nureyev, David Blair, Julia Farron, the Royal Ballet Company and the orchestra of the Royal Opera House, Covent Garden.
Press for Time *PC*: Ivy. *P*: Robert Hartford-Davis, Peter Newbrook. *D*: Robert Asher. *S*: Norman Wisdom, Eddie Leslie. *C*: Norman Wisdom, Derek Bond, Angela Browne, Derek Francis.
The Quiller Memorandum *PC*: Ivan Foxwell. *P*: Ivan Foxwell, Sydney Streeter. *D*: Michael Anderson. *S*: Harold Pinter. *C*: George Segal, Alec Guinness, Max Von Sydow, Senta Berger.
Deadlier than the Male *PC*: Santor. *P*: Betty Box, Bruce Newbery. *D*: Ralph Thomas. *S*: Jimmy Sangster, David Osborn, Liz Charles-Williams. *C*: Richard Johnson, Elke Sommer, Sylva Koscina, Nigel Green.
Don't Lose Your Head *PC*: Adder. *P*: Peter Rogers. *D*: Gerald Thomas. *S*: Talbot Rothwell. *C*: Sidney James, Jim Dale, Kenneth Williams, Charles Hawtrey.
Maroc 7 *PC*: Cyclone. *P*: John Gale, Leslie Phillips, Martin Chute. *D*: Gerry O'Hara. *S*: David Osborn. *C*: Gene Barry, Elsa Martinelli, Leslie Phillips, Cyd Charisse.

1967

The Magnificent Two *PC*: Rank. *P*: Hugh Stewart. *D*: Cliff Owen. *S*: Sid Green, Dick Hills, Michael Pertwee. *C*: Morecambe and Wise, Margit Saad, Virgilio Texeira.
Stranger in the House *PC*: De Grunwald. *P*: Dimitri de Grunwald. *DS*: Pierre Rouve. *C*: James Mason, Geraldine Chaplin, Bobby Darin, Paul Bertoya.
The Long Duel *PC*: Rank. *PD*: Ken Annakin. *S*: Ernest Bornemann, Peter Yeldham, Geoffrey Orme. *C*: Yul Brynner, Trevor Howard, Harry Andrews, Andrew Keir.
The Trygon Factor *PC*: Rialto/Preben Philipson. *P*: Ian Warren, Brian Taylor. *D*: Cyril Frankel. *S*: Derry Quinn, Stanley Munro. *C*: Stewart Granger, Susan Hampshire, Cathleen Nesbitt, James Culliford.
Follow that Camel *PC*: Adder. *P*: Peter Rogers. *D*: Gerald Thomas. *S*: Talbot Rothwell. *C*: Phil Silvers, Jim Dale, Peter Butterworth, Charles Hawtrey.
Carry On, Doctor *PC*: Adder. *P*: Peter Rogers. *D*: Gerald Thomas. *S*: Talbot Rothwell. *C*: Frankie Howerd, Sidney James, Kenneth Williams, Charles Hawtrey.

A helping hand for Yul Brynner in *The Long Duel*.

Hell is Empty *PC*: Dominion. *P*: Michael Eland. *D*: John Ainsworth, Bernard Knowles. *S*: John Ainsworth, Bernard Knowles, John Fowler. *C*: Martine Carol, Anthony Steel, James Robertson Justice, Shirley Anne Field.
Two Weeks in September *PC*: Francos/Quadrangle/Pomereu/Kenwood. *P*: Francis Cosne, Kenneth Harper. *D*: Serge Bourgignon. *S*: Vahe Katche, Pascal Jardin, Serge Bourgignon. *C*: Brigitte Bardot, Laurent Terzieff, Jean Rochefort, James Robertson Justice.

1968

Carry On Up the Khyber *PC*: Adder. *P*: Peter Rogers. *D*: Gerald Thomas. *S*: Talbot Rothwell. *C*: Sidney James, Kenneth Williams, Charles Hawtrey, Roy Castle.
Nobody Runs Forever *PC*: Selmur/Rank. *P*: Selig Seligman, Betty Box. *D*: Ralph Thomas. *S*: Wilfred Greatorex. *C*: Rod Taylor, Christopher Plummer, Lilli Palmer, Camilla Sparv.
Subterfuge *PC*: Intertel/VTR. *P*: Trevor Wallace, Peter Snell. *D*: Peter Graham Scott. *S*: David Whittaker. *C*: Gene Barry, Joan Collins, Richard Todd, Tom Adams.

1969

Carry On Camping *PC*: Adder. *P*: Peter Rogers. *D*: Gerald Thomas. *S*: Talbot Rothwell. *C*: Sidney James, Kenneth Williams, Joan Sims, Charles Hawtrey.
Some Girls Do *PC*: Ashdown. *P*: Betty Box. *D*: Ralph Thomas. *S*: David Osborn, Liz Charles-Williams. *C*: Richard Johnson, Dahlia Lavi, Beba Loncar, James Villiers.
Ring of Bright Water *PC*: Brightwater/Palomar. *P*: Joseph Strick. *D*: Jack Couffer. *S*: Jack Couffer, Bill Travers. *C*: Bill Travers, Virginia McKenna, Peter Jeffrey, Roddy McMillan.
Carry On Again, Doctor *PC*: Adder. *P*: Peter Rogers. *D*: Gerald Thomas. *S*: Talbot Rothwell. *C*: Kenneth Williams, Jim Dale, Sidney James, Joan Sims.
Twinky *PC*: World Film Services. *P*: John Heyman, Clive Sharp. *D*: Richard Donner. *S*: Norman Thaddeus Vane. *C*: Susan George, Charles Bronson, Trevor Howard, Michael Craig.
The Royal Hunt of the Sun *PC*: Royal/Benmar/Security. *P*: Eugene Frenke, Philip Yordan. *D*: Irving Lerner. *S*: Philip Yordan. *C*: Christopher Plummer, Robert Shaw, Nigel Davenport, Michael Craig.
Mister Jericho *PC*: Incorporated Television. *P*: Julian Wintle. *D*: Sidney Hayers. *S*: Philip Levene. *C*: Patrick MacNee, Connie Stevens, Herbert Lom, Marty Allen.

1970

Carry On Up the Jungle *PC*: Adder/Ethiro. *P*: Peter Rogers. *D*: Gerald Thomas. *S*: Talbot Rothwell. *C*: Frankie Howerd, Sidney James, Charles Hawtrey, Joan Sims.
Doctor in Trouble *PC*: Welbeck/Rank. *P*: Betty Box. *D*: Ralph Thomas. *S*: Jack Davies. *C*: Leslie Phillips, Harry Secombe, Angela Scoular, Irene Handl.
Carry On Loving *PC*: Adder/GT. *P*: Peter Rogers. *D*: Gerald Thomas. *S*: Talbot Rothwell. *C*: Sidney James, Kenneth Williams, Joan Sims, Hattie Jacques.
Toomorrow *PC*: Lowndes/Sweet Music. *P*: Harry Saltzman, Don Kirschner. *DS*: Val Guest. *C*: Olivia Newton-John, Benny Thomas, Vic Cooper, Karl Chambers.
Countess Dracula *PC*: Hammer. *P*: Alexander Paal. *D*: Peter Sasdy. *S*: Alexander Paal, Peter Sasdy, Jeremy Paul. *C*: Ingrid Pitt, Nigel Green, Maurice Denham, Sandor Eles.
Carry On, Henry *PC*: Adder. *P*: Peter Rogers. *D*: Gerald Thomas. *S*: Talbot Rothwell. *C*: Sidney James, Kenneth Williams, Joan Sims, Charles Hawtrey.
The Firechasers *PC*: ITC. *P*: Julian Wintle. *D*: Sidney Hayers. *S*: Philip Levene. *C*: Chad Everett, Anjanette Comer, Keith Barron, Joanne Dainton.

1971

Assault *PC*: Peter Rogers. *P*: George H. Brown. *D*: Sidney Hayers. *S*: John Kruse. *C*: Frank Finlay, Suzy Kendall, James Laurenson, Lesley-Anne Down.
Carry On at Your Convenience *PC*: Peter Rogers. *P*: Peter Rogers. *D*: Gerald Thomas. *S*: Talbot Rothwell. *C*: Sidney James, Kenneth Williams, Charles Hawtrey, Joan Sims.
Hands of the Ripper *PC*: Hammer. *P*: Aida Young. *D*: Peter Sasdy. *S*: L.W. Davidson. *C*: Angharad Rees, Eric Porter, Dora Bryan, Jane Merrow.
Quest for Love *PC*: Peter Rogers. *P*: Peter Eton. *D*: Ralph Thomas. *S*: Terence Feely. *C*: Tom Bell, Joan Collins, Denholm Elliott, Laurence Naismith.
Revenge *PC*: Peter Rogers. *P*: George H. Brown. *D*: Sidney Hayers. *S*: John Kruse. *C*: Joan Collins, Sinead Cusack, James Booth, Ray Barrett.
Twins of Evil *PC*: Hammer. *P*: Harry Fine, Michael Style. *D*: John Hough. *S*: Tudor Gates. *C*: Madeleine and Mary Collinson, Peter Cushing, Kathleen Byron.

1972

All Coppers Are . . . *PC*: Peter Rogers. *D*: Sidney Hayers. *S*: Allan Prior. *C*: Nicky Henson, Martin Potter, Julia Foster, Ian Hendry.
Carry On Abroad *PC*: Peter Rogers. *P*: Peter Rogers. *D*: Gerald Thomas, *S*: Talbot Rothwell. *C*: Sidney James, Kenneth Williams, Barbara Windsor, Hattie Jacques.
Carry On, Matron *PC*: Peter Rogers. *P*: Peter Rogers. *D*: Gerald Thomas. *S*: Talbot Rothwell. *C*: Sidney James, Kenneth Williams, Charles Hawtrey, Terry Scott.
Kidnapped *PC*: Omnibus. *P*: Frederick Brogger. *D*: Delbert Mann. *S*: Jack Pulman. *C*: Michael Caine, Lawrence Douglas, Trevor Howard, Jack Hawkins.
Rentadick *PC*: Rank/Paradine/Virgin. *P*: Ned Sherrin. *D*: Jim Clark. *C*: James Booth, Richard Briers, Julie Ege, Donald Sinden.
Vampire Circus *PC*: Hammer. *P*: Wilbur Stark. *D*: Robert Young. *S*: Judson Kinberg. *C*: Adrienne Corri, Laurence Payne, Thorley Walters, **John Moulder Brown.**

Ingrid Pitt and Sandor Eles in *Countess Dracula*.

1973

The Belstone Fox *PC*: Independent Artists. *P*: Sally Shuter. *DS*: James Hill. *C*: Eric Porter, Jeremy Kemp, Rachel Roberts, Bill Travers.
Bless This House *PC*: Peter Rogers. *D*: Gerald Thomas. *S*: Dave Freeman. *C*: Sidney James, Diana Coupland, Terry Scott, June Whitfield.
Carry On, Girls *PC*: Peter Rogers. *P*: Peter Rogers. *D*: Gerald Thomas. *S*: Talbot Rothwell. *C*: Sidney James, Joan Sims, Barbara Windsor, Kenneth Connor.
Father, Dear Father *PC*: Sedgemoor/MM Films. *PD*: William G. Stewart. *C*: Patrick Cargill, Natasha Pyne, Ann Holloway, Noel Dyson.
Nothing But the Night *PC*: Charlemagne. *P*: Anthony Nelson-Keys. *D*: Peter Sasdy. *S*: Brian Hayles. *C*: Christopher Lee, Peter Cushing, Diana Dors, Georgia Brown.

1974

Carry On, Dick *PC*: Peter Rogers. *P*: Peter Rogers. *D*: Gerald Thomas. *S*: Talbot Rothwell. *C*: Sidney James, Barbara Windsor, Kenneth Williams, Bernard Bresslaw.
Don't Just Lie There, Say Something *PC*: Comocroft. *PD*: Bob Kellett. *S*: Michael Pertwee. *C*: Brian Rix, Leslie Phillips, Joan Sims, Joanna Lumley.
Soft Beds, Hard Battles *PC*: Charter. *P*: John Boulting. *D*: Roy Boulting. *S*: Leo Marks, Roy Boulting. *C*: Peter Sellers, Lila Kedrova, Curt Jurgens, Gabriella Licudi.
That's Your Funeral *PC*: Hammer. *D*: John Robins. *S*: Peter Lewis. *C*: Bill Fraser, Raymond Huntley, David Battley, Dennis Price.

1975

Carry On Behind *PC*: Peter Rogers. *P*: Peter Rogers. *D*: Gerald Thomas. *S*: Dave Freeman. *C*: Elke Sommer, Kenneth Williams, Windsor Davies, Liz Fraser.
That Lucky Touch *PC*: Gloria. *P*: Dimitri de Grunwald. *D*: Christopher Miles. *S*: John Briley. *C*: Roger Moore, Susannah York, Lee J. Cobb, Shelley Winters.

1976

Bugsy Malone *PC*: Bugsy Malone Productions. *P*: Alan Marshall, Alan Parker. *DS*: Alan Parker. *C*: Jodie Foster, Scott Baio, John Cassisi, Florrie Dugger.
Carry On, England *PC*: Peter Rogers. *P*: Peter Rogers. *D*: Gerald Thomas. *S*: Jack Seddon, David Pursall. *C*: Kenneth Connor, Patrick Mower,

Windsor Davies, Judy Geeson.

1978

The Shout *PC*: Recorded Picture. *P*: Jeremy Thomas. *D*: Jerzy Skolimowski. *S*: Jerzy Skolimowski, Michael Austin. *C*: Alan Bates, John Hurt, Susannah York, Robert Stephens.
The 39 Steps *PC*: Rank. *P*: Greg Smith, James Kenelm Clarke. *D*: Don Sharp. *S*: Michael Robson. *C*: Robert Powell, Karen Dotrice, John Mills, Eric Porter.
Tomorrow Never Comes *PC*: Classic/Montreal Trust/ Neffbourne. *P*: Michael Klinger, Julian Melzack. *D*: Peter Collinson. *S*: David Pursall, Jack Seddon, Sydney Banks. *C*: Oliver Reed, Susan George, Raymond Burr.
The Uncanny *PC*: Cinevideo/Tor. *P*: Claude Heroux, Milton Subotsky. *D*: Denis Heroux. *S*: Michael Parry. *C*: Peter Cushing, Donald Pleasence, Samantha Eggar, Ray Milland, Susan Penhaligon, Joan Greenwood.
The Wild Geese *PC*: Richmond. *P*: Euan Lloyd. *D*: Andrew V. McLaglen. *S*: Reginald Rose. *C*: Richard Burton, Roger Moore, Richard Harris, Hardy Kruger.
Wombling Free *PC*: Rank. *P*: Ian Shand. *DS*: Lionel Jeffries. *C*: David Tomlinson, Frances de la Tour, Bonnie Langford, Bernard Spear.

1979

The Lady Vanishes *PC*: Rank/Hammer. *P*: Michael Carreras, Tom Sachs. *D*: Anthony Page. *S*: George Axelrod. *C*: Cybill Shepherd, Elliott Gould, Ian Carmichael, Angela Lansbury.
The Riddle of the Sands *PC*: Rank/Worldmark. *P*: Drumond Challis. *D*: Tony Maylam. *S*: Tony Maylam, John Bailey. *C*: Michael York, Simon MacCorkindale, Jenny Agutter, Alan Badel.
Tarka the Otter *PC*: Tor/ Rank/NFFC. *PD*: David Cobham. *S*: Gerald Durrell, David Cobham. *C*: Peter Bennett, Edward Underdown, Brenda Cavendish, John Leeson.
The Eagle's Wing *PC*: Rank/Peter Shaw. *P*: Ben Arbeid. *D*: Anthony Harvey. *S*: John Briley. *C*: Martin Sheen, Sam Waterston, Harvey Keitel, Stephane Audran.

1980

Bad Timing *PC*: Rank/ Recorded Picture Company. *P*: Jeremy Thomas. *D*: Nicolas Roeg. *S*: Yale Udoff. *C*: Art Garfunkel, Theresa Russell, Harvey Keitel, Denholm Elliott.
Silver Dream Racer *PC*: Rank/David Wickes. *P*: René Dupont. *DS*: David Wickes. *C*: David Essex, Beau Bridges, Cristina Raines, Harry H. Corbett.
The Sea Wolves *PC*: Richmond/Lorimar/Varius. *P*: Euan Lloyd. *D*: Andrew V. McLaglen. *S*: Reginald Rose. *C*: Gregory Peck, Roger Moore, Trevor Howard, David Niven.

1982

The Boys in Blue *PC*: Rank/MAM/Apollo Leisure. *P*: Greg Smith. *DS*: Val Guest. *C*: Cannon and Ball, Suzanne Danielle, Eric Sykes.
Nutcracker *PC*: Jezshaw. *P*: Panos Nicolaou. *D*: Anwar Kawadri. *S*: Raymond Christodolou. *C*: Joan Collins, Carol White, Paul Nicholas, Finola Hughes.
Who Dares Wins *PC*: Rank/Richmond Light Horse. *P*: Euan Lloyd, Raymond Menmuir. *D*: Ian Sharp. *S*: Reginald Rose. *C*: Lewis Collins, Judy Davis, Ingrid Pitt, Richard Widmark.

1983

Educating Rita *PC*: Acorn. *PD*: Lewis Gilbert. *S*: Willy Russell. *C*: Julie Walters, Michael Caine, Michael Williams, Maureen Lipman.
Heat and Dust *PC*: Merchant/Ivory. *P*: Ismail Merchant. *D*: James Ivory. *S*: Ruth Prawer Jhabvala. *C*: Julie Christie, Christopher Cazenove, Greta Scacchi, Shashi Kapoor.

1984

The Bostonians *PC*: Merchant/Ivory. *P*: Ismail Merchant. *D*: James Ivory. *S*: Ruth Prawer Jhabvala. *C*: Christopher Reeve, Vanessa Redgrave, Madeleine Potter, Jessica Tandy.
Not Quite Jerusalem *PC*: Acorn. *PD*: Lewis Gilbert. *S*: Paul Kember. *C*: Joanna Pacula, Sam Robards, Kevin McNally, Todd Graff.
The Chain *PC*: Quintet. *P*: Victor Glynn. *D*: Jack Gold. *S*: Jack Rosenthal. *C*: Maurice Denham, Warren Mitchell, Nigel Hawthorne, Bernard Hill, Leo McKern, Anna Massey.
Secret Places *PC*: Skreba. *P*: Simon Relph, Ann Skinner. *DS*: Zelda Barron. *C*: Marie-Thérèse Relin, Tara McGowran, Claudine Auger, Jenny Agutter.

1985

Defence of the Realm *PC*: Enigma. *P*: Robin Douet, Lynda Myles. *D*: David Drury. *S*: Martin Stellman. *C*: Gabriel Byrne, Denholm Elliott, Greta Scacchi, Ian Bannen.
The Girl in the Picture *PC*: Antonine. *P*: Paddy Higson. *DS*: Cary Parker. *C*: John Gordon-Sinclair, Irina Brook, David Mackay, Gregor Fisher.

1987

The Fourth Protocol *PC*: Fourth Protocol Films. *P*: Timothy Burrill. *D*: John Mackenzie. *S*: Frederick Forsyth. *C*: Michael Caine, Pierce Brosnan, Joanna Cassidy, Ned Beatty.

Pierce Brosnan and Joanna Cassidy in *The Fourth Protocol*.

Acknowledgements

My grateful thanks to everyone who helped me with this book and without whom it would not have been possible. For their generous recall: Keith Robertson, Olive Dodds, Cornel Lucas, Cyril Howard, Norman Martlew (who also allowed me access to his *Cleopatra* material), Betty Box, Peter Rogers, Joan Collins, Norman Wisdom, Jerry Juroe, Geoff Labram, Charles Staffell, Andy Knapman, Paddy Bennett, Alan Marshall and Peter Noble. For their invaluable research: Colin Vaines, Deborah Fulham and Norma Simpson. To Brian Davison, for designing the book, and Val Sillery, for supplying the titles index. Generally, to: the British Film Institute, Pinewood Studios, Screen International, The Hollywood Reporter, Tim Whittingham and Maggie Corke.

For photographs: Rank Film Distributors, Eon Productions, Columbia Pictures, Twentieth Century-Fox, Universal Pictures, MGM-UA, ITC Film Distributors, Warner Brothers, the National Film Archive, John Dark and the *Sky Bandits* team.

Grateful acknowledgement is also made to the writers and their works who have been quoted in the text.

Bibliography

Mr Rank by Alan Wood (Hodder & Stoughton); *Snakes and Ladders* by Dirk Bogarde (Chatto & Windus); *Movies for the Millions* by Gilbert Seldes (Batsford); *In Search of Gandhi* by Richard Attenborough (Bodley Head); *Reflected Glory* by Peter Noble (Jarrolds); *More or Less* by Kenneth More (Hodder & Stoughton); *Forever Ealing* by George Perry (Pavilion/Michael Joseph); *Past Imperfect* by Joan Collins (W.H. Allen); *Peter Finch – A Biography* by Trader Faulkner (Angus & Robertson); *The British Film Catalogue, 1895–1970* by Denis Gifford (David & Charles); *The Great Movie Stars (The Golden Years* and *The International Years)* by David Shipman (Angus & Robertson); *British Films 1971–81* (BFI Library Services); *A Night at the Pictures – Ten Decades of British Films* by Gilbert Adair and Nick Roddick (Columbus Books); *Cinema in Britain: An Illustrated Survey* by Ivan Butler (Barnes/Tantivy); *The Contemporary Cinema 1945–1963* by Penelope Houston (Penguin); *The Carry On Book* by Kenneth Easthaugh (David & Charles); *Movies from the Mansion* by George Perry (Pavilion/Michael Joseph).

Index

Illustration references are in bold type, filmography references italic.